The Church on British Television

Marcus Harmes
Meredith Harmes • Barbara Harmes

The Church on British Television

From the Coronation to *Coronation Street*

Marcus Harmes
Open Access College
University of Southern Queensland
Toowoomba, QLD, Australia

Meredith Harmes
Open Access College
University of Southern Queensland
Toowoomba, QLD, Australia

Barbara Harmes
Open Access College
University of Southern Queensland
Toowoomba, QLD, Australia

ISBN 978-3-030-38112-7   ISBN 978-3-030-38113-4   (eBook)
https://doi.org/10.1007/978-3-030-38113-4

Cover illustration: Alan Mather / Alamy Stock Photo

This Palgrave Macmillan imprint is published by the registered company Springer Nature Switzerland AG.
The registered company address is: Gewerbestrasse 11, 6330 Cham, Switzerland

To Tosca

Acknowledgements

Associate Professor Richard Scully, Dr Catriona Mills and Dr Jeremy Patrick read parts of the manuscript and we are grateful for their time and suggestions. Staff at Lambeth Palace Library, the Church of England Records Centre and the National Archives have provided much appreciated assistance in research. Edwin Apps and Alvin Rakoff both generously shared memories and reflections of their respective television programmes.

POST-WAR ARCHBISHOPS OF CANTERBURY

Geoffrey Fisher 1945–1961
Michael Ramsey 1961–1974
Donald Coggan 1974–1980
Robert Runcie 1980–1991
George Carey 1991–2002
Rowan Williams 2002–2012
Justin Welby 2013–

CONTENTS

Abbreviations

ABC   Associated Broadcasting Company
ACCM   Advisory Council for the Church's Ministry
ATV   Associated Television
BBC   British Broadcasting Corporation
BCC   British Council of Churches
CERC   Church of England Record Centre
CRAC   Central Religious Advisory Committee
HTV   Harlech Television
IBA   Independent Broadcasting Authority
ITA   Independent Television Authority
ITV   Independent Television
LPL   Lambeth Palace Library
RTV   Church of England Radio and Television Council

Introduction

Coronation Street began in December 1960 with an argument about the Church of England. Ena Sharples barged into the corner shop and into the world of the soap opera and immediately began to quarrel with the new shopkeeper about churchgoing. Early years of *Coronation Street* were steeped in religion. Sharples was caretaker and harmonium player of the Glad Tidings Mission, where Leonard Swindley was lay preacher. Their nonconformity evoked a particular Northern religiosity with long antecedents, including the Lantern Yard community in George Eliot's *Silas Marner* (1861), and was a religious identity at odds with the Church of England's establishment status. In *Coronation Street* episode one, Sharples demanded to know where the new shopkeeper went to church. The shopkeeper's vague response that she is not especially religious made Sharples jump to the conclusion she must be 'C of E'. Further disparagement of the national Church then followed, Ena deriding her sister-in-law for social climbing by becoming Anglican: 'Oh it's like my sister's husband', who said '"we're civic dignitaries now. We must head for church"'. Within a week they were received, christened, and confirmed and within a fortnight she was sitting up all night sewing surplices'. Ena's assumption was that the Church of England stood for class, status, snobbery and lukewarm belief. Seven years earlier, at Elizabeth II's Coronation, television viewers watched the highest echelons in the Empire gathered around the archbishop of Canterbury, presenting a vision of the Church and elites also evoked by Ena Sharples' tirade. *Coronation Street* and the Coronation are

© The Author(s) 2020
M. Harmes et al., *The Church on British Television*,
https://doi.org/10.1007/978-3-030-38113-4_1

indicative of the many ways, that the Church of England has been a significant presence in British television. The Church as subject matter and setting traverses changes in a number of disparate areas: in policy and legislation, in taste and aesthetics, and in production methods and scheduling priorities.

Off screen and in reality the Church in the twenty-first century may have a dwindling influence and shrinking number of worshippers, but it remains a compelling source for drama and human interest. The institution, including its liturgy, discipline, organisations and doctrines, has inspired decades of comedy and drama. Its people, from humble vicars to bishops, as well as the spouses and children of the parsonage, and the laity, are part of this television content.

This study examines both fictional and non-fictional television involving the Church of England. In Part I: Shaping the Medium, we consider the Church's own efforts to shape television through means such as script approval, efforts to produce a professional looking and sounding body of clergy to appear on television, and lobbying broadcasters and ministers through its Radio and Television Council. Key moments in the history of British television, from the launch of the television service itself, the development of second, third and fourth terrestrial channels and commercial advertising will be seen anew from the perspective of influential voices from within the Church. But we will also see that influence decline.

In Part II: Shaped by the Medium, we look at the opposite, the Church not as shaping but as a creation of the media, and consider the discursive constructions of the Church on the screen and how the television industry itself, including people with no connection to the Church, have shaped perceptions of it through their programmes. In Part II, each chapter examines television programmes showing the Church's interactions with specific organisations, institutions and occasions: with the marches of the Campaign for Nuclear Disarmament, with the high politics of Downing Street, with inner-city communities decaying under Thatcherism, and with the law. In each case, specific programmes raise questions about how these interactions inform the place of the Church in modern society.

These programmes and broadcasts traverse genres and approaches. There is no 'canon' as such of Church of England programmes. Television programmes about the Church or programmes that highlight it in some way have appeared across all genres, types, schedules and channels. There are sitcoms, science fiction serials, soap operas and broadcasts of actual events such as weddings and funerals. Broadcasters have longstanding commitments to the broadcasting of Church's own key moments such as the enthronement of archbishops. Sometimes the broadcasting is lavish and large scale and sometimes intimate, such as the short serious talks delivered by vicars in the epilogue.

This analysis centres on core organising questions. First, as the real-life Church grows ever more remote from the daily lives of many people, what are the implications for its place in public consciousness of being on the small screen, the most intimate and immediate form of broadcasting? Second, as television shows different aspects of the Church while fewer people engage with the real-life institution, what impressions are created, what distortions are propagated, and what is the influence of iterations of popular culture on shaping relationships between people and the national Church? Third, in what way are these televisual texts part of a wider social discourse around religion? In short, what are the stories that television tells about the Church, and what televisual entities have emerged to take the place of real-life engagement with organised religion?

This study encompasses some of the most enduring television programmes that appear on British television. Studying the Church and television together is rare in scholarly writing. There are isolated instances of academic study of some of the programmes under scrutiny, including *The Vicar of Dibley*, *Yes, Prime Minister* and major examples of non-fiction broadcasting including the 1953 Coronation and *Panorama*. However, there have been limited attempts to explore the longer history of the Church of England as both a participant in and the subject of broadcasting. The large-scale *Oxford History of Anglicanism* gave limited attention to broadcasting or mass media. There are studies of organised religion and broadcasting in other national contexts: one important parallel approach is Richard Wolff's *The Church on TV*, a study of multiple Christian denominations on American television (2010). His text explored both intersections and distinctions relating to fictional representations and actual churches, but aside from the American focus, its range of denominations and traditions was eclectic. In recent years, scholarly monographs have examined important aspects of television history. The ubiquitous adaptations of Agatha Christie's crime fiction on British television are the subject of Mark Aldridge's 2016 monograph *Agatha Christie on Screen*. A broader study of British television by Lez Cooke appeared in 2003 and Gavin Schaffer's *The Vision of the Nation* (2014) examined race and multiculturalism on British television.

While religion and broadcasting have separately received scholarly and journalistic attention, on television, the Church of England vicar is ubiquitous. He or she is taking drugs on *Coronation Street*, solving crime in *Rev*, getting murdered in *Midsomer Murders* or critiquing television itself on *Gogglebox*. An institution that is integral to popular culture warrants a study of its principal means of interaction with popular culture, particularly how the small screen has been shaped by and in turn mediates the Church for mass consumption.

It is important to clarify major aspects of the approach taken here: why the Church of England and why television? By law, the Church of England is the established church. Its clergy, especially its bishops, speak publicly as befits their status as the leaders of the national Church. Television seems the most effective medium for them to reach wider audiences. In early chapters of this study, we will especially see Geoffrey Fisher, archbishop of Canterbury from 1945 to 1961, as a shaper of the medium in ways hitherto unconsidered by television and church historians and even his own biographers. Establishment makes the Church of England more than just another denomination, giving it unique privileges and a unique place in public life, but also posing distinctive challenges. Until the later twentieth century, it was also the largest religious denomination in the British Isles and it remains the Church that marries royals and maintains the cathedrals that are major tourist drawcards.

It is however *English*, whereas broadcasting covers the entire British Isles. Even when considering regional independent franchises such as Harlech (HTV) or Yorkshire Television, as well as the BBC's own history of regional broadcasting from Pebble Mill or BBC Scotland, the Britishness of this broadcasting can be deceptive. For most of the period covered by this book, the BBC's base of operations for its television production was the Television Centre in White City and before that Lime Grove, Riverside and Alexandra Palace, supported by the rehearsal facilities in Acton. Until 1994, the Department of Religion and Ethics remained centrally located (Noonan 2012, 367). Independent companies were more widely distributed but frequently still London-centric, including the studios in Teddington and the use of production facilities at Elstree and Shepperton in the Home Counties. Much of the drama output of the period covered by this book is accordingly not just English in accent and emphasis, but southern English. That bias, as well as the consolidation of technical and creative personnel in the capital, had implications for religious broadcasting. Churches and cathedrals in London were convenient and obvious centres to broadcast hymns and sermons.

Methodologically, the English Church and its refractions and recreations on television alone provide an important focus. One focus is the Anglicanism. Further volumes could fill with other expressions of British religion, including the Scottish Presbyterian Church, the Irish Catholic Church, and the Welsh Independent and Methodist congregations, not to mention non-Christian communities.

That is not to say that this wider vista is irrelevant: the Church of England on screen should be contrasted with the dramatic treatment of other expressions of religious life. Another is the medium of television. Expansion to the many appearances of the Church in film, radio or new social media would fill volumes. Vicars and their churches abound in cinema. Yet television raises distinctive issues and asks us to pose distinctive questions precisely because it is an intimate and domestic medium and, by being so, it has a curiously direct and challenging relationship with churchgoing. Indeed, the Church in many ways made television happen in postwar Britain though the televising of the Coronation, the grandest and most important church service of all. The Church created a competitor for the time and attention of the populace. One of the most notable successes of the BBC in the 1960s was the dramatisation of John Galsworthy's *The Forsyte Saga* (1967). Some historians of popular culture credit it with ushering in a major sociological change by ending Sunday evening church going. At the very least, it contributed to a change in the patterns of daily activity as more people opted to buy a television licence and watch their sets on Sunday evenings than go to Evensong. Television served as one aspect of a wider set of leisure industries competing with Sunday church attendance (Morris 2003, 973) so *The Forsyte Saga*'s impact was not absolute. Clergy also found they faced stiff competition from *Sunday Night at the London Palladium* and from the 1950s it became increasingly clear that people would rather be at home watching television than in church on Sunday evening (Moran 2013, 175). The sociological and historical understandings of religion in Britain from the 1960s onwards received a sharp refocus in Callum Brown's *The Death of Christian Britain*, published in 2000. Brown, repudiating several decades of scholarship, pinpointed a notable shift not merely in churchgoing but in patterns of belief from the 1960s, later than his scholarly predecessors suggested (Brown 2000, 27). The interplay between the Church, television, and belief or its absence, lead to key themes that apply throughout this study.

Key Themes

Denominationalism

Throughout this book, the terms Church of England and Anglican are mostly used interchangeably, but the former term carries particular connotations not captured by the latter. 'Anglican' denotes a denomination, but 'Church of England' encompasses the establishment status and national character of the Church. The Church is established by law and has been since the sixteenth century. Some of its bishops are legislators in the House of Lords. The Church of England also proclaims itself by its internet strapline to be a 'Christian presence in every community', linking its establishment status to expectations of serving the wider community.

That establishment status has implications for the broadcasting and dramatisation of religion on British television. A spectacular event such as a coronation is a once in a lifetime occasion, but British people tuning into a broadcast of a Remembrance Service, a royal wedding, a national thanksgiving occasion, a state funeral or even a typical episode of *Songs of Praise* are going to see Anglican clergy in charge of proceedings (Cumper and Edge 2006, 617). That participation is stretched to absurdity in the sharply observant political comedy *Yes, Prime Minister*. In *A Diplomatic Incident* (1987), the Prime Minister's predecessor has just died, necessitating a gathering of world leaders at Westminster Abbey for his state funeral. PM Jim Hacker is delighted by the opportunity the broadcast will provide to appear statesmanlike, and he understands the Church of England funeral service as being a party political opportunity. 'Plenty of room for television cameras, won't there?' he asks anxiously, before learning with outrage that he cannot have a camera conveniently positioned in the pulpit and trained on his pew because 'it won't leave a lot of room for the archbishop'. 'There is always the High Altar, but I think the archbishop may need that as well', suggests the bureaucrat Sir Humphrey Appleby, leading to Hacker's annoyed observation 'Who does he think he is?'.

Who indeed. The dialogue is a valuable entry point to the broadcast of a national and established church, to the blurred distinctions between politics, religion and national identity. The Church's internet strapline, proclaiming itself part of 'every community' is ambitious. Set against it is the landmark 2013 UK census, which was the first to register a higher proportion of 'no religion' compared to 'Christian', or specifically Church of England among the British. Being part of every community is more than a statement of geographic presence however, and draws theologically from the Church of England's identity as grounded in society. That would include the Church, especially its bishops, expecting to speak authoritatively to society and to shape social values. In doing so, their actions and their Church transcend denominationalism to permeate the body politic and society in general. It also carries an expectation of 'C of E' being normative within society and the shared values of society (Cumper and Edge 2006, 602), something the 2013 census for the first time subverted.

These issues have recently and controversially been highlighted in *That Was the Church That Was*, a 2016 book jointly authored by the Anglican academic Linda Woodhead and the columnist Andrew Brown, who had written in the past for the Church of England's *Church Times*. The book was sufficiently controversial to be withdrawn and pulped and, when finally available to read, to have been negatively reviewed in some quarters, including the *Church Times* (July 26, 2016). Even its critics have conceded some merit in the broader arguments, while disliking the tone, the methodology, some breaches of privacy in reporting conversations, and more specific claims. Woodhead and Brown pinpoint 1986, about the half-way point of Archbishop Robert Runcie's primacy, as being when the Church of England 'lost' the people. Here, they suggest, is when 'C of E' ceased to be normative, in that a majority of people once had even a fairly Anglican nebulous identity, based not so much on regular church attendance but at least on a nominal attachment, and certainly an absence of hostility to the established Church. These issues raise questions of importance for considering the Church of England as an entity brought onto the screen in fictional and non-fictional programmes and as a behind the scenes influence on broadcasters and other key personnel responsible for television, such as the postmaster general. This broader population after all is also the audience for television programmes, who saw and see the Church of England on the screens in various fictional and documentary guises; attitudinally, this audience shifted over decades from one more broadly familiar to the Church and supportive of it, to one largely unchurched.

This shift prompts a study of the ways it has guided the presentation of the Church as a televisually mediated institution. Church leaders expected to morally instruct the people on the use and development of television, and they expected to be part of the process of shaping the purpose, content and tone of first the BBC Television Service, then ITV, BBC2 and

Channel 4, but we will see where influence shifts from the authoritative to the beleaguered. There are tensions between a denomination, bounded by confessional limits and marked by an inward focus, and a national Church, that theoretically should have no boundaries and be part of each community. These tensions are central to studying the Church on television. As the audience's familiarity with the institution waxes and wanes, the tone and content of what is broadcast must change, and the contribution of the Church will also change as it declines from being a nationally familiar institution.

Secularism

As a study of the Church of England on television, this work is therefore a study of an institution and so relates more to people's external activities than intangible interior beliefs. The Church on television brings into focus the tangible and visible. If some recent studies have suggested that 'God may still be part of everyone's life, but for increasing numbers of people the institutional church no longer is' (Hall 2014, 729), the study of the institution does not necessarily include the study of belief. Indeed in *Yes, Prime Minister* the disjunction between the institution and belief is clearly marked out. When discussing the ideal characteristics of a Church of England bishop, civil servants put religious belief far down the list of desirable qualities because God is 'what's known as an optional extra', compared to essentials such as good breeding and correct table manners as well as the Queen's role as the Supreme Governor. Through the medium of television, senior churchmen, especially John Robinson, the bishop of Woolwich in the 1960s, and David Jenkins, the bishop of Durham in the 1980s, provoked storms of controversy about belief, or rather its absence. Broadcasting that asked challenging questions about faith and belief or offered affronts to doctrine is also suggestive of secularism (Wallis 2016, 669). *Yes, Prime Minister* offers droll commentary on churchmen who will wear gaiters to garden parties but scarcely recognise a word of scripture.

The cultural trajectory of the Church of England across the twentieth century also brings the institution into a framework involving secularism. Before liturgical reform in the latter part of the century and the replacement of the universally used 1662 *Book of Common Prayer* by a variety of alternatives, the Church of England had spoken with a mostly uniform voice in its worship. As Melvyn Bragg points out, the Church of England was also where 'people went for guidance in their journey through life', and in doing so 'they received a not dissimilar range of messages' (Bragg 2006, 59). As the national Church, its public worship largely achieved national uniformity, a descriptor that can also be applied to British broadcasting, and the intentions of Lord John Reith in particular for the BBC to provide intellectual leadership matched by moral and tonal consistency. The historian of broadcasting David E. Morrison points to the collapse of this uniformity in the 1960s, and the loss of 'any overarching cultural meaning acceptable to society as a whole' (2009, 117). Morrison suggests that the fragmentation of the cultural assumptions underpinning British broadcasting occurred as the medium 'lost its claim to speak for an identifiable set of values drawn from cultural assumptions about Britain as a Christian nation' (2009, 117). Likewise, Bragg sees the Church as displaced by a 'new Church', the media, but a body devoid of a consistent message or essential meaning (2006, 59). Morrison marshals a number of landmark legislative and cultural changes including the Wolfenden Report and the subsequent decriminalisation of homosexuality for consenting adults in the Sexual Offences Act in 1967, and the changes brought to family and married life by the Divorce Reform Act in 1969. Morrison sees these 1960s changes as diminishing the authority of the Church and from there the diminution of cultural certainties in broadcasting. But Morrison's point needs further nuance. The Church of England has been subject to the forces of secularism but the Church and secular impulses are imbricated and even mutually reinforcing. As Morris points out, the notion that secularism causes a decline in belief and institutions is 'deceptively simple' (Morris 2003, 964). It is important to remember that rather than being passively subject to cultural changes, the Church actively engaged in major acts of social change, including deliberations about crime and sin that led to the Wolfenden report (Grimley 2009). Churchmen were decisive participants in landmark moments of social change, such as Bishop John Robinson's testimony in the trial about *Lady Chatterley's Lover* in 1960 in favour of its publication (Mews 2012). Churchmen made contributions that materially shaped secular changes, such as conceptualising the distinction between a sin and a crime, which proved to be an important distinction for lawmakers needing ways to end prosecutions for homosexuality without making it normative (Grey 2011, 90; Johnson and Vanderbeck 2014, 47).

Sociologists, historians, scholars of religious studies and demographers offer a range of interpretations of British secularism, many providing data showing the retreat of religious affiliation and observance, especially of the

Anglican kind. Census data as well as in-depth surveys of religion regularly mark a decline in denominational membership. The number of people identifying as 'religious' in some way, or believing in God, remained higher than people self-identifying as belonging to a denomination, but that figure too declined (Davie 1990, 404).

Genres

Tone and content bring a focus to another core theme in this study: genre. Religious broadcasting, while a legislative requirement for public and commercial television and guided by internal regulations, also defies definition. It is not enough to consider it as anything non-secular (Harrison 2000, 7). Broadcasting producers, particularly in the BBC's religious department, had traditionally been ordained clergy, although that tradition has now faded. Religious broadcasting has long held itself to a non-denominational approach as well as being educative rather than evangelising. The very lack of a stable definition explains why productions are diverse rather than canonical. In Part II of this book, the chapters are organised around genres. Across these genres, the Church is not a constant presence. However, considering genre enables a study of the way programme makers deliberately included the Church in the diegesis.

Limitations of the Study

For a study of the Church on television, one compelling limitation is the absence of the sound and image of many important broadcasts. Neither the BBC nor the independent companies introduced a consistent archiving policy until long after drastic purges of content had taken place. While the *Radio Times* and *TV Times* document the casts and timing of broadcasts, little survives of early television. Instead there are the 'ghost texts' (Jacobs 2000, 14). These are the memories of lost broadcasts, where the sound and image are gone but written traces remain. The survival rate for British television improves for the 1970s and after, but many programmes made before then are now accessible only as a written discourse (Jacobs 2000, 14). *Our Man at St Mark's* and *All Gas and Gaiters* are especially drastic losses from the archives of Associated Rediffusion and the BBC respectively; in both cases, only a few episodes survive to represent entire series. Very little remains of once popular non-fictional religious broadcasting such as *Stars on Sunday*. The losses raise major issues, in that interpreting

several years of programme making depends on using the remaining fragments. Thus it is unsafe to draw conclusions in case surviving episodes may
not be typical entries or wholly representative of the entire series but partial impressions can be supplemented by wider evidence.

Therefore, while this book is a study of the Church in a visual medium,
the written as well as the visual are key modes of interpretation. Our
approach will be that of interpreting the television programmes in terms
of both their production and their content, and placing them within a
framework built out of the documentary sources for the social and political history of the twentieth and twenty-first centuries. The content of television programmes form one source of analysis but there are also extensive
written records in archives of Lambeth Palace Library, the Church of
England Record Centre and the National Archives. These include formerly confidential notes, letters and reports that were inbound and out-
bound from bishops' palaces, rectories and government offices, including
correspondence with the postmaster general. Handwritten annotations
sometimes supplement the typewritten reflections. What the television
programmes suggest about the Church is based on a number of elements:
the content of the programmes themselves; contemporary historical
records; reviews of programmes in the trade papers and press; and production paperwork.

OUTLINE

Chapter 2 places the 1953 broadcast of the Coronation in a wider context,
not only of the BBC's earliest religious broadcasting but the way clergy
pondered the intersection of sacred religious events with the intrusive
electronic technology and the meaning they bestowed on the passive cameras as participants in worship. Chapter 3 fills out this context with the
Church's active participation in the shaping of broadcasting, the expansion to a second and commercial channel and Chap. 4 moves clergy out
from behind the scenes to in front of cameras and the ongoing, intentional
training undertaken by clergy to appear on the small screen. Chapter 5
considers the Church's coordinated responses to government and industry via the Radio and Television Council but charts the suave confidence
of the Council's engagement with the Pilkington report to its uncertainty
before Mrs Mary Whitehouse's purity campaigns.

In Part II and Chap. 6, a particular turning point is noted as coming in
the middle of the 1960s. Occasional appearances of clergy characters in

comedy and drama changes to the more regular, when first *Our Man at St Mark's* and *All Gas and Gaiters* opened up sustained plots involving the clergy. In Part II, the focus shifts from clergy being the drivers of television policy and debates to being the object of attention. Firstly, attention is given to drama, from the fantastic to the realistic and the elite to the quotidian. Landmark works in comedy in Chaps. 6 and 7, science fiction in Chap. 8, soap opera and period and crime drama in Chaps. 9 and 10 present different aspects of the Church. Finally, in Chap. 11, fiction and non-fiction converge in #Vicargate on *Newsnight*, a moment in the Brexit debate that brings together a long televisual history of the Church of England, vestiges of popular knowledge about the Church, and the nation's future.

REFERENCES

NEWSPAPERS, PERIODICALS AND TRADE PAPERS

Church Times

PRINTED SECONDARY SOURCES

Aldridge, Mark. 2016. *Agatha Christie on Screen*. London: Palgrave Macmillan.

Bragg, Melvyn. 2006. The Media and the Church. In *Public Life and the Place of the Church: Reflections to Honour the Bishop of Oxford*, ed. Michael Brierley. Ashgate.

Brown, Callum. 2000. *The Death of Christian Britain: Understanding Secularisation, 1800–2000*. Cambridge: Cambridge University Press.

Brown, Andrew, and Linda Woodhead. 2016. *That Was the Church That Was: How the Church of England Lost the English People*. London: Bloomsbury Continuum.

Cooke, Lez. 2003. *British Television Drama: A History*. BFI Publishing.

Cumper, Peter, and Peter Edge. 2006. First Among Equals: The English State and the Anglican Church in the 21st Century. *University of Detroit Mercy Law Review* 83: 601–623.

Davie, Grace. 1990. "An Ordinary God": The Paradox of Religion in Contemporary Britain. *The British Journal of Sociology* 41 (3): 395–421.

Grey, Antony. 2011. *Quest for Justice: Towards Homosexual Emancipation*. Random House.

Grimley, Matthew. 2009. Law, Morality and Secularism: The Church of England and the Wolfenden Report, 1954–1967. *Journal of Ecclesiastical History* 60: 725–741.

Hall, Gary. 2014. The Purpose of Cathedrals. *Anglican Theological Review* 96 (4): 727–736.

Harrison, Jackie. 2000. A Review of Religious Broadcasting on British Television. *Liberal Theology in the Contemporary World* 41 (4): 3–15.

Jacobs, Jason. 2000. *The Intimate Screen: Early British Television Drama.* Clarendon Press.

Johnson, Paul, and Robert Vanderbeck. 2014. *Law, Religion and Homosexuality.* Routledge.

Mews, Stuart. 2012. The Trials of Lady Chatterley, the Modernist Bishop and the Victorian Archbishop: Clashes of Class, Culture and Generations. *Church History* 48: 449–464.

Moran, Joe. 2013. *Armchair Nation: An Intimate History of Britain in Front of the TV.* Profile Books.

Morris, Jeremy. 2003. The Strange Death of Christian Britain: Another Look at the Secularization Debate. *Historical Journal* 46 (4): 963–976.

Morrison, David E. 2009. Cultural and Moral Authority: The Presumption of Television. *Annals of the American Academy* 625: 116–127.

Noonan, Caitriona. 2012. The BBC and Decentralisation: The Pilgrimage to Manchester. *International of Cultural Policy* 18 (4): 363–377.

Wallis, Richard. 2016. Channel 4 and the Declining Influence of Organized Religion on UK Television. The Case of *Jesus: The Evidence. Historical Journal of Film, Radio and Television* 36 (4): 668–688.

Wolff, Richard. 2010. *The Church on TV: Portrayals of Priests, Pastors and Nuns on American Television Series.* Bloomsbury Publishing.

Shaping the Medium

In Part I, we will see that aspects of British broadcasting that are now axiomatic were originally contested and uncertain. Should there be a second, then a third and fourth terrestrial channel? Should there be commercials? Should an additional channel be solely educational? These were areas of broadcast policy debate where the Church of England made authoritative contributions in the House of Lords, through its Radio and Television Council, and through close connections with key industry players. We can track these contributions through private correspondence and official testimonies. The role of the Church was not merely to shape the tone and content of religious broadcasting but to plan entire schedules for new channels and to traverse all manner of programme types. Here archival records, both secular and ecclesiastical, show where discussion between bishops, clergy and prominent lay intellectuals on one side, and government representatives including postmasters general and civil servants on the other, were the means for Church to participate in policy debates.

Being on Television Part One: Broadcasting the Institution

In this chapter, shaping the medium means endowing it and its technology with meaning and purpose, sacralising and even at times even anthropomorphising the technology and decisively influencing the tone and content of broadcasts. Archbishop Geoffrey Fisher, one of the key decision makers about the 1953 Coronation, will emerge across this chapter and those following in a guise hitherto unconsidered by his biographers or by historians of Church and state in the twentieth century, as a shaper of the growing medium. As sensed by Archbishop Fisher in 1953, television would shine glaring lights (literally and figuratively) on the sacred mysteries of the Church. In actuality, the 1960s was the first decade since the end of the war when church attendance began to decline and where instead of congregations seeing actual clergy in church, audiences saw fictional clergy on the small screen.

The Church Visible: Sound and Then Vision

John (later Lord) Reith, the general manager of the British Broadcasting Company and then the first director general of the British Broadcasting Corporation (BBC), placed God at the centre of British broadcasting. Former employees remembered an interviewing style that disconcerted and intimidated as Reith demanded answers to a key question: 'Did they accept the fundamental teachings of Jesus Christ?' (*Daily Mail* July 12, 2014). The question was the most important, sitting at the heart of Reith's

© The Author(s) 2020
M. Harmes et al., *The Church on British Television*,
https://doi.org/10.1007/978-3-030-38113-4_2

intentions for the BBC, his determination that it would inform, educate and entertain as a Christian institution broadcasting to a Christian nation. Lord Reith emphatically disregarded television's potential (McIntyre 1993, 209) but departed the Corporation by the end of the 1930s, by which time the BBC's engineers had experiments underway with both John Logie Baird's mechanical television apparatus and the Marconi electronic equipment. The story of early television has been well told by Asa Briggs (1995b, 479, 481), including the Corporation's decision to adopt the Marconi technology, driven by Marchese Marconi's own visionary enthusiasm for technology as he predicted, 'I can visualise the time very soon when television across the Atlantic will be very simple' (*Evening Telegraph* November 12, 1934, 5). Then there was the sudden shutdown of the fledgling television service when the Second World War broke out.

Post-war television was a mixture of variety, education and occasional drama. The BBC's Television Service broadcast a great deal of cricket, along with educational programmes and some light music. Part of the post-war mixture was also religion. On Christmas Day 1949, the BBC Television Service broadcast a service from the Royal Hospital Chapel, Chelsea conducted by the military chaplain G.V. Riley. Thereafter across the early 1950s Harvest Festivals, Evensongs, documentaries about historic churches, organ recitals and comforting talks by vicars before the epilogue brought the church onto the small screen and kept it there.

Around the time of the first mechanical and electronic experiments by Baird and Marconi (Briggs 1995a, 14), the Church of England was unsure about television. In 1928 (two years after Baird had demonstrated his apparatus) the bishop of St Alban's made a speech stating 'I make no secret of the fact that I view with great trepidation the coming of the day when by television my morning ablutions at St Albans will be reflected on a screen in New York for the entertainment of the American cinema public' (*Scotsman* March 13, 1928, 5). Other clergy reiterated his fears in following decades, if in less colourful terms. A year before the 1953 Coronation, the vicar of St Paul's in Warwick blamed television for causing anti-social behaviour when some boys broke the church windows with an air pistol. 'Such things, he said, were notorious for encouraging that type of offence' and the boys' previous good characters had decayed from too much TV (*Coventry Evening Telegraph* February 27, 1952, 5). Naughty boys also caused problems for the vicar of Holy Trinity in Attleborough, Nuneaton, whose choirboys walked out on strike after an argument with the organist. 'This is one of the unfortunate consequences of television' the vicar told a congregation whose service suddenly contained much less music than normal. He pinpointed the source of his choirboys' disobedience in their imitation of television. 'Recently there was a television play in which choirboys went on strike' he told the congregation (*Birmingham Post* March 12, 1962, 3). Looking at the television listings from the days before the incident, the naughty boys on television could have been either from *Billy Bunter of Greyfriars School* or *The Fifth Form of St Dominic's*, both on BBC Television in February 1962.

While a vicar warning against the perils of television becomes a trope, the medium also won converts. The Reverend Alan Holt, the vicar of Streetly, had called television a 'time waster and anti-social'. When his own parishioners clubbed together and purchased him a television set, his attitude softened, yet ironically, he also became living proof of his own warning. Now that he and his wife could watch the Goodwood races, the vicar admitted in a press interview that reading good books, writing sermons and writing the parish newsletter had all taken a backseat (*Birmingham Post and Gazette* April 30, 1958, 4).

The Coronation

These are small-scale and intriguing cameos of the churchmen and its clergy reacting to something new in post-war England. Where and when the Church's part in the revival and then expansion of the post-war television service becomes spectacular but contested is 1953, the year of the Coronation. The first mass television audience for a Church of England service: the 1953 Coronation of Queen Elizabeth II. The television broadcast of the 1953 Coronation of Queen Elizabeth II apparently provided a major impetus for the purchase of television sets and licences in post-war Britain and as having consolidated widespread television ownership in the British Isles. Although accurate figures are not possible for 1953, television historians suggest over 50 per cent of the population watched Elizabeth's Coronation and the television footage also appeared overseas (Crisell 1997, 75).

The broadcast of the Coronation is an aspect of early television that historians of the medium have told well, but the significance of this landmark broadcast and its focus on the established Church, is subject to debate. Did it actually cause television ownership to soar? It was an all-day event and papers everywhere provided the schedule from the start of the broadcast at 10:15 am outside Buckingham Palace to the close of broadcast at 11:15 pm with fireworks (see for instance *Motherwell Times* May 29, 1953, 9). Regional presses throughout Britain carried similar advertisements for television sets and licences, although the Coronation was not unique in being a vehicle to promote television ownership. Terry-Thomas's popular comedy series *How Do You View* (1949–1953) had earlier been a means to encourage consumer behaviour, as word spread about its appeal (McCann 2008, 61). Television retailers used Terry-Thomas's face to encourage purchasers. Sport was also a clear impetus for people to watch television, as was the funeral of George, VI; before 1953, millions of people had already been watching (Moran 2013, 72–73).

What is clearer is the technical leap forward the Coronation forced on television engineering inside and outside Westminster Abbey (in the parlance of the time, the people controlling the cameras and the rediffusion technology were engineers). Based on the experience of American technicians broadcasting Eisenhower's Inauguration, BBC engineers managed interesting and special shots, such as a zoom on Prince Charles as the crowning happened (Briggs 1979, 426). The technology televising the Coronation attracted admiration for the astounding statistics: 'there will be in action a total of 250 sound and television engineers....engineers of the General Post Office will provide at least 400 television and sound circuits. With some 800 extensions for microphones, cue lights so that commentators can be switched on smoothly... Some 80 commentary points will be installed along the processional route... Sound Broadcasting will be under control from the Head Verger's room within Westminster Abbey itself' (*Burnley Express and News* May 16, 1953, 8).

Social histories of the 1950s and histories of British broadcasting note as a conventional narrative that the Coronation made television sets and television viewing from the home more commonplace. Less familiar in academic discussion is the experience of television as mass participation in a sacred event. Some clergy took measures to transform the television experience into something sacred. The bishop of Chelmsford wrote to his clergy suggesting that 'where practicable', televisions should be set up in churches to allow people to feel they were participating in the events in Westminster Abbey (*Coventry Evening Telegraph* January 2, 1953, 1). He also instructed that no church should schedule anything that would conflict with the time of the Coronation broadcast (*Coventry Evening Telegraph* January 2, 1953, 1). One cleric took matters literally, spending months building a television set in his garden shed so his parishioners could see the Coronation (*Mercury and Herald* February 20, 1953, 5).

One of the 'stars' of the Coronation, Archbishop Geoffrey Fisher, had in 1952 declared that the world would be a happier place without television (Moran 2013, 74). Fisher exemplified the tension inherent at this time, where the Church received a wide audience but viewed television with distaste. In 1953, the BBC needed to overcome the reluctance of the Prime Minister, Winston Churchill, Fisher, and the Queen to get their cameras not just inside the Abbey but also inside the choir, where the main action took place. Simultaneously creative, technical and sacerdotal decisions brought the sacred onto the screen. There was a range of objections to the BBC's sustained pressure to allow the event to be broadcast. Churchill thought a broadcast would demean the event by turning it into theatre. Some suggested the technical aspects would be too challenging, that the lights would put the Queen under strain, or the cameras would capture any mistakes for posterity (Tossell 2013). Archbishop Fisher had sacerdotal concerns: what if people watching the Coronation were also drinking beer? (Balmer 2017, 62). In fact, Mass-Observation reports of working-class audiences watching the broadcast captured a range of irreverent comments including suggesting the Queen looked like she needed a 'quick one' (Örnebring 2007, 177).

Fisher emerges as a decision maker of importance. His distaste for the idea of televising the Coronation gave way to a positive sense that after all it had gone very well. He went as far as praising 'the marvel of television', and the fact that he 'had received letters of gratitude from all over the world' for the televised Coronation fuelled his generous comments (*Hastings & St Leonards Observer* June 20, 1953, 10). As the entire BBC recording of the service survives, it is possible to watch Fisher in action and sense that he thoroughly enjoyed himself. His powerful voice, the product of decades of experience as a public school headmaster and officiating and preaching as a clergyman, sounded impressive inside the Abbey and was a distinctive type of chanting and declaiming 'parsonical' voice. The episcopal biographer Edward Carpenter thought that Cosmo Lang had done a better job at George VI's Coronation in 'lifting a ceremony into a world of drama and mystery' in front of the cameras, but judged Fisher still presided with spiritual and interpersonal impact (Carpenter 1997, 509).

In many respects Fisher was also the most dynamic and visible participant in the ceremony; the BBC's camera angle during the crowning even meant that the back of Fisher's head blocked the view of the Queen. His part in the proceedings was larger and more important than the archbishop of York, other bishops, the moderator of the Church of Scotland or the representative of the Free Churches, and there were no Catholic dignitaries. The other lords temporal were simply a great mass of people. Even Queen Elizabeth II was more passive and silent than Fisher and was a recipient of actions such as anointing and crowning rather than an active doer of anything.

For Fisher, the Coronation was an extended moment of triumph. Epistemologically, it captured for a mass audience what Fisher knew to be the imbrication of the Church with the state. His careful planning brought onto the screen what the divinity professor E.C. Ratcliffe had already rhapsodised as the '*sub specie Christianitatis*', meaning the happy union in the English people of 'Sovereign, Church and People' (cited in Le Roy 2010, 118). Personally, it showed Fisher as a great man of the state, barely eclipsed in the proceedings by the Queen herself. If his positive views seem a turnaround from an earlier opposition, we can read them another way, including the positive impression made on him by his successful appearance. His engagement with television is an action aligned with the core priorities of his primacy. It is important to remember that Fisher became archbishop in 1945 with a clear identity bound up with an equally clear agenda. His reputation was as an energetic administrator whose brief was to modernise the Church of England. That reputation, as a practical man rather than a scholar or prophet, brought him to Canterbury instead of more intellectually esteemed contemporaries such as George Bell of Chichester (Chandler 2016, 126). Fighting against Germany in the Second World War had meant articulating what they fought against but also what the British were fighting for, in a positive sense. Ideas that emerged during the War ranged, says Philip Coupland, from the fantastical to the practical but they revolved around a common theme that postwar life would be different from the older world as people moved on and modernised. Fisher tackled a host of overdue reforms including to Canon Law and church finance, his actions taking place as a socially reforming Labour Government came to power with plans for social changes in welfare, education and health (Chandler 2006, 478). A modernising and energetic primate aligns with these broader national visions and Fisher engaged with the new medium as one aspect of the newer and more modern world that he wanted the Church to be part of.

A massive audience saw Fisher when he crowned Elizabeth II. It was far from being the last or only time television audiences would see him. A modernising archbishop was willing and able to step into the futuristic environment of the electronic television studio and to work with television engineers to make creative production decisions. Even that year, the Queen gave permission for the BBC to televise part of Mary of Teck's funeral, including the procession to Westminster Hall where Archbishop Fisher was waiting to receive the Queen (*Dundee Courier and Advertiser* March 27, 1953, 5).

SACRED TECHNOLOGY

Fisher's concern about appropriate decorum for broadcasting a religious ceremony, in fact the most glorious and important ceremony he would ever be involved in, can seem quaint now. However he was not the first and would not be the last person to ponder the nature of the interaction between a sacred act shown on television and people watching in their homes, and the technology in the middle mediating this encounter. As we will soon see, other clergy thought deeply about whether showing the sacred on screen turned an audience into participants and congregants or whether they remained merely television viewers. Then there was the electronic equipment itself, which seemed to be passively viewing events but in the eyes of theologians could be recast as dynamic participants, and could even be sacralised.

The Coronation marked not only technological but also theological advancement. Churchmen, producers and engineers collectively considered how the camera could participate in worship. Producers and technicians had already moved towards some understanding of this possibility of the television apparatus being almost anthropomorphised as an intrigued but respectful witness to the sacred. The Austrian producer and editor George Hoellering made *Message from Canterbury* in 1944, including footage of Archbishop William Temple preaching inside the war-damaged cathedral. Playing on the centuries of history of Chaucer's pilgrims making their way to the cathedral, an opening commentary described the act of filming as a religious pilgrimage, where 'here the camera comes like a pilgrim to see the life of its people and the Cathedral'.

In 1951 the BBC Television Service broadcast Evensong from Leeds Parish Church. The broadcast was significant for both churchmen and television engineers. For the technicians, the broadcast from within the church's gothic interior provided a good test of the capacities of their cameras and lights and the good reception for London viewers of the events in Yorkshire was a most satisfactory demonstration of the expansion of the Service and its signal strength. The churchmen, who on this occasion included the vicar of Leeds, the provost of Bradford and the church's precentor, found the television engineers and their equipment to have been discreet, barely intruding on the service. The van containing the outside broadcast remained unobtrusively out of sight. Inside, only the brighter than usual lighting indicated a television broadcast underway. Together, the churchmen and the engineers thought about the liturgical implications of broadcasting divine service and how viewers could interact with the congregation they saw on the television. One camera pointed at a copy of the prayer book so people at home could follow the service and join in if they wished. The vicar and provost also made a brief allusion to the television audience in their addresses, praying for them but also making clear that watching a church service was no substitute for attending one. 'You are only partially sharing in this service' said the provost, and 'you cannot completely worship God unless you take the trouble to bring your body to church' (*Yorkshire Post and Leeds Mercury*, October 15, 1951, 1).

Between them, the technical achievements in bringing services onto the screen and the theological reflections included in the broadcast from the officiating clergy are early statements of what would be recurring preoccupations and questions. Would televising church become a substitute for going to church? Were audiences in front of a television also congregants? The Evensong from Leeds was a less participatory type of worship that did not include the Sacrament of the Eucharist. Clergy also felt relief that the equipment could be discreetly used inside the church. Two years later, inside Westminster Abbey for the Coronation, there was a striking aesthetic contrast as the large and cumbersome lights and cameras peered out from behind gothic screens and pinnacles (Briggs 1979). This vast effort for the transmission of something sacred, together with contemporary responses, aligns the technical achievements with the sacred mystique of the church service. Part of the admiration was enabling participation in a religious ceremony. In previous coronations from the early Middle Ages onwards, the only participants were the people inside the Abbey. But now, the most important moment of the ceremony, when the archbishop of Canterbury showed the new Queen to the assembled peers and sought their acclamation, would be experienced in real time throughout the country. 'For the first time in history people in all parts of the British Isles will be able to acclaim their Queen at the same instant that she is, in actual fact, "shown" to them by the magic eye of the television cameras' (*Burnley Express and News* May 16, 1953, 8).

Excursus: Television Afterlives of the Coronation

The drama of televising the Coronation has also lingered in television consciousness and we will detour forwards first to 1977 and then to 2016 to consider two contrasting ways modern television revisited the Coronation.

The Princess Has Mounted the Archbishop

Twenty-five years after the actual Coronation, the comedy trio *The Goodies* offered their own highly irreverent portrayal of the monarchy, the government, pageantry and the Church of England in the *Royal Command* episode of their television series. In the 30-minute story, the royal family becomes bored by the usual Royal Variety show and demands more violent and drastic entertainment. They eventually participate in the show 'The Amazing Tumbling Royals on Ice', breaking every bone in their body and needing the Goodies to impersonate them when the Chancellor of the Exchequer decides to milk American tourists for more money by re-mounting the Coronation. The episode also speculated about what would happen if the royal family gained influence over television. As the royal family gains control first of the Royal Variety and then all broadcasting, religious programmes undergo a metamorphosis, with the royals' favourite equestrian pastimes inserted in all possible genres. Thus on *Stars on Sunday* the archbishop of Canterbury has to take the water jump on horseback, while Moira Anderson sings 'bless this horse' rather than 'bless this house'. Later in the episode, we see the remounted Coronation, which is set against the actual financial crises of the later 1970s and is accordingly shoddy. Cardboard cut-out choirboys and mannequins instead of actual visiting heads of states passively watch the proceedings and *Zadok the Priest* plays on a gramophone record. Then more horsing around happens when the archbishop of Canterbury is himself used as a steed by the man impersonating Princess Anne.

The episode is prescient in what it suggests of royalty's future relationship with television as it declined from the reverent to the boisterous. A further decade on from 1977, the BBC showed *It's a Royal Knockout!*, involving Princes Andrew and Edward and Princess Anne and the Duchess of York as team captains of celebrities performing humiliating and dangerous stunts to raise money for charity. Ivan Waterman and Daniel Roseman have since called the broadcast a 'watershed' moment for the monarchy, but in the sense of being a disaster that broke the spell of monarchy (*Independent* April 21, 1996). That spell had survived the lights and cameras of 1950s television and indeed flourished because of the televised Coronation guided by Archbishop Fisher's stern demands. *The Goodies* showed how, by 1977, the royal family, religious broadcasting and television culture were more mutually reinforcing and assimilated with each other as television favourites such as *Stars on Sunday* and the Newmarket racing merged, and their parody stretched to ludicrous lengths to show a matured world of royal and religious broadcasting.

Poetry Not Prose

The planning and broadcasting of the 1953 Coronation also came back to life and back to the screen in the Netflix drama *The Crown*, particularly the 2016 episode *Smoke and Mirrors*. The episode dramatised the tensions between the royal family, the government, the BBC and the press about televising the event. The episode highlights Prince Philip as the agent of change, a misleading account of the actual Coronation Committee, which under Philip's leadership had implacably opposed letting cameras any further than the quire screen (Moran 2013, 73). The episode weaves together a number of strands related to the broadcasting of religious ceremony. Geoffrey Fisher is one of the characters portrayed by an actor, and in a scene where the archbishop bears the news to the Duke of Windsor (ex-King Edward VIII) that the Duchess of Windsor cannot attend the Coronation, he is berated with the rhyme 'My Lord, Archbishop, what a scold you are. And when your man is down, how very bold you are. Of Christian charity, how very scant you are, You Auld Lang Swine, how full of cant you are'. The rhyme has actual historical provenance, having been devised to chastise Archbishop Cosmo Gordon Lang after he broadcast on the BBC following Edward VIII's abdication in 1936 and made comments condemned as needlessly uncharitable (Beakin 2012, 137; *Church Times* October 19, 2012; Grimley 2004, 189). In *The Crown* the broadcasting history associated with one archbishop comes back to life to become part of the fabric of drama of exclusion and exile preceding the Coronation involving another archbishop. In the 2016 drama, the actual history of broadcasting becomes part of a fictionalised encounter between two historical figures, in a deft weaving of the Church's experiences with broadcasting and the dramatisation of its history.

Smoke and Mirrors further weaves together the analogue sound and vision captured by the analogue television engineers of 1953 and the digital television making of 2016. On screen, historic television equipment is pressed back into service to recreate the recording and transmitting of the Coronation and the episode shows us footage on black and white monitors coming from the old Marconi cameras. On screen, actors portraying the BBC technicians and contemporary viewers including the Duke and Duchess of Windsor peer at the black and white monitors' 405 line transmission. Viewers of *The Crown* themselves watch these characters watching the Coronation. Supplementing that is what the high definition technology of 2016 can achieve, such as close-ups. The fictionalised recreation of the past, seen by characters in the diegesis on the flickering black and white monitors, interacts with what the viewers of 2016 see in the finished programme. In *The Crown*, audiences see a purportedly faithful recreation of the Coronation through the old technology mixed with the new. Archbishop Fisher's dawning awareness that the Queen's person in front of him is changed and sacralised after the anointing, and tensions between the Queen and Prince Philip about Philip bowing in homage are fictional extensions to the Coronation.

The cameras in 1953 showed events in blurry longshot and the cameras of 2016 show a high definition vision of the same, providing close-ups and reactions impossible in the earlier medium. The moment of the crowning itself is heady. Handel's Coronation Anthem *Zadok the Priest* grows louder and louder and the archbishop's sense of wonder greater as the crown descends on the young queen's head, and once in place the archbishop throws up his arms ecstatically. Watching from exile, the Duke of Windsor provides commentary not merely for the guests in his house but for the audience watching *The Crown*, remarking that the ritual, the music and the wonder of television together are providing 'poetry' rather than 'prose' to the watching population. The magic he sees on screen and evoked in *The Crown* distils the capacity churchmen found in the unblinking cameras to not only show but also participate in worship. The Coronation tends to overshadow other television events of the 1950s but it also has an intellectual and social context, as the clergy sought to understand not simply television's technical implications but more importantly its ontology: was it sacrilegious or was it a powerful means of reaching audiences? Was it appropriate to watch a television in a church or to watch a church service in one's home?

BROADCASTING CONTEXTS

The Coronation broadcast has generated these contrasting afterlives which found both the ludicrous and the sacred in what took place. Other contemporary broadcasts contextualised the Coronation. In 1953, the new bishop of Lichfield was sufficiently enamoured of television to invite a crew to capture parts of his enthronement in Lichfield Cathedral. On this occasion, reports of the interaction between the technology and ceremony are brash, suggesting not so much a happily discreet presence but a notable contrast between ancient rituals and the intrusive arc lights beaming down on the large congregation. There is also an early sign of awareness that television images, because of editing, could be manipulated and made to look better than reality. On the day of the enthronement it poured with rain in Lichfield and the new bishop, other bishops, hundreds of clergy, the lord mayor, and their wives, all elaborately dressed, were drenched. On screen however for the Monday evening newsreel on the BBC, the footage did not show the rain and the pomp and splendour looked better than it had for real (*Birmingham Gazette* October 24, 1953, 5).

Early broadcasts foregrounded other aspects of the Church. An informative 1956 documentary made on film investigated the Anglican monastic community at Mirfield, and in Christopher Mayhew's production, the film cameras peered daringly into an enclosed and spiritual world (*Motherwell Times* March 16, 1956, 6). Thereafter, the sober vision of documentary cameras continued to turn towards the Church from time to time, especially to illuminate social and welfare issues. The 1959 documentary *Building Afresh* examined pastoral welfare in post-war housing estates. *The Good, the Bad and the Indifferent* on Yorkshire Television in 1976 continued that trend in later decades, and surveyed the Church's social contribution.

The Church of England appeared on a grander scale the Television Service in July 1958 when the BBC broadcast the opening service of the Lambeth Conference from Canterbury Cathedral. The 'cast' on this occasion was the archbishop of Canterbury, hundreds of bishops, and the cathedral itself, with Richard Dimbleby providing a reverential and erudite description of the unfolding scene. Fisher had been available for a personal appearance and he was the focal point of a BBC special on the conference, taking questions from Dimbleby about the conference (*Coventry Evening Telegraph* June 25, 1958, 2). The next year, the construction of Guildford Cathedral was the subject of a *Meeting Point* documentary. This latter programme also testifies to the continuing expectation within the BBC that the Corporation staff would include Anglican clergy as being responsible for religious content. The producer of *Meeting Point*, John Elphinstone-Fyffe, was a chaplain who churned out a steady stream of ecclesiastical content, from documentaries about the Bible in Anglo-Saxon and Tudor England to programmes about Moses.

Especially so in the late 1950s, these broadcasts are part of a context where churchmen had some reason to feel positive about their Church. Archbishop Fisher was a vigorous and energetic leader, presiding over the expansion of the global Anglican Communion. Domestically, church-based activity such as parents enrolling their children in Sunday school and baptising their infants rose after the war (McLeod 2007, 62).

Yet television could compete. As noted earlier, a television folktale has it that *The Forsyte Saga* was responsible for killing off Sunday evening worship but the complaints about competition with Evensong predated that programme by at least a decade. The vicar of All Saints in Rockwell 'blamed Sunday evening television for the decrease in evening church attendances' (*Somerset County Herald* April 19, 1958, 4). There are some documented cases of clergy changing service times to suit viewing schedules, and even going further and having television sets in their churches, with an additional layer to the experience in having the officiating vicar also appearing on the small screen. The vicar of St Leonard's Church in Bilston changed his evening service time by half an hour and installed four television sets, so that his congregation could attend Evensong *and* watch a documentary made about their district in which the vicar himself appeared (*Birmingham Post* January 15, 1963, 6). A decade later the vicar of Craghead in County Durham changed his main service, because he found people were staying up late on Saturday nights as 'many of the best programs are shown in the late evening' (*Evening Chronicle* February 5, 1968, 7). These are impressionistic accounts of clergy responding to the inroads made by television but they span the country and cover decades.

Other clergy grappled with the theological implications of the medium and not always in negative terms. Daringly, the congregation of St Peter's Church in Belper, Derbyshire, installed several sets in their church and sat down to watch a service happening in Kew. St Peter's at the time had no vicar and, in an intriguing example of making do, a congregation of 500 people watched their former vicar officiating on television in another church, an eloquent interaction between religious fulfilment and the television. 'Some people thought the idea of television sets in a church sacrilegious but we explained the plan and most of them, I believe, turned up', said a churchwarden to a local reporter (*Birmingham Gazette* March 26, 1951, 1).

The connection between the medium, the technology and the church became even closer in some instances. In 1959 the curate at St Peter's Church in Crawley stepped down from his pulpit and made place for a television set there. As reported in *The Times*, 'instead of a sermon the congregation saw the first of the B.B.C. series of programmes for World Refugee Year' (November 30, 1959, 6). The significance of the action taken by the curate and his congregation is their joint experience of the medium as an active rather than a passive aspect of their worship. Instead of merely sitting and watching something, the Reverend Philip Turner intended that television during a service would be mobilised as a dynamic and participatory force in prayer and worship. The documentary 'made vivid and real the thing for which we are working and praying' and the congregation collectively 'moves straight from the television set to prayer, and from there, one would hope, to action' (November 30, 1959, 6).

In an extension from having televisions in churches, some church buildings became broadcast venues. After World War Two, the BBC and the Diocese of London found an innovative use for All Hallows London Wall. Like many other city churches, it was no longer needed for regular worship. Instead, the church became a television studio for broadcasting religious programmes, doing so in ways that ensured the eighteenth-century ecclesiastical interior remained intact and became part of the fabric of the studio and the broadcasts (*The Times* September 28, 1963, 5). All Hallows assumed a notable role as the venue for *Seeing and Believing*, a creatively formatted religious programme on BBC Television from 1960 to 1976 and the church-cum-studio played host to a range of character actors including Roger Delgado, Michael Gough, James Grout and Gwen Watford who enacted religious dialogues and participated in readings from scripture and religious classics.

SACRED TECHNOLOGY REVISITED

The interfaces between divine service, the building where it was taking place, the officiating clergy, their congregation and engineers remained a source of both concern and measured theological reflection. A few clergy developed their own confidence not just with interacting with the technology and crews but also in the theological integrity of bringing the Church onto television. Canon Bryan Green had (in terms of the age of the medium) early become an authoritative commentator on the Church on television, including the intrusion of technology into a church service. His reputation also made appearing with him on television seem daunting to other clergy. There were few other clergy as familiar as Green with television studios and their apparatus. He was an adroit user of all media. In addition to successful television appearances, he also wrote columns for *Woman's Illustrated* and in the press for a Birmingham newspaper (*Independent* March 20, 1993).

More than any other clergyman, Green reasoned through the sacerdotal, ecclesiastical, pastoral, technical and missional implications of the Church being on television. He was televisually literate, in particular aware of how the technology and apparatus of broadcasting could intrude if a service were broadcast and disconcert the minister but also how an effective partnership could be achieved by the clergy and congregation and the technical crew. Addressing whether or not services of Holy Communion should be broadcast, he acknowledged that 'I wondered whether it was possible for those who were taking part in the actual service so to forget the lights, the television cameras and all the etceteras that they could offer a genuine and spontaneous act of worship to God' (*Birmingham Daily Post* January 3, 1959, 17).

Green also considered the implications of having technology in the church which would allow the producer and director to mix shots, track, and zoom, and he wrote with a mixture of both wonder and pragmatic technical literacy of how 'I was particularly interested in the mobile camera moving up and down the centre aisle. Having made careful enquiries, I find that its work was done so simply and unobtrusively that it hardly disturbed at all the worship of the congregation' (*Birmingham Daily Post* January 3, 1959, 17).

In time, other clergy also became confident appraisers of the interaction between ancient gothic structures and modern technologies. Confidential notes prepared in the bishop of Manchester's household in 1966 advised on the television coverage planned for an ordination service on Trinity Sunday the next year. The bishop agreed to allow a live broadcast from inside his cathedral, and the meeting raised important points about the use of technology inside a medieval building. As noted, the cathedral 'is a wide and open building, but the Ordination has to take place in the Choir—and this means a certain amount of "enclosure and cramp". The Chapter is well aware of the need for effective co-operation with the TV Authority concerned'. Meanwhile, another local church had already proved perfect for broadcasting, as a meeting participant noted of St Philip's Salford: 'I visited the Church and realise that it is admirable for TV. There are spacious galleries and a very open Sanctuary and movement is easy in chancel and sanctuary'. (CERC ACCM/VP/SEC/9). An expert eye could be wielded, which could see with precision where and how an older building could be a suitable venue for the cumbersome technology.

The combination of modern technology with an ancient building not designed to be a broadcasting venue was not always so happy. Across the 1950s and into the early 1960s, we see both success and failure as technical crews and churchmen worked together to bring services to the screen. In 1961, the dean of York Minster slapped a one year ban on all television cameras from entering the Minster 'owing to a certain amount of damage' caused to the medieval fabric of the cathedral during the broadcast of wedding of the Duke and Duchess of Kent (*Stage and Television Today* June 29, 1961, 9). Despite the dean's annoyance, other clergy found television cameras and a congregation could happily occupy the same physical space. Broadcasting both ordinary services and grander affairs such as royal weddings soon become commonplace. After the Kents' wedding in 1961, Princess Alexandra's wedding to Angus Ogilvie in Westminster Abbey in 1963 took place in front of television cameras. Ten years after the Coronation and the negotiations then over what was too sacred for the cameras to capture, the use of the technology continued to be moderated by decorum and religious scruple. While the wedding appeared on television, the technicians worked with the stipulation that 'the television cameras will not be tracking the faces of the bride and bridegroom until after the service' (*Liverpool Echo* April 5, 1963, 1).

Despite occasional controversies, Green could report on positive experiences with BBC technicians. As a churchman with a widespread reputation for missional expertise, his views on the evangelical potential of the medium carried weight and reassured other clergy that the sacred and the technical could happily come together. Green's comments are a significant behind the scenes glimpse of the Church and the television crew preparing and working together. That includes rehearsing in the church with the clergy and congregation and the creative and technical decisions made on the spot about where and when to place emphasis during the broadcast (*Birmingham Daily Post* January 3, 1959, 17).

The broadcasts of religious occasions also kept pace with developments in television technology. Originally Pathé and Movietone film cameras captured great occasions such as the enthronements of the archbishops of Canterbury. As patterns of cinema schedules changed and the once familiar concatenation of B film, news reels, advertisements and cartoons and the A film disappeared, so did Pathé and Movietone. The BBC instead broadcast significant religious ceremonies in their entirety and contextualised them with a wider array of programmes, such as an in-depth interview with Michael Ramsey broadcast on *Panorama* (June 26, 1961) on the eve of his broadcast enthronement in Canterbury. However, their place and appeal were contestable rather than certain. Ramsey's enthronement in 1961 conflicted with Wimbledon and consequently Associated Rediffusion and Associated TeleVision pushed Ramsey's enthronement to late night and broadcast edited highlights (*Daily Mirror* June 23, 1961, 11). However, the independent channels did show their commitment to Ramsey's enthronement by putting his face on the cover of *TV Times*'s June 25th edition. Inside the listings of the magazine, an article boasted of the technical achievement of the ITV crews in bringing the ceremony onto television and the service also became available for international transmission. Although not as large as the BBC's engineering achievement at Westminster Abbey in 1953, the technology in 1961 included an impressive 'one mile of cable and half a mile of scaffolding' as well as ten cameras to cover the ceremony inside and outside the cathedral. The *TV Times* matched discussion of the technology with a piece on Ramsey himself, giving a personal insight to his working methods and personal life, including anecdotes of what it was like moving from one episcopal palace into another. Archiepiscopal enthronements continued to keep pace with and reflect changes in the medium. In 1975, the enthronement of Donald Coggan was the first to be broadcast in the newer medium of colour television (*Birmingham Post* January 24, 1975, 2).

Televising church services also meant understanding the recalibration of the concern that television was a competitor. That competition had meant the beguiling small screen in general would keep people at home rather than in church. Canon Green, in reporting on the experience of a successful broadcast of an actual church service, now introduced a different note. Could television, by broadcasting services, keep people away from church by making it possible to participate vicariously from their sitting rooms? Green thought not, suggesting instead that both studio-based discussions and televised services could be mutually reinforcing, for 'if evangelism is to be properly done we must show to others what it means to worship as a Christian' (*Birmingham Daily Post* January 3, 1959, 17). In the next decade, clergy responsible for devising religious broadcasting and inculcating industry-standard levels of professionalism and presentation took these points further. The Reverend Paul Wigfield, the Anglican Assistant Director of the Churches' Television Centre, discussed in writing the sort of content that could best fill up the hours available for religious broadcasting, proposing that documentaries rather than broadcast services best served the Church's purpose. 'Why should this be so?' he asked. 'I think that's because although many people have lost interest in going to church, they still have an interest in religion', and documentaries provided a means to provide answers people had about it. (CERC ACCM/ VP/SEC/9). The intention of religious broadcasting therefore was not evangelising but at least providing the opportunity for the interested but not religious to remain informed about aspects of the Church's activities.

Some clergy also remained technically literate. The Reverend Lorys Davies, vicar of Moseley, revealed himself as being so when drawing a series of parallels between envisioning Christ and making television. In a 'theme for the day' column in the *Birmingham Post* he described how the term 'vision on' was parlance in the television industry for indicating that transmission had started. He then considered that while the producer and director play essential roles in the form and character of the transmitted programme, 'a good deal depends on the receiver. Technical faults may give a distorted picture. Even when the picture which reaches the set is that decided by the director, much depends on the attitude of the individual receiver'. From there, Davies worked his analogy into a meditation on the biblical verse 'How blest are those whose hearts are pure; they shall see God', in which Christ is a broadcast vision, and people are the receivers or viewers of that vision. These comments are in fact remarkable in the cross-over the vicar finds in the creation, broadcasting and reception of television and the eyes of faith seeing God (June 25, 1975, 6). Not only was the Reverend Davies literate in the terminology and technology of television, but he provided the theological meaning in its broadcasting.

Many of the broadcasts discussed in this chapter were 'big picture' occasions in line with the Coronation, where the cameras were directed at large numbers of people participating in corporate worship. To achieve that had included working out and through the use of technical equipment in a sacred space. However a further strand of the Church's shaping of the medium is in close up, both literally and figuratively. Clergy stepped into television studios to be interviewed but possibly also intimidated by the experience and to say things they later regretted. These broadcasts lead us to actions the Church took to hone skills for up close religious broadcasting. The next chapter moves to examine the smaller scale focus on individuals.

References

Newspapers, Periodicals and Trade Papers

Birmingham Daily Post
Birmingham Gazette
Birmingham Post
Birmingham Post and Gazette
Burnley Express and News
Church Times
Coventry Evening Telegraph
Daily Mail
Daily Mirror
Dundee Courier and Advertiser
Evening Chronicle
Evening Telegraph
Hastings & St Leonards Observer
Independent
Liverpool Echo
Mercury and Herald
Motherwell Times
Scotsman
Somerset County Herald
Stage and Television Today
The Times
TV Times
Yorkshire Post and Leeds Mercury

ARCHIVES

CHURCH OF ENGLAND RECORD CENTRE (CERC)

ACCM/VP/SEC/9

PRINTED SECONDARY SOURCES

Balmer, John M.T. 2017. *Foundations of Corporate Heritage*. London: Taylor and Francis.
Beakin, Robert. 2012. *Cosmo Lang: Archbishop in War and Crisis*. London: I.B. Tauris.
Briggs, Asa. 1979. *The History of Broadcasting in the United Kingdom: Volume IV Sound and Vision*. Oxford: Oxford University Press.
———. 1995a. *The History of Broadcasting in the United Kingdom: Volume I: The Birth of Broadcasting*. Oxford: Oxford University Press.
———. 1995b. *The History of Broadcasting in the United Kingdom: Volume II: The Golden Age of Wireless*. Oxford: Oxford University Press.
Carpenter, Edward. 1997. *Cantuar: The Archbishops in Their Office*. A & C Black.
Chandler, Andrew. 2006. *The Church of England in the Twentieth Century: The Church Commissioners and the Politics of Reform, 1948–1998*. Boydell.
———. 2016. *George Bell, Bishop of Chichester: Church, State, and Resistance in the Age of Dictatorship*. Wm. B. Eerdmans Publishing.
Crisell, Andrew. 1997. *An Introductory History of British Broadcasting*. London: Routledge.
Grimley, Matthew. 2004. *Citizenship, Community, and the Church of England: Liberal Anglican Theories of the State Between the Wars*. Oxford: Clarendon Press.
McCann, Graham. 2008. *Bounder! The Biography of Terry-Thomas*. London: Aurum Press.
McIntyre, Ian. 1993. *The Expense of Glory: A Life of John Reith*. London: HarperCollins.
McLeod, Hugh. 2007. *The Religious Crisis of the 1960s*. Oxford University Press.
Moran, Joe. 2013. *Armchair Nation: An Intimate History of Britain in Front of the TV*. Profile Books.
Örnebring, Henrik. 2007. Writing the History of Television Audiences: The Coronation in the Mass-Observation Archive. In *Re-Viewing Television History: Critical Issues in Television Historiography*, ed. Helen Wheatley, 170–183. London: I.B. Tauris.
Tossell, David. 2013. *The Great English Final: 1953: Cup, Coronation & Stanley Matthews*. ebookpartnership.com.

DISSERTATIONS

Le Roy, Doris. 2010. Anglicanism, Anti-communism and Cold War Australia. PhD diss., Victoria University, Melbourne.

CHAPTER 3

Being on Television Part Two: Broadcasting the Individual

A television studio in the 1950s or 1960s was awe-inspiring and intimidating. The studios themselves were like large barns. Hot lights shone down from the lighting grid and enormous Marconi electronic cameras, with teams of crewmembers operating them and their sound apparatus, stared impassively at the people in front of them. Apart from the occasional use of film inserts and telecine, early television was live from a studio, and for those involved it was a nerve wracking and intense experience.

Clergy stepped into this space with increasing frequency from the 1950s, especially to broadcast about religion in the 'God slot', the quarantined space in the schedule for religious content. This chapter traverses the 1950s to the 1980s and explores broadcasting of individual clergy, especially bishops, highlighting them as individual performers. The reasons to bring clergy onto television, the opportunities and pitfalls of appearing, and remedial efforts to create star television performers are considered as ways the Church shaped the medium, along with explorations of Anglican broadcasting efforts in the United States and Australia to provide comparative examples.

Where this chapter begins in the 1950s is when television was largely new to most people. The BBC was constructing the gigantic new Television Centre in White City to create state-of-the-art television facilities. Actors were discovering that theatre acting was inappropriate for the smaller scale television and were learning to adjust, and both the BBC and the newer

© The Author(s) 2020
M. Harmes et al., *The Church on British Television*,
https://doi.org/10.1007/978-3-030-38113-4_3

independent companies needed to train engineers and technicians. The Church discovered that its star performers also needed training to acclimatise to the studio.

BEING ON TELEVISION

Why did the clergy appear on television? Sometimes it was because television producers found them interesting in their own right. One instance is Dr Hewlett Johnson, the 'red dean' of Canterbury (from 1931 to 1963) and who throughout the Second World War and post-war eras attracted wide levels of controversy for his sympathetic interest in the Soviet Union (Kirby 2012, 136). Granada Television's *Head On* profiled Johnson and the broadcast was a full hour of guests including Johnson and his wife and ranging from the bishop of Southwark to the Secretary of the British Communist Party (*Coventry Evening Telegraph* March 7, 1962, 2). In being so controversial he was an attractive subject for television.

A related but entirely different example of why programme makers put clergy on the screen is the Church's then leader, Geoffrey Fisher (who to his chagrin was sometimes mistaken for Hewlett Johnson). We have already encountered Fisher as the guiding force behind the 1953 Coronation, including setting in place the limits on what the television camera could and could not show. We will return to him later as a vigorous debater in the House of Lords about the Television Bill and when studying the use made of the Church of England in science fiction, owing to his startling comments on atomic warfare.

Fisher reveals himself as a major but neglected player in the maturing of post-war television in documentaries, news, comedy and science fiction. For Fisher, television meant having the opportunity to offer sustained observations and defence of Church doctrine. By the late 1950s, he could be sure that a television studio would be a respectful and respectable environment. It was not until 1965 that Kenneth Tynan said the 'F' word on television, and even that remained a startling one-off for years afterwards (Yates 2011). Before then, Fisher was sure of a decorous environment from which to speak authoritatively to the nation.

To an extent overlooked by his biographers, Fisher emerges as a major figure in 1950s and 1960s television, including as an interpreter of royalty, monarchy, the Empire and religion to mass audiences. One implication of Fisher's appearances was to bind the Church and the State into a unified televisual entity. For example, before the Coronation, Fisher participated in a broadcast called *What is the Crown* (May 25, 1953), explaining to viewers the heritage and structure of the service they would soon see.

From seeing his surviving appearances, it is also clear that Fisher got better at television. In 1950, he participated (for film not television) in a Movietone News report on his visit to Australia and New Zealand. After footage of his reception in Sydney, Fisher appeared on film from his study at Lambeth Palace and delivered a lecture from his notes. His demeanour was that of the stern headmaster, an impression reinforced by the wood panelled study, the desk and the notes. Ten years later, footage survives of Fisher's appearances on ITN news. By now, the notes are gone, and seated in the studio rather than the study, an altogether more relaxed and twinkly archbishop appears. His use of the medium transcended boundaries. He appeared on British television and on television in the United States when travelling there (Hein 2008, 59). In 1958, Fisher appeared on an ITV interview programme and took the opportunity to defend the Church's teaching on divorce and the H Bomb (*Birmingham Post* June 30, 1958, 1).

Other occasions gave Fisher an opportunity to show his comfortable demeanour before the cameras, combined with rapid but clear diction and a sharp wit. In August 1957, the peer Lord Altringham had called the Queen's manner of public speaking a 'pain in the neck' in *The National and English Review* (Shawcross 2002, 75). Fisher appeared on the late night ITN bulletin, speaking direct from London Airport (as it then was) after returning from the United States. Like many commentators ranging from the prime minister of Australia to most leading articles in the English press, Fisher was appalled by Altringham's comments, but in attacking them he also slipped in a small joke. Altringham had said the Queen's public speaking was like 'a priggish schoolgirl, captain of the hockey team, a prefect, and a recent candidate for Confirmation'. Fisher, grinning broadly, riposted 'if I might dare say so, I'm not sure that the thoughts of a young girl at aren't on the whole more pleasant thoughts than the thoughts of Lord Altringham many years after his confirmation!'.

In April 1961, again at London Airport, Fisher recorded an interview with the journalist Brian Widlake, explaining his plans for retirement. Fisher again showed he was relaxed enough in front of a camera to make a joke. 'Will you speak in the House of Lords?' asked Widlake. 'That depends entirely on what the House of Lords is speaking about!' Fisher shot back.

Fisher's biographers and historians of British cultural and television heritage have rarely considered Fisher's appearances before the camera, but for 1950s Britain they offered astonishing vistas and diversity and visions that were publicly impressive or domestically intimate. For Movietone, he first appears in the war-damaged but still impressive Canterbury Cathedral, surrounded by bishops, politicians and royalty when enthroned as the archbishop. In 1945 the Movietone cameras also showed him in his sitting room at Lambeth Palace, doing a crossword (the 'harder they are the more he enjoys them', the voiceover informs viewers), knocking out his pipe in the fireplace and gazing at portraits of his mother and father. A BBC outside broadcast unit again captured the domestic image of Fisher in *At Home* in November 1955, when both Fisher and Mrs Fisher appeared from Lambeth Palace. Mrs Fisher also became a competent broadcaster for occasions when a homely female voice was suitable, such as a talk for the epilogue on March 28, 1954, when she spoke on Mothering Sunday about the importance of mothers.

A notable characteristic of Fisher's archiepiscopate was his travel; to an extent unmatched by his predecessors, Fisher travelled to dioceses in Africa, America and Oceania to meet Anglicans and world leaders. His biographers note his travel, but what is also significant is that the cameras went with him. For British viewers, Fisher's black-clad figure in gaiters, apron and homburg became their guide to far-flung locations. He pointed to the torrential waters of the Devil's Cataract, which connected North and South Rhodesia. He walked through the streets of Rome on his way to meet the Pope, sailed into New York Harbour, and enthroned an archbishop in Tanganyika amongst other globetrotting activities captured on camera. Both film and television cameras followed him around the world. Before meeting the Pope in 1960 (an occasion the Roman Catholic Church would not allow to be shown on camera), the BBC accompanied Fisher to Rome and broadcast a programme from inside the Vatican on the significance of the first meeting between Canterbury and Rome in 600 years (*Coventry Evening Telegraph* December 1, 1960, 2). The commentaries also introduced Fisher the man. Even if seen in a grand setting such as a cathedral, viewers were reassured: 'Dr Fisher's geniality quickly dispels any remoteness one might expect from one in his high office'. It is also clear that Fisher enjoyed hamming it for the cameras, such as standing outside a church in Dar-es-Salaam brandishing a Massai shield and rungu.

Fisher's travelling and his willingness to before on camera was emulated by his successors, but they only continued what Fisher had started. Fisher also brought a wider religious vista onto the small screen. His global travels were usually to provinces in the Anglican Communion, about which he could preach and speak and which he could interpret.

The presentation of Anglican Churches around the world sparked televisual imaginations in curious ways. *The Little Wonders*, a 1964 episode of crime and fantasy series *The Avengers*, is an outlandish television iteration of the global Anglican Communion. The members of a crime syndicate called 'Bibliotek' carry out their business disguised as respectable clergymen in gaiters, frock coats and silk hats (Phillips 2018, 138) but the global reach of their crime syndicate is possible because of the global spread of the Church of England. They carry out their activities under such aliases as the Bishop of Winnipeg, the Vicar of Toowoomba, the Archdeacon of Bangkok and the Dean of Rangoon. The clerical identities are bogus, but this family of clerics in early 1960s drama follows oddly but creatively in the trajectory of Fisher using television to introduce British audiences to exotic but Anglican locations around the world.

Television also became a key medium for Fisher to explain the Church to the nation. That could include lecturing on the Coronation ritual, explaining the creeds, or discussing the Lambeth Conferences, as he did on a visit to the Liverpool Associated Television studios to appear on *Whose World*. The next night the BBC hosted Mervyn Stockwood, the vicar of Great St Mary's in Cambridge, who agreed to appear and answer the questions of young people about the Church of England (*Liverpool Echo* June 28, 1958, 6). The broadcast was on a Sunday evening, the traditional time for the BBC to show a religious show.

One further contribution Fisher made to the Church was his choice of bishops; Fisher was himself largely preoccupied with administration and Canon Law (De La Noy 1993, 237), and his choices of clergy for bishops rested on forthright administrators not theologians. In the television age, that initially meant a bench of bishops who could speak unflappably and without complexity and ambiguity on television. Fisher did not want the university theologian Michael Ramsey as his successor and it is notable that with Ramsey, a less confident and more ambiguously academic approach prevailed in archiepiscopal broadcasts. That is apparent because, notwithstanding his deficiencies as a broadcaster, broadcasters kept inviting him onto their shows. Even before his enthronement, Ramsey was wanted for television and appeared on *Panorama* on the eve of his enthronement in Canterbury. Another early appearance was on ITV's *Three Archbishops* with the interviewer Kenneth Harris from the *Observer* (*Birmingham Post* June 5, 1961, 4). In keeping with talk-based formats of the era, an appearance meant a sustained and detailed discussion, which in Ramsey's case also meant revealing his eccentricities of speech and appearance. What Ramsey said in interviews was of a depth and detail without concessions to a television audience. Both interviewer and guest presupposed that a detailed discussion of liturgical and prayer book reform, ceremonialism and ecumenism would be understood by a wider audience.

Ramsey's archiepiscopate is significant in broadcasting history in showing an Anglican leader as a mainstream television presence but also one where programme makers critically and at times caustically reviewed his performances, his ease or otherwise with the technical environment of the television studio and a gradual improvement in his appearance. A note in BBC files, written from the perspective of someone with expertise in how a person came across on screen, sadly noted how Ramsey had 'a curious habit of grunting, nodding, and blinking'. Producers also knew that technical and editing processes could control any unfortunate mannerisms, whereby 'His hesitations can be edited out and he can be made to sound more fluent' (quoted in Chadwick 1990, 122–123).

Ramsey and Fisher are instructive contrasts. Fisher on screen was brisk, concise and headmasterly. Ramsey was scholarly, making rambling explanations of theological abstractions and asking interviewers such as David Frost if they were keeping up with him, as though they were befuddled undergraduates. In 1968 he took a 'crash course' on dealing with a television camera and learning how to interact with this static item (Chadwick 1990, 123).

Ramsey's biographer Owen Chadwick also pinpoints an uneasy sense as to whether an archbishop should even be on television and the question of whether something sacred should be overexposed. That suggestion, though, is out of time. Fisher had already authoritatively demonstrated that an archbishop could safely appear on television. Indeed, it was hard to keep Fisher away from the camera. The transcripts of Ramsey's television appearances are coherent, whereas the combination of words, sound and vision was less so, as Ramsey wriggled, grunted, gurned and spluttered his way through interviews. These traits are on display in surviving footage from Ramsey's 1966 appearance on the *Frost Programme* to discuss the Dead Sea Scrolls and evidence for the historical Jesus. The question was not so much if archbishops and television were an appropriate conversation but if Ramsey made a sacred office look less effective under the glare of a television studio than had Fisher. Robert Runcie similarly failed to master television, and his son, the writer James Runcie, described his appearances on television as 'particularly bad, where he came across as weak and unsure' (quoted in Carpenter 1996, 372).

Ramsey would also find that television could dangerously intrude into internal Church controversies, especially if a bishop inexperienced with the medium made loose comments on live and unedited television. Ramsey gradually became better at his television appearances, but in an unguarded comment during the public controversy over John Robinson's *Honest to God* he criticised his fellow bishop on television and called the book 'utterly wrong', and thus opened to public view the spectacle of bishops arguing with each other (Webster 2016). John Robinson was a far better television performer than Ramsey and the church historian Hugh McLeod describes him as 'seldom far from a TV studio in the 1960s' (McLeod 2007, 228).

The fallout from these public arguments surfaced in odd places on television. To step ahead for a moment to the science fiction and fantasy later chapters is to see distillations of Ramsey's fears. He had feared that Robinson's book would confuse in their minds the 'Imagery of God held by Christian men, women and children'. One of the oddest signs of the confusion is a moment in the 1971 *Doctor Who* serial *The Dæmons*, in which an alien criminal the Master is impersonating the vicar of a West Country village. While posing as the Reverend Magister, the Master also infuriates a member of his congregation with the languid observation 'The soul as such is a very dated concept', and by arguing for a more 'existential' understanding of the traditional theology. As we have noted elsewhere (Harmes 2017, 181), the moment is a curiosity, suggesting an alien criminal has made time to read some examples of the trendy works dubbed Southbank religion (Peart-Binns 1990, 157). The scene also dramatises exactly what Archbishop Ramsey feared would happen if clergy were influenced by Robinson, and upset and confused the 'ordinary' churchgoer (McGrath 1997, 108).

The controversies Robinson unleashed leaked through into other television productions. *Penda's Fen*, an oblique and enigmatic drama from 1974 portrayed a scholarly country rector who has come to hold, and is writing about, unorthodox views on biblical scholarship. David Rudkin's screenplay in charged with resonances of unorthodoxy. A classroom discussion on Manichaeism, an oriental dualistic religion that was an early rival to Christianity (and deemed heretical), precedes a scholarly discussion between the rector and his son on the meaning of paganism. The script's choice of language also plays with the impulses realised by Robinson and the fraught level of debate it engendered, when the rector defensively writes in his manuscript *The Buried Jesus* of being blasphemous that it was 'worse that the name of this life-enhancing revolutionary Jesus should now be dangled like a halo above a sick culture centred on authority and death'. The vicar's manuscript asserts multiple layers of fabrication in the Gospels and again is a distillation of the controversy about *Honest to God* that television amplified. Robinson's smoother television performances outclassed Ramsey's and in retrospect Ramsey also regretted the vehemence of his own reaction to *Honest to God*.

Make Me a Star: Pupil Parsons and Charm School

The appearance of the archbishops of Canterbury in broadcasts testifies to an emerging trend, which is the appearance of not just clergy but senior clergy appearing on television to discuss matters of note, doing so either with polish or with awkwardness. During a debate in Church House in Westminster in 1961, clergy had lamented that 'we are getting a little tired and irritated by being occasionally depicted as affected, ineffectual and unable to understand the simplest human problems' (*Birmingham Post* November 9, 1961, 6). But there was also the possibility that the clergy had only themselves to blame, with one speaker in Church House saying 'There is still a little too much of the parsonic voice on the air and on the screen. We want a wider selection of clergy and laity available for radio and television' (*Birmingham Post* November 9, 1961, 6).

A number of implications emerge from these views. If some clergy complained that television mocked them, others had sufficient insight to realise that the clergy made themselves easy targets by appearing on television with an inadequate understanding of what they would look and sound like when mediated into people's homes via lights, cameras and television sets. In 1958 the Church Assembly (a forerunner of the General Synod) accepted the logic of statements made by George Reindorp that more people watched television than attended church, and accordingly clergy needed the skills to appeal to television audiences. Canon R.L. Hussey from Salford agreed but also indicated that not all clergy were suitable and some were downright 'impossible'. 'We have got to try to find clergy who speak with a natural voice' rather than the fruity parsonical voice, was his advice (*The Times* June 19, 1958, 6).

It must not be forgotten what a pitiless medium 1950s' television was. Television sets were bulky items but had tiny screens; those appearing on the box were seen in unedited close up. For all public figures, the development of television technology and then television formats such as the interview and discussion programme meant that specific communication skills became essential. Some took to the new medium with grace and aplomb. While little actually survives of 1950s television, enough remains to show how well or how poorly public figures learned to perform on the small screen. The few surviving episodes of *Animal, Vegetable, Mineral?* (1952–1959) show the archaeologist Sir Mortimer Wheeler's easy grace and authoritative charm in front of the cameras, compared to some of his shyer academic colleagues such as Vere Gordon Childe. Possibly the most notorious instance of an unsuccessful transition to the small screen was Anthony Eden's broadcast during the 1956 Suez Crisis. While an event of compelling seriousness, one eccentric way people remember the crisis is because Anthony Eden's moustache became invisible when in front of the BBC lights and cameras, accentuating his apparent weakness and ill health. As told in Quentin Falk's collection of strange television moments, Lady Eden had to whip out her own mascara to darken the hair on his upper lip (Falk 2014).

Into this pitiless space stepped a few courageous churchmen aside from Fisher, who were prepared to be a television presence. Canon Charles Crowson, a Midlands vicar, experimented with a new medium and a new identity when he accepted the invitation to become the first 'TV padre' on Independent Television (*Birmingham Post* April 4, 1957, 1). His slot was only a two-minute reflection, but around it swirled a number of sudden debates and concerns, including attempts to foretell the type of religious content that would work on the new medium and efforts to re-align the reputation of Independent Television. Canon Crowson admitted a degree of nervousness and bafflement as to what he was actually going to do in his two-minute slot. 'Exactly how we shall do it, I don't know. It is an experiment, and obviously I have been chosen as the guinea pig' (*Birmingham Post* April 4, 1957, 1).

Even for two minutes, the possibility of being the TV padre made Canon Crowson consider possible changes to message and content that would be necessary to broadcast Christianity. 'We must get away from the ordinary form of service. I am convinced that anything that is out of the ordinary in the presentation will attract attention.' What the Canon delivered has not survived in the archives, but his willingness to think that being on television meant changes from the ordinary to the different is an early sign of clergy grasping the potential of television.

From the other side, the Canon's participation was valuable to the Independent Television executives. Having an Anglican priest in their schedule gave a touch of class to their company. That was a particularly sensitive issue for Independent Television, which was a newcomer and perceived in some quarters as tawdry. Far from it, argued the Controller of Television, who complained: 'It is a misconception that we descend to strip-tease and blue jokes, and people do not realise that in the more serious things of life such as religion we are doing more than B.B.C. in the Midlands' (*Birmingham Post* April 4, 1957, 1).

By 1957, making television was new for the independent companies and still relatively new for the BBC. Reputations and a competing urge to be seen as quality and tasteful made the Church useful. How therefore did churchmen adapt to the new medium and become more professional rather than uncertain and experimental? Dawning awareness that television was expanding into more channels and into more homes registered with clergy who wished to become proficient television performers and who saw the medium as both a challenge and a possibility, where the standard of performance and appearance would need to be lifted (Green 2011, 290). Its possibilities, according to the Reverend L.G. Tyler, an Anglican clergyman who served as advisor to the Associated British Corporation (ABC), was how clergy used television for 'the ventilation of moral and social problems'. As a result, 'People who were right outside any contact with the Church are beginning to be interested' (*Birmingham Daily Post* April 17, 1959, 4). The view is a contrast to those more often encountered where the Church and television met, and the possibility seemed to be the loss of congregations to the lure of the new medium.

One ecumenical effort saw Roman Catholics, Free Churches and the Church of England undertake a type of finishing school for television performing. Plans for this 'charm school' were underway by November 1958, when the bishop of Manchester, who was also the chairman of the Central Religious Advisory Committee (CRAC), and the MP Sir Eric Fletcher, a prominent Anglican layman, announced its inauguration. According to Fletcher, the clergy would learn 'the technique of television', such as 'how to write scripts and the art of appearing before cameras' (*The Times* November 19, 1958, 12). Surviving accounts of what happened in 1959 indicate a vigorous 'vetting' process to find the right calibre of performers and then the week-long courses they trained in. According to the *Daily Mirror*, aspiring clergy went through 'stringent TV camera tests at private closed-circuit auditions at ABC's Birmingham studio' (April 17, 1959, 7).

Inside a studio, clergy sat at a table, with a large Marconi camera and its operators looming over them.

It is worthwhile considering in more detail what they were attempting. By 1959, the BBC had lost its broadcasting monopoly, meaning that the training of these 'pupil parsons' was ecumenical industrially as well as religiously. While the commercial company ABC was hosting the event, one of the trainers was the BBC's head of Religious Broadcasting, Canon Roy McKay, and the clergy graduating from their training, were free to appear on any network. More channels meant more opportunities to participate in religious broadcasts. The somewhat ramshackle technicalities of post-war television were in turn giving way to slicker and more polished broadcasts in drama and in non-fiction (Thumim 2004, 121) such as *What the Papers Say* (on Granada from 1956) and *The Brains Trust* (on the BBC from 1955). What is noteworthy therefore is the realisation of some clergy to adapt to the newer standards and increased professionalism of the medium and to become performers.

The reactions of both the clergy and the media yield important insights. The clerical point of view situates the television training in a wider context of the Church seeking to lift the standard of its communication. Almost coterminous with the charm school came the establishment of a 'college of preachers', chaired by Donald Coggan the bishop of Bradford. The college, a loose gathering of experts and trainees doing a course rather than a formal institution, sought to raise the standard of delivery and theological content of Anglican sermons (*The Times* June 3, 1960, 9). Also from the point of view of the clergy, their willingness to audition, learn and present themselves to the camera in the charm school indicates a level of professional insight into the importance of the new medium. The media reporting on their efforts characterised their actions within what amounted to a series of show business clichés such as a 'star was born'. According to the *Daily Mirror* the standout performer at the auditions was the Scottish episcopal bishop Edward Easson. He not only had a confident television manner and natural talent, but he had the looks to match and according to the report bore an uncanny resemblance to movie star Yul Brynner. The writer couched the report in a gushing tone about how the bishop 'made an immediate impact on everyone who saw him. He was so completely at home in front of the TV cameras and he is so like Yul Brynner!'.

The clergy who participated the in-house camera auditions were then put through their paces in an intensive five-day course. The *Daily Herald* picks up the story at this point, again with the Yul Brynner look-alike from

Aberdeen. We learn that among the skills acquired by the clergy was the importance of getting their make-up right before appearing on screen (as per the disastrous Eden broadcast during Suez). Looking like Yul Brynner of course meant that the Bishop of Aberdeen was totally bald and his picture in the make-up chair accompanied the story of him 'getting tips from TV make up girl Jean McKenzie which may take him to stardom on millions of television screens' (May 8, 1959, 3). The make-up tips were part of what the paper described as a 'school to teach churchmen the way to hold a TV audience'.

The *Coventry Evening Telegraph* took a more serious tone about the 'school' and displayed local pride in the selection of two ministers. It soberly reported that ABC, which had a weekend franchise and therefore a particular interest in Sundays, had committed to lifting the standard of the content and presentation of religious talk programmes (*Coventry Evening Telegraph* April 16, 1959, 12). It also emphasises the seriousness of the enterprise. To maintain the clergy's dignity, the test broadcasts were private, but the ABC's executive level viewed and seriously critiqued them and provided feedback to the clergy. The Anglican Church was sufficiently committed to send two bishops, the bald bishop of Aberdeen and the suffragan bishop of Middleton.

It is possible to follow some of the successes of the 'charm school'. Some clergy became closely associated with the medium and a small number of clerical identities could be reconfigured around television work. The Reverend Edward J. Parkinson became known in the press as the 'TV parson'. Parkinson was a missioner and an evangelist. He had completed the 'charm school' and had mobilised television as a means of reaching large audiences (*Belfast Telegraph* February 2, 1959, 5). Clergy who were naturally adept at being on television were effective communicators through other channels.

While Parkinson was the 'TV parson', the Reverend George Reindorp was known as the 'Church of England television broadcaster' and from the mid-1950s had been keenly interested in using television for religious broadcasting (Crozier 1958, 181). His profile on the BBC Television Service was high, including as a panellist on the *Mainly for Women* discussion programme, as a preacher from televised services in his parish church of St Luke's Westminster, and then in Southwark Cathedral, where he was provost, and as an interpreter of both the Gospel and modern social problems in shorter slots such as the Epilogue and *Viewpoint*. In addition to television work, Reindorp had a flair for communication across media.

He stringently trained his curates to be good preachers and wrote accessible works interpreting doctrine and the Church, such as *What About You?* (1956) and *No Common Task: An Outline of a Parish Priest's Job* (1960), that put his name and face into wide circulation.

The charm school's efforts also lived on into the following years. Lord J. Arthur Rank, a teetotal Methodist, put his material support behind a 1961 effort by the BCC to run courses for clergy to be on television. Rank provided the studio and the equipment. Clergy from the Anglican and Free Churches then learnt not only 'the techniques of the media, but to try to find out what part of the Gospel message can effectively be conveyed through these media' (*Birmingham Post* May 21, 1960, 6). This effort, therefore, was not identical to the ABC's 'charm school' of 1959, which had emphasised appearance and technique. Here, with Lord Rank's support, knowledge of how to look good on television combined with serious thought as to what parts of scripture were most readily suitable for broadcasting.

Lord Rank also intended to give a solid institutional foundation to these efforts to ensure continuity and the Churches' Television Centre (CTVC) provided technical facilities and training. A brochure for the facilities in a converted country house in Bushey noted the three Marconi cameras in a '3 camera closed-circuit TV lay out with control desk and monitor racks, tele-cine and twin video tape recorder, with an 8 way sound channel, transcription decks and tape recorders'. Lord Rank's generosity had provided up to date technology and more was on its way, including a 16-mm film unit. (ACCM/VP/SEC/9)

The Centre was ecumenical, not exclusively Anglican, although the Anglican clergy participating in the training course noted a peculiarity of the Church of England's engagement with and understanding of television by the early 1960s. In short, and ironically, they knew very little about religious broadcasting on either the BBC or ITV. The BBC in particular had a 'God slot' on Sunday evening, at precisely the time when parish clergy were unable to watch television. Canon Bryan Green, chairing the courses, wrote of this irony: 'It has always seemed to me singularly unfortunate that the main religious programme on a Sunday is at 7 o'clock, when ministers are at their evening services' (*Birmingham Post* May 21, 1960, 6). The course therefore built not only skills but also basic familiarity with what religious broadcasting looked and sounded like for the part of the population, the clergy, who knew less about it than anyone else.

Green's observations testify to an emerging type of broadcasting. Green recognised this type of programming as comprising 'televised religious programmes which are aimed at drawing those outside towards the Christian Faith' (*Birmingham Daily Post* January 3, 1959, 17). More efforts were made to give a professional gloss to clerical broadcasts. In 1962 the Church of England's RTV, chaired by Bishop Cockin and run in practical terms by the energetic David Skinner, held a two-day Radio and Television Conference. In reality the conference was all television with no radio, and reflects the reality of the Council itself which just two years into its existence was preoccupied largely with television. Skinner's organisation drew together clergy and industry professionals for two days of work at the Church's TV Centre. Professionals including the Reverend Douglas Stewart, the assistant head of Religious Broadcasting at the BBC, Penry Jones, ABC's Religious Advisor, and Gordon Reece, a religious content producer for Associated Television each did a demonstration a five-minute presentation before the cameras. They also offered studio practicals and there was an Audio-Visual Aid Display and 'advice from the staff on tape-recorders, film and film strip projectors, and non-projected visual aids'. Cumulatively the two days would allow the presenters to be in a studio, de-mystify its technology, and see other clergy who were broadcasters demonstrate how to be on camera (ACCM/VP/SEC/9).

The Specialists

The schools and conferences had ambitions that extended beyond clergy looking and sounding good and encompassed building up a commentariat with specialist areas. David Skinner dubbed his conference the 'Specialists' course', signalling the intention of building up a body of Anglican clergy who would be ready and able to offer both news and information before the cameras and provide 'responsible, specialist information'. 'Specialist' carried another meaning in this context (CACEC/SEC/10). In 1962 when the Council was planning the Conference, Bishop Cockin wrote to David Paton stating that the 'specialists' conference' was 'of particular importance' and was part of a considered broadcasting strategy that realised 'the most effective way of presenting the Christian faith to the general public is not so much by talks and discussion as by programmes which illustrate the Church actually at work in one or other sphere' (CACEC/SEC/10).

The specialists therefore were clergymen from the Youth Council, the Overseas Council and others who could show different aspects of the

Church's activity. The same intention continued to inform the Church's formal and organisational efforts to produce television-ready clergy. The training had not met its intended purpose by the next year. Cockin, who had become the chairman of the Council at Archbishop Fisher's direct request because of his specialist insights into broadcasting, found 'our greatest weakness as a Church consists in the fact that we have got no comprehensive survey of the men and women in various parts of the country specially competent' for broadcasting (CERC CIO/RTV/1).

For Cockin, strategic development included planning for broadcasting not only on religious programmes but also on other subjects, and his future planning entailed building up and knowing who the specialists were. These efforts did ensure continuity. In 1970 the latest Television Training Course took place in November, still under the financial patronage of Lord Rank's Foundation for Christian Communication and the CTVC, or the Churches' Television Centre. The training programme still comprised a mixture of seeing and hearing from experts, touring a working television studio and participating in mock-interviews, which were then played back for appraisal.

The rise of the specialists resonated in negative ways through the wider Church. A hint of envy registers among some clergy about how religious broadcasting had been almost a closed shop for a few smooth-voiced and well-trained clergy. There was after all only one 'TV parson' and only a few such as Canon Green who could engage with the medium on its own terms, as a technologically alert participant in a broadcast.

The work of the CTVC continued from the 1960s into the 1970s and attracted the interest of senior Anglicans as offering them important resources. The Centre itself continued to offer courses that merged the theoretical with the practical. In November 1970 the latest batch of clergy received their instructions for the Television Training Course. Their bundle of notes and instructions included tips such as 'Be as natural and relaxed as possible. Both the microphone and the television camera are quick to reveal artificiality and tension' (ACCM/VP/SEC/9). The course went deeper and offered 'as much background about the place of the mass media in our culture as is possible in the brief time available' (ACCM/VP/SEC/9).

At the same time, awareness that the Church had to engage with television professionals more widely is also apparent. Extensive planning notes survive in the private papers of Archbishop Donald Coggan for his large-scale television broadcasts. These included three special episodes of *Seeing and Believing* in 1975, planned by the Rev. R.T. Brooks, an Anglican clergyman who was a producer in the BBC's Religious Broadcasting Department. Correspondence between the BBC and Lambeth Palace swapped planning ideas. The camera scripts for the broadcast, which contain not only the spoken content but the technical direction for the camera crews, provide evidence of Coggan's assiduous preparation for a complex broadcasting occasion and his ability to interact with the outside broadcast crew, follow prompts, follow his cue, and deliver to screen alongside a cast of actors, singers and presenters (LPL Coggan 6).

The Church of England's leadership remained actively involved in planning broadcasting involving individual clergy throughout the 1970s. In February and March 1977 a trail of correspondence between Church House, Westminster, the bishop of Portsmouth, the archbishop of York and the recruitment officer in the diocese of Durham was in train, attempting to mobilise support for the Church's engagement with external television companies. The recruitment officer reported hopefully on a meeting with R. Maxwell Deas, the head of religious broadcasting at Tyne Tees Television. An interplay of different expectations informed the discussion. On one level, its offers the reminder that both the BBC and the IBA continued to receive input from their Anglican religious advisors, with Stephen Purvis, the diocesan recruitment officer, hoping that the Reverend Colin Still, the recruitment secretary at Church House, could see if the 'religious advisors to the TV networks might have been prepared to actively encourage this venture' (ACCM/VP/SEC/9). The Reverend Still in turn mobilised at the episcopal level, and sought help from the archbishop of York and the bishop of Portsmouth (then the chairman of the ACCM) to write to Maxwell Deas encouraging him to proceed to make programmes that the Church could use for recruitment purposes. Meanwhile the Church's Information Officer mobilised Wakefield, another bishop. Collectively the Church's intention was to encourage Tyne Tees to make one or more programmes that could then be cannibalised for the Church's own use, as a programme could 'provide some useful visual-aid material, which could be harnessed to recruitment' (ACCM/VP/SEC/9). Overall they suggest in microcosm the Church's engagement with television, from the expectation that the intervention of one or more bishops may impress a producer, to the role of the specialist advisors, the efforts to gently shape the content, as Colin Still politely suggested to the bishop of Portsmouth that they were looking for positive programmes.

Excursus One: The Church on American Television

The early broadcasts by clergy on television were not uniquely British and it is worthwhile looking further afield to developments in other broadcasting contexts when clergy not only appeared on television but also actively and creatively shaped the medium. American religious broadcasting has benefitted in major ways from the oratorical and broadcasting skills of many evangelical preachers and American network television established and early consolidated the place of the preacher on screen. Before that, some clergy had harnessed radio as an effective means to reach beyond their physical churches. One such was Dr Norman Peale, a long-standing minister of New York's Marble Collegiate Church whose media impact extended from radio broadcasts in 1935 to attracting tycoons such as Donald Trump to his church in the 1980s.

The Federal Communications Commission obliged the post-war American television networks to include religious content in their schedules. Both *The Hour of Decision* (1951–1954) and *The Billy Graham Crusade* (1957–1959) presented the famous evangelical preacher. Roman Catholic perspectives were provided by Bishop Fulton J. Sheen in *Life Is Worth Living* (1951–1957). Sheen's broadcasts and personal appearances caused sensations including when he visited Britain and tens of thousands saw 'America's television bishop' (*Yorkshire Post and Leeds Mercury* April 4, 1953, 5).

The Episcopal (or Anglican) Church in the United States was and is numerically small but has a high profile. Thus it was that alongside Graham and Sheen, a third successful religious broadcaster of the 1950s was Dr James Pike, who hosted the *Dean Pike* show from his study in the close of St John the Divine Cathedral in New York and sometimes from within the cathedral itself.

Pike was a university academic, then the dean of St John the Divine and finally the bishop of California. Pike's later career in both the Church and the media was colourful to the point of being controversial. Before dying mysteriously in the Palestinian desert in 1969, Pike had numerous times faced charges of heresy and eventually left not only his position of Bishop of California and but also the Episcopal Church (Stringfellow and Towne 2007, 18, 197). He was also immortalised in the science fiction writer Philip K. Dick's 1982 novel *The Transmigration of Timothy Archer* (Dick 2010, 134). The existential Anglican bishop who was the title character was an analogue of Bishop Pike and his controversial theology.

The suggestions of unorthodoxy that swirled around Pike's career in the Church also make sense of his style of broadcasting. Graham preached with massive evangelical fervour. Bishop Sheen lectured and even had a blackboard on the studio set. Pike, however, discussed, debated, questioned and doubted (Wolff 2014, 84). Later in this book, we will consider the extent to which Anglicanism's reputation for 'believing everything and nothing' reflected its television presentations, or was even a product of them. For now, it is notable to consider Pike's American contribution. On a visit to Britain in 1966, Pike featured in the press in terms of his brilliance as a television performer and furthermore one who used the medium to expound radical views and court controversy. He 'has plainly said that he does not believe that a belief in the literal virgin birth for Jesus Christ is essential for Christian faith... He is a strong supporter of family planning and contraception' (*Birmingham Post* March 5, 1966, 7). There is an insight to that assessment in Pike's reception when he was described as the American version of the 'Bishop of Woolwich', meaning John Robinson, the author of *Honest to God*.

For the moment, to remain with Pike, it is instructive to consider the complex interplay in his appearances between controversy and tradition. On one level, Dean Pike appeared on screen in ways semiotically coded as traditional. Little footage survives of his programme but some shows him striding across the lawns outside his cathedral vested in cassock, surplice, tippet, bands and academic hood. He presented from inside his study like a scholarly gentleman of leisure and sometimes from within the gothic beauty of St John the Divine. But there were sweeping and diverse intellectual discussions beneath the traditional surface. His guests included Ivy League professors, religious scholars from different faiths, atheists and sometimes his own children. Topics were avant garde for 1950s' television, such as race relations and the Civil Rights movement, freedom of religion, and secularism (Wolff 2014, 85).

Excursus Two: The Church on Australian Television

Like Pike mobilising the medium with flair, confidence and success, another cathedral dean made a considerable impact on early television. Television came later to Australia than to Britain and the United States. When it did arrive in 1956 to Sydney and 1959 to Brisbane, it broadcast to a country that retained political and cultural sympathies with the mother country. Prime Minister Robert Menzies was an ardent monarchist. While

Menzies was not himself Anglican, the Church of England in Australia was the largest Christian denomination in the country, at least in nominal membership (Rayner 1962, 280) and one clergyman saw its potential and achieved success on the fledgling medium.

William Baddeley was the dean of St John's Cathedral in Brisbane from 1958 to 1967. He was the natural son of a French singer and the half-brother of Angela Baddeley and Hermione Baddeley, both famous actresses, the latter especially so for her appearances in *Brighton Rock* and *Mary Poppins*. When he died in 1998, the *Independent* obituarised him as 'the epitome of the worldly West End Anglican priest' with a rich and melodious speaking voice (cited in Holland 2006, 76). He also was appointed to the cathedral in Brisbane in an era when the Church of England in Australia still drew many of its senior clergy from England and at the same time many performers on Australian television either were British or aspired to sound British (McKee 2001, 72).

Baddeley was a pioneer in both format and medium. On Australian television he became a TV host and led a monthly show *What Do YOU Think?* on Channel 9. His format was simple and the Dean answered questions sent in advance by his viewers. The church historian Jonathan Holland notes Baddeley's 'flair for communication, good looks, charm and resonant voice', attributes which made him a popular preacher in his cathedral and a successful television host. An odd but telling anecdote of Baddeley's success as a television host is that his decision to wear half-moon glasses on the air led to a run on this design among optometrists (Holland 303).

Baddeley was not a lone Anglican clerical presence on Australian screens. Channel 7 devoted an entire programme to the Church of England called *Anglican Magazine*. Some of the earliest Australian television broadcasts included worship, such as the 1956 service marking 100 years of responsible government in New South Wales (*Church Chronicle* LXVI, 790, 1956). The Australian Broadcasting Corporation televised services from St John's Cathedral, starting with the Christmas service in 1959. However, Baddeley shone as a star performer.

Importantly, Baddeley's television success was not simply a product of natural charm or good looks. Baddeley's own comments on the medium make clear he worked on a carefully considered theory and approach to broadcasting, as a channel of religious interaction. According to Baddeley, as a clergyman on the screen he was taking advantage of a mass medium that enabled individual communication. His obituary in *The Times* recalled:

'He considered giving personal guidance to individuals to be of far greater value than dealing with them *en masse*' (cited in Mackenzie-Smith 2008, 329). For Baddeley, television was a mass medium but one where viewers felt they had been addressed individually (Mackenzie-Smith 2008, 329).

Baddeley also took keen professional and technical interest in television. He wrote about the medium in the diocesan newsletter (*Church Chronicle* LXIX, 823, 1959). He insisted on his own broadcasts being of high quality and recognised that television was a form of propaganda reaching deep into people's lives. He was the chairman of the Anglican TV committee (Mackenzie-Smith 2008, 330). It is tempting to think of Baddeley's efforts in this realm as indebted to a theatrical upbringing and actorly instincts for communicating with an audience, not least as Baddeley caused a storm in secular domains such as the race track and on game shows. However, personal comments and public statements reinforce Baddeley's shrewd awareness that religion on the small screen would be competing with other more secular topics but that the medium was also distinctively expressive and influential. Apart from some such as Bryan Green and George Reindorp, it is also hard to find such a developed and successful approach to broadcasting among his contemporaries back in England.

Trial by Television

Unlike Baddeley but like Pike, television was a place where clergy could make controversial statements. English clergy appeared on television because they could be newsmakers themselves when they were prepared to be controversial. One example is from a 1957 edition of *Panorama* with Richard Dimbleby interviewing the Reverend William Weir, the rector of Kirton (*Evening News* October 7, 1957, 9). Weir was newsworthy because he had officiated at the wedding of not only a divorcé but a divorcé who was also a clergyman and he had incurred the displeasure of Archbishop Fisher and the Convocation (*Lawton Constitution* September 23, 1957, 9).

The willingness of bishops to speak out on controversial topics also meant television placed churchmen in unusual configurations and juxtapositions. In 1962, Donald Coggan, the archbishop of York got more than he bargained for when he complained publicly that the pop singer Adam Faith 'tells youngsters that the meaning of life is sex, the propagation of the species….he tells us nothing about the life hereafter, or why we are here at all'. In response, the BBC cancelled its normal Sunday evening religious broadcast and brought Faith and Coggan together to debate sex, life and the hereafter (*Birmingham Post* January 25, 1962, 1). Adam Faith treated the interview as a serious opportunity to ask questions about belief, whereas Coggan was determined to seem 'right on' by moving the conversation onto sex, including assuring viewers that 'I'm not one of those who belong to the generation who thought it was a sort of smutty thing that you only talk about hush-hush'. The guise of the progressive bishop seemed unconvincing to some viewers and the *Guardian* soon parodied Coggan with the 'right on' bishop of Twicester, who advocated 'rocking and rolling' (Sandbrook 2015).

Alternatively, bishops could be startlingly authentic. A 1960 television interview with Dr Cuthbert Bardsley the bishop of Coventry on *Meeting* seemed uncomfortably revealing. The interview piqued the interest of the television correspondent of Bardsley's local paper, who wrote with considerable televisual literacy about what he saw, including 'intimate and incisive' camerawork, perfect for a one-on-one interview in which the bishop talked intimately about his childhood, his father's early death and his formative experiences as a young clergyman (*Coventry Evening Telegraph* December 12, 1960, 10). Some of his own clergy criticised the bishop for the appearance for being in competition with his own denomination as the broadcast clashed with Evensong. Then there was the concern that the bishop was unusually revealing. Bardsley's response, which he repeated in a sermon the evening after the broadcast, was 'with 41 million people who do not come to church, do you not think that we ought to go out and meet them?'. His answer reiterated the point made by George Reindorp, but added a further reflection overlapping with concern that there was a bit too much of the parsonical voice on the screen. Bardsley explained he had not only chosen to be on television but to talk on a personal level because 'people regarded the parson as somebody quite unnatural', so therefore people should 'invite him into their homes and get to know him'.

Bardsley's response toyed with different levels of meaning. As a clergyman who notably seized any and all opportunities for evangelism (Beeson 2003, 202), television was seen to be one such tool, and the notion of being invited into the home positioned television as an intimate and domestic medium. Bardsley also pre-empted what was later taught as sound television practice to clergy participating in training with the CTVC. Notes disseminated by its director Leslie J.M. Timmin in 1970 advised: 'Always imagine you are talking to one, or at the most, two people in an average living room. You have been invited into their home'. The advice was partly to help settle nerves and make being on television less daunting but also to ensure the clergyman on television came over as a vicar visiting a parishioner.

Clergy who were particularly involved with the mass media gave further intellectual coherence to these ideas. The Reverend Paul Wigfield, the Anglican Assistant Director of the Churches' Television Centre, saw the possibility for an interaction between the 'electronic parson' on the television screen and the flesh and blood version. Acknowledging that no amount of polish or rehearsal could make a 'talking head' on the small screen the same type of intimate experience as a home visit, the one could interact with and reinforce the other. 'Yet, opportunity also knocks, because the unanswerable "talking head" of the previous night's electronic parson on the Epilogue might have said something that can well be followed up by the visiting minister' (CERC ACCM/VP/SEC/9).

Bardsley therefore sought to turn a television appearance into an opportunity for intimate engagement; in a later decade, the bishop of Durham, David Jenkins, offered complex thoughts on the resurrection and virgin birth that opened a storm of controversy that endured throughout his episcopate. Accounts of Jenkins' television appearances bring together an interplay of ideas about the Church and television, including the possibility of the former exploiting the latter, the intersection between a physical pulpit and electronic ones, and the way a senior ecclesiastic could assume a specific televisual identity. Thus it was that Jenkins became in television parlance the 'doubting bishop', and as such an exploitable commodity in television.

Curiously, in earlier decades and before his combative relationship with television in the 1980s, Jenkins caught the attention of Bishop Cockin of the Church's Radio and Television Council who had earmarked him as a rising talent who would make a useful future member of the Council (CERC CIO/RTV/1). He was also known as an unambiguously left-wing bishop, a circumstance registering in popular culture in the short-lived comedy *Hell's Bells* (1986), a vehicle for Derek Nimmo to play a clergyman. In this series, he was the conservative cathedral dean coping with a new socialist bishop.

Wider events ensured Jenkins' profile remained high. Questions in the House of Commons about the possible ordination of women to the priesthood included 'if the unfortunate day comes when women are ordained, they will at least be ordained by Bishops who believe in God?', asked of Sir

William van Straubenzee, the Second Church Estates Commissioner (*House of Commons Hansard* June 25, 1984, vol. 62, col. 679).

Jenkins' appearance in 1984 on *Credo* came prior to his consecration as the bishop of Durham and a major fire in York Minster caused by lightning and attributed in some quarters to God's anger. The television episode proved to the first indication of a controversial television trajectory. Jenkins himself records the sense he felt of needing to adjust not a message but a manner when appearing on television. Jenkins swiftly realised that not what he said but how he said something would need to be changed to work in front of the camera. Like other clergy in earlier decades who became technologically literate and realised that being on television meant effective interaction with cameras and lighting equipment, he soon noticed that 'lighting kills the twinkle in the eye. The television camera gives the illusion of familiarity without the face-to-face encounter' (Jenkins 2003, 32).

According to the trade paper the *Stage*, the Tyne Tees Television producer Paul Black rejoiced in his cleverness in getting Jenkins on television over Easter to express doubts about the physical resurrection. 'It won't do our viewing figures any harm', he said shortly after Jenkins appeared on Tyne's show. Black was also especially proud that 'this is the first time ever the BBC used my programme in the opening slot of the 9 O'Clock News (*Stage and Television Today* April 6, 1989, 17). Like Fisher some decades earlier, Jenkins broke free from the confines of the 'God slot' and began to reach a wider television audience through more diverse television appearances. Jenkins could say once and to millions what would have been heard by a few had he spoken from a physical pulpit. His ecclesiastical and televisual identities therefore became complex, even contradictory, as the 'doubting bishop' was also the cause of immense popular discussion of Christianity, making him 'one of the greatest evangelists in history', according to the producer Paul Black.

The comment is hyperbolic however television now could also make or break ecclesiastical careers. By appearing on television and becoming known with a specific controversial identity, it was out of the question that Jenkins could ever become an archbishop. In 1990, the little-known bishop George Carey became the new primate. The Jenkins controversy prefigures the impact of another cleric who made an uneasy transition from scholarly debate at Oxbridge, where nuance and subtlety were expected, to the harsh glare and simplification of television. Rowan

Williams' 2008 speech to Temple Foundation did not say that Sharia Law should be introduced as a parallel jurisdiction in British law. In the media, however, that seemed to be exactly what he had said and the resulting international furore reportedly shook Williams although it was largely detached from what he had really said. Once again, ideas that were complex rather than clear created a level of controversy that the archbishop was unable to control (Cranmer 2008, 4–5). Jenkins' contemporary, Canon D.W. Gundry, knew both worlds, as he came from academia but wrote professionally for the *Telegraph* as their church correspondent. He therefore could comment authoritatively that what Jenkins could get away with saying as a 'donnish gadfly' would not work in the wider world, especially not on television (*Telegraph* July 10, 1984, 16).

Jenkins's comments caused an authentic crisis in the Church's association with the state. Apart from the questions in the House of Commons, he met with protests against his consecration, including one vicar in Essex soliciting over a thousand letters questioning Jenkins' beliefs (*Telegraph* July 10, 1984, 16). Clergy in his own diocese formed an Evangelical Fellowship to coordinate public statements questioning the Bishop's faith in traditional teachings (*Telegraph* October 1, 1984, 1).

The controversy also drew in the wider episcopate, showing them as susceptible to media manipulation and allowing television producers to pit bishops against each other on television. Jenkins' original controversial comments were made on the April 29, 1984, edition of *Credo*. A follow-up episode on June 24 that year got first bishops and then the programme's editor into difficulty. It featured the canvassed opinions of other Anglican bishops about doctrine, views which when broadcast pitted other bishops against Jenkins and suggested they attacked his doctrinal orthodoxy while also sounding inane and simplistic. The episode subsequently drew complaints from the archbishop of York that the researchers for London Weekend Television obtained the interviews via deception and distorted the bishops' responses, meaning the bishops underwent 'trial by television' (*Telegraph* August 31, 1984, 12).

As the television service expanded from the 1950s onwards, the participation of clergy behind the scenes as advisors to the BBC and the independent companies remained consistent. In front of the cameras, clergy, both senior and humble, appeared with regularity. For some, gloss and poise came courtesy of charm school training, but training and infrastructure could not preclude controversial and uncontrolled content. A one-on-one discussion or an address to camera merited the same theological reflection as broadcasting a service and clergy pondered its missional and evangelical potential. Television also came to participate directly in clerical careers and Church-state relations, with some clergy like Geoffrey Fisher appearing on the small screen as one of the greatest men in the British Empire but David Jenkins as the evangelist of doubt. Appearances on television were simultaneous with the growth of the service and in the next chapter we turn back to clergy behind the scenes as players in policy debates about the future of the medium.

References

Newspapers, Periodicals and Trade Papers

Belfast Telegraph
Birmingham Post
Church Chronicle
Coventry Evening Telegraph
Daily Herald
Daily Mirror
Evening News
Lawton Constitution
Liverpool Echo
Stage and Television Today
Telegraph
The Times
Yorkshire Post and Leeds Mercury

Government Sources

UK Parliament. 1984. *House of Commons Hansard*, vol. 62, col. 679

Archives

Church of England Record Centre (CERC)

ACCM/VP/SEC/9
CIO/RTV/1
CACEC/SEC/10

LAMBETH PALACE LIBRARY (LPL)

Coggan 6 ff 162–270

PRINTED SECONDARY SOURCES

Beeson, Trevor. 2003. *The Bishops*. Hymns Ancient and Modern.
Carpenter, Humphrey. 1996. *Robert Runcie: The Reluctant Archbishop*. Sceptre.
Chadwick, Owen. 1990. *Michael Ramsey: A Life*. Oxford: Oxford University Press.
Cranmer, Frank. 2008. The Archbishop and Sharia. *Law & Justice* 160: 4–5.
Crozier, Mary. 1958. *Broadcasting: Sound and Television*. Oxford: Oxford University Press.
De La Noy, Michael. 1993. *The Church of England: A Portrait*. London: Simon and Schuster.
Dick, Anne R. 2010. *The Search for Philip K. Dick*. Tachyon Publications.
Falk, Quentin. 2014. *Television's Strangest Moments: Extraordinary but True Tales from the History of TV*. Pavilion Books.
Green, S.J.D. 2011. *The Passing of Protestant England: Secularisation and Social Change, C.1920–1960*. Cambridge University Press.
Harmes, Marcus K. 2017. *Roger Delgado: I Am Usually Referred to as the Master*. Fantom Films.
Hein, David. 2008. *Geoffrey Fisher, Archbishop of Canterbury 1945—1961*. Eugene, OR: Pickwick Publications.
Jenkins, David. 2003. *The Calling of a Cuckoo: Not Quite an Autobiography*. A&C Black.
Kirby, Dianne. 2012. The Church of England and the Cold War. In *God and War: The Church of England and Armed Conflict in the Twentieth Century*, ed. Stephen G. Parker and Tom Lawson, 121–145. Ashgate.
Mackenzie-Smith, John. 2008. Dean WP Baddeley in Brisbane 1958–1967. *Journal of the Royal Historical Society of Queensland* 20 (7): 321–336.
McGrath, Alister E. 1997. *J.I.Packer: A Biography*. Baker Books.
McKee, Alan. 2001. *Australian Television: A Genealogy of Great Moments*. Oxford University Press.
McLeod, Hugh. 2007. *The Religious Crisis of the 1960s*. Oxford University Press.
Peart-Binns, John Stuart. 1990. *Bishop Hugh Montefiore*. Quartet Books.
Phillips, Michael Scott. 2018. *Quite Quite Fantastic! The Avengers for Modern Viewers*. Lulu.com.
Sandbrook, Dominic. (2007) 2015. *White Heat: A History of Britain in the Swinging Sixties*. 2 vols. Hatchette.
Shawcross, William. 2002. *Queen and Country: The Fifty-year Reign of Elizabeth II*. London: Simon and Schuster.

Stringfellow, William, and Anthony Towne. 2007. *The Bishop Pike Affair: Scandals of Conscience and Heresy, Relevance and Solemnity in the Contemporary Church.* Wipf and Stock Publishers.

Thumim, Janet. 2004. *Inventing Television Culture: Men, Women, and the Box.* Oxford University Press.

Webster, Peter. 2016. *Archbishop Ramsey: The Shape of the Church.* Routledge.

Wolff, Richard. 2014. The *Dean Pike* Show: An Examination and Comparative Analysis of Bishop James A Pike's 1950s Television Program. *Journal of Media and Religion* 13 (2): 82–96.

Yates, Nigel. 2011. *Love Now, Pay Later?: Sex and Religion in the Fifties And Sixties.* SPCK.

DISSERTATIONS

Holland, Jonathan. 2006. The Past Is a Foreign Country: A History of the Church of England in the Diocese of Brisbane, 1950–1970. PhD diss., University of Queensland.

Rayner, Keith. 1962. The History of the Church of England in Queensland. PhD diss., University of Queensland.

CHAPTER 4

Policy and Possibilities Part One: The Commercial Channel

What were the policy and industry contexts for these appearances of the institutional church, its services, and individual clergy on television? On screen, they were often in the 'God slot', a product of broadcasting policy that both guaranteed religion a place in the schedule and placed it in a ghetto. It meant that the slot confined religious content to a time and day (70 minutes of broadcasting time on Sunday evenings) that in the 'television ecology' kept it away from peak broadcasting slots (Harrison 2000, 6). Despite the limitations intrinsic to the God slot, Church of England clergy broke out of that confinement and sought not only to appear on television (as seen in the previous chapter) but also to actively shape the future of the medium. This chapter considers their efforts in two crucial areas: the emergence of commercial television and then the launch of a second BBC channel (the 'third' terrestrial channel to be part of British television). Broader histories of television have largely overlooked their participation but it was significant; at times, it included prophetic commentary on the universal spread of the television set into homes and the contribution of clergy to debates at key moments in the development of television.

Clergy, both senior and parochial, actively shaped the medium's future. The Beveridge Committee handed down its report at the start of the 1950s, recommending the BBC keep its broadcasting monopoly. The fall of the Labour Government and the election of the Conservatives reversed this outcome, and the 1954 Television Act paved the way for a second

© The Author(s) 2020   65
M. Harmes et al., *The Church on British Television*,
https://doi.org/10.1007/978-3-030-38113-4_4

channel that would be commercial (Holmes 2005, 113). This chapter considers how the Church engaged with the wider vista that opened up as the monopoly ended. Through organs including the House of Lords, the British Council of Churches (BCC) and the Central Religious Advisory Committee (CRAC), the latter two both ecumenical but dominated by Anglicans, we see the Church forcefully interacting with stakeholders including the postmaster general and shaping the limits and definitions of what was recognised as appropriate religious content. Outside of policy debates in Whitehall, churchmen learnt more about the technology itself, with an increase in technological literacy.

Future Potential: Converting the Nation

The shutdown of the television service at the start of the Second World War was only temporary. Even before transmissions recommenced in 1946, senior Church of England clergy began planning nothing less than the conversion of the entire country via mass media. The Commission on Evangelism produced a monumental and ambitious report in 1945, proposing an 'adventure into Christian education' through any means possible, including cinema and radio, but also television. Their suggestions were far-sighted. By 1945, television had been off the air for the entire duration of the War and even before 1939 had been a fledgling and limited service. Yet the bishops overseeing this report speculated as to its future as means of mass communication and had no doubt there would be a television in every home. Seeing its potential, bishops wished not to repeat the mistakes of the recent past when 'The original desire and drive for religious broadcasting came from the B.B.C. The only opposition (and it was at times very great) came from the Church. Will history repeat itself when television enters every home?' (*The Scotsman* June 19, 1945, 7).

These reflections on the growth of the first service put into perspective the emergence of second and third terrestrial channels and the Church's interventions in these stages. The Church of England became intrinsic to the development of television policy as well as content. Geoffrey Fisher's comments that television was 'another means of wasting time' caused dismay at the BBC in 1952 and the Director of Television Broadcasting took the step of addressing the BCC, in Fisher's presence, about the potential of the infant national service (*Hartlepool Northern Daily Mail* September 24, 1952, 1). Another bishop, Cockin of Bristol (of whom more later) had early on had cause to watch with interest the development of broadcasting because he was chairman of the CRAC. His appearances before the Beveridge and the Pilkington Committees were marker stones for him of evolving and emerging attitudes. 'I watched with very great interest the gradual "come around" of various Churches to the idea that it was not only permissible but a good and wise thing to present shall I say services of Holy Communion or confirmation services on the screen', as a way to reach 'people who would never have come near the thing live' (CERC CIO/RTV/1).

These comments are a window into a period when the nature of a national television service remained uncertain, together with what it would show, and the moral implications of a universally available medium. It was however becoming clearer that the Church was central to the development of a national Television Service.

Geographically, the Church of England is a marker of the spread of the BBC's transmission; one by one, local papers reported the 'first' broadcast of a church service from their district. Often, the transmission of a church service would be the first occasion when broadcast engineers appeared in a regional community and sometimes the desire for a religious transmission gave impetus to the spread of the Television Service. In 1952 a complicated lash up of cables, microwave gear and radio along with a TV Mobile Control Unit gave a further push to what the Television Service could deliver and enabled the 'longest "hop" yet to be achieved by TV outside broadcast unit in the Midlands', reported the *Mercury and Herald* proudly (October 10, 1952, 8). Equally proudly, the *Birmingham Gazette* reported on the first televised service from Aston in 1952.

The BBC retained a monopoly on television broadcasting until September 1955. The Church had concerned itself with the political and public debate over its form and the type of the second channel. After the Coronation, Archbishop Fisher was more at home with television as something to appear on and actively contributed to the debate about a second channel. More broadly, Fisher spoke out against the different uses for television. He abhorred the BBC's experiments with using television as a medium of instruction, trialled in 1952 in six London schools (*Daily Mirror* March 7, 1952, 1). The creation of an independent channel raised questions, many of them disturbing for broadcasting stakeholders, such as what would happen to BBC revenues, or if a second channel would be state sanctioned and open to political manipulation. Fisher called the debates 'thorny and difficult' but his voice cut into them with a type of direct authority that he notably brought to the exercise of his office and which made many feel they were being addressed by their headmaster. Fisher declared the need for a fine line, between the too strict control of a medium which was so 'socially powerful', but having it controlled by responsible people not bounden to political influence (*Yorkshire Post and Leeds Mercury* July 1, 1953, 5).

Senior clergy therefore sought to predict into the near future how television would influence society in general as well as to consider its religious impact. Archbishop Cyril Garbett of York followed the 1945 evangelism report with his own judgements on the potential of the medium. In 1952, he told a diocesan conference that television could be either good or evil and he laid out his own terms for how it could be the latter. Garbett especially feared television becoming commercialised rather than remaining an exclusively public medium, but found that a national service provided the means to reach a large and unchurched body of people (*Coventry Evening Telegraph* November 6, 1952, 7). Garbett also found the BBC to be a willing worker with the Church in thoughtfully devising out 'how best television could be used for religious purposes'. By 'religious purposes', Garbett thought of not only televised services but also more imaginative presentations such as religious drama (*The Times* November 7, 1952, 3). Like Fisher, Garbett had seen the televising of the Coronation from the inside out and was impressed by the BBC's sensitivity in dealing with the Abbey authorities and the sacred elements of the ceremony. He regarded the BBC's coverage not merely as a technical success but as a sacerdotal one as well, as television had enabled millions of people to be part of 'a great act of dedication and worship' (*Yorkshire Post and Leeds Mercury* June 29, 1953, 5).

Garbett's anxieties about television were more specific than a pious concern that the medium would keep people away from church or prove a time waster. His concerns turned sharply on the question of control and the implication of breaking the BBC's monopoly with a commercial channel. Ironically, the BBC's extended moment of triumph in televising the Coronation was tempered by the challenge to its monopoly as policy makers and politicians began considering a second and commercial channel. By November 1953, the postmaster general presented Parliament with a memorandum on Television Policy, following on from a white paper and spelling out the future contours of British broadcasting. The government envisaged 'some element of competition', on the basis of what both churchmen and politicians were recognising as the increasing spread of television not just in geographical terms, as more and more homes across the United Kingdom began to receive signals, but also in its influence on people. The memorandum recognised that 'television has great and increasing power in increasing men's minds', and this power 'should not remain in hands of a single authority, however excellent that may be' (CERC BCC/7/1/9/2/1).

Garbett had specific grounds for his concerns and believed that commercial television in America represented the very worst of what could happen when commercial companies filled the screens with 'sex, murders and violence', whereas a national and monopolising public service needed to be concerned only with 'education and standards of culture' (*Yorkshire Post and Leeds Mercury* June 29, 1953, 5). A few days after circulating these comments in print, Garbett restated them to a clergy conference and repeated his linked fears of a rupture of the monopoly by commercial television, for 'Commercial television simply means advertising by television and the supreme end of the advertiser was to persuade people to buy what they would not otherwise want' (*Yorkshire Post and Leeds Mercury* July 3, 1953, 5).

Garbett's comments to his diocesan conference are a mixture of the eschatological and the practical, showing himself to be far from unworldly about commercial practice and television licensing while also fearing for the state of the nation's soul if people started watching commercial television. Fearing spiritual degradation caused by commercial television, Garbett foresaw a terrible future filled with 'pictures of horror' that would entice viewers and make money. In strictly practical terms, Garbett also worried that a second channel would dilute standards as the BBC would be drained of resources and quality personnel and businesses unable to afford television advertising would close down (*Coventry Evening Telegraph* July 2, 1953, 5).

For the Church, a commercial channel raised a distinctive concern: would religion be among the commodities for sale? That concern led to animated discussion and strategising among members of the BCC, focusing on Anglicans in leadership roles (and Geoffrey Fisher was the president at the time). In notes from June 1954 marked 'strictly confidential' members received reassurance that the 'Postmaster General repeated assurances he had previously given that it would be impossible for religious bodies to "buy time"' (CERC BCC/7/1/9/2/1). The BCC also moved to ensure that religious broadcasting on the new commercial channel would take on two particular characters. One was that it would represented the 'main streams' of British religion, meaning largely Anglican but with input from the Church of Scotland, the Methodist Church, the Free Church and the Congregationalists. It did not embrace Catholicism or non-Christian groups (CERC BCC/7/1/9/2/1). The other was that the CRAC, which already existed to advise the BBC, should serve the same function for the IBA, rather than each channel having their own panel.

The various positions expressed in the White Paper, the memorandum and the British Council of Churches' internal paperwork were the outcome of vigorous and sustained pressure although they were met with resistance in some cases. The government of the day stood firm on some issues. One was bringing in commercial television at all. The Beveridge Committee had received submissions from churchmen on the desirability of 'broadcasting under public corporation', a view that was ignored (CERC BCC/7/1/9/2/1). Fisher expected that as the archbishop of Canterbury he was entitled to speak to and advise the Queen, the Prime Minister and the government. For the last of these, his was a far from token presence in the House of Lords. Instead, he spoke forcefully, often, and at length on the implications of commercial television. In July 1954 he rose in the Lords to describe the Television Bill as a 'bad bill', and one where 'almost every organisation concerned with religion, education and social welfare also regards it as a bad Bill' (*House of Lords Hansard* July 1, 1954, vol. 188, col. 346).

Fisher's contribution to debates on the White Paper records a distinctive ecclesiastical contribution to the emergence of commercial television. Fisher's involvement was to weigh up and provide guidance on the moral implications of advertising on television. Central to this issue was the function of the medium itself. The usually polite tone of the Lords debate occasionally broke down, especially so when one peer, Lord Brand, suggested that 'the new commercial television must be almost entirely entertainment, a point of view which naturally will receive plaudits from the noble Viscount, Lord Hudson, who thinks that the tremendous instrument of television should be entirely used for entertainment' (*Hansard* July 1, 1954, vol. 188, col. 361). While Viscount Hudson denied the comment, the deeper implication of the debate was how to think of a broadcaster that did not balance the informative, educational and entertainment intentions, as did the BBC.

The House of Lords debates around the White Paper are significant for showing an evolution in people's perceptions of television. Apart from Fisher, the chamber in the 1950s contained a range of notable intellects including Lord Beveridge, the economist and social reformer, who found himself profoundly moved by Fisher's cautions about commercial television and who commented 'that television is too precious to be entrusted to the wrong hands, to persons interested in selling other things. Television is a voice and a presence in every home. It is a new means of influencing men's minds, influencing their thoughts, their enjoyments, their whole lives'. Beveridge noted that the Committee advocating for a second channel had reached exactly the same conclusion about television's potent influence, but Beveridge took the point in the opposite direction, determining that its potency should not be cheapened (*House of Lords Hansard* November 25, 1953, vol. 184. col. 590).

Fisher's headmasterly authority did not always go unchecked and some of his contemporaries saw limitations in his experience and authority, which included the incongruity of a religious leader seeking to influence the future of commercial television. Lord Brabazon, the Conservative peer, spoke in favour of the White Paper on independent broadcasting and placed Fisher as one of the 'curious collection of people we have against us'. Seeking to limit the Church's sphere of influence, Brabazon declared: 'I look upon him more as an expert in education than in entertainment, and although I would certainly go to any church service that he had organised, I do not know whether I would go to any music-hall entertainment that he had organised' (*House of Lords Hansard* November 25, 1953, vol. 184, col. 551). Beneath a robustly humorous comment lay a deeper insinuation that was rejecting Fisher's repeated demand that a second channel should be an educational enterprise. In the lower house, Fisher's suggestion 'that licence fees and advertising revenue might be shared between the B.B.C. and the new corporation' received a knock back from Sir Ian Fraser, the Conservative MP who was also a Governor of the BBC (*House of Commons Hansard* December 14, 1953, vol. 522, col. 113).

Likewise, Archbishop Fisher's suggestion in the House of Lords to have two public corporations did not find its way into the White Paper or the Television Bill, which legislated for 'programme contractors' to provide content (CERC BCC/7/1/9/2/1). The Council itself accepted that the extension of CRAC's advisory role across both channels was what the government itself wanted (CERC BCC/7/1/9/2/1) and happily they all thought alike. The Council sought to qualify and clarify that role for both, and in doing so demonstrated an awareness of appearance and the need to navigate reputation and public expectations. It urged that CRAC should advise not merely on policy but also on content, and further it should become involved 'at an early stage in the planning of any scheme of religious programmes so that there may be no danger of the Committee appearing to censor programmes rather than advise upon them' (CERC BCC/7/1/9/2/1).

In the BCC's archives are some hand scribbled notes of 'assurances received' and the writer was following closely the passage of the television legislation and the details in schedules and clauses through the Commons and Lords. Among the assurances are 'no religious body "buy time"' and "I.T.A. to have C.R.A.C"' (CERC BCC/7/1/9/2/1). The postmaster general, Lord De La Warr, was also compelled to reassure them, more than once, that commercial television would not lead to inter-denominational competition to 'buy' adherents through buying advertising. Although the British Council of Churches was an ecumenical body, any possibility that religious organisations could have bought advertising time was a denominationally sensitive issue for the Church of England in particular, anxious to safeguard its position as the largest and most influential religious body in England. The Postmaster General reassured Bishop Cockin in a letter from June 10, 1954 that 'it would be quite impossible for any religious body to "buy time" on the air' (CERC BCC/7/1/9/2/1).

In the early 1950s, the Church of England counted around 60 per cent of the general population as its membership, and remained sensitive to preserving relative denominational percentages in the content of broadcast religion. When the Church of England's Radio and Television Council (RTV) was in its early planning stages, one function highlighted for it was to 'watch over the "proportion of the faith"' (CERC CIO/RTV/1). In addition, it was to 'watch the denominational balance' and to 'watch for sectional propaganda'. Ecumenical bodies such as the British Council of Churches did not mitigate against Anglican awareness of both their numerical strength and their establishment status.

The postmaster general also responded to the sustained expressions of Anglican concern and explicitly promised 'NO advertisements whatever are to be allowed to be televised during a religious programme or within a stated period before or after such a programme' (CERC BCC/7/1/9/2/1). The ban made its way into the Second Schedule of the Television Bill (2 & 3 Eliz. 2, 1954). The ban also speaks to an additional layer of meaning in Anglican concerns about a commercial channel competing with the BBC. Another early function intended for the RTV was to 'coordinate Anglican work in the B.B.C. and television companies' (CERC CIO/RTV/1) because 'There is naturally strong competition between the B.B.C. and television companies where secular programmes are concerned. The tendency for this competition to creep into the religious sphere must be resisted at all costs' (CERC CIO/RTV/1). Advertisements could potentially make the independent channel's broadcasting more enticing and more competitive, a trend to be resisted.

The Church of England, including two heavy weights, William Wand the bishop of London and Frederick Cockin the bishop of Bristol (CERC BCC/7/1/9/2/2), spearheaded the interactions between the BCC and the government. The latter remained an active participant in committees and advocacy for the Church in government circles for years to come. However the primary channel of communication was though the Reverend R.D. Say. Say later acquired a considerable reputation for expertise in broadcast communications policy and procedure, and by the mid-1960s Cockin of the RTV thought of him as an authoritative judge on succession planning for the chairmanship of the Council (CERC CIO/RTV/1). It was Say who provided the Government with ecclesiastical perspectives. The assistant postmaster general David Gammans wrote to Say on January 11, 1954, noting the Government's commitment to the White Paper, but acknowledging that 'Many of the details, however, remain to be discussed', therefore opening up the space for negotiation into which the Church of England specifically and the BCC generally could step in order to shape policy and content. Gammans positively invited the Church to be involved, writing to this effect to the Reverend Say that 'Your Committee may have suggestions they would wish to make on the general subject of religious broadcasting, and if so the Postmaster General or I would much appreciate the opportunity of a discussion with them' (CERC BCC/7/1/9/2/2).

Say's correspondence is significant for showing the leadership of the Church of England in the BCC in organising itself to lobby, cajole and influence the government. Say pulled together a delegation to meet the postmaster general in February 1954. Again, these efforts were ecumenical but the ecumenism was tempered in two ways. One was that leadership was axiomatically Anglican. The other was that the Church of Scotland subsequently went 'rogue', organising its own meeting with De La Warr and prompting confusion among Anglican clergy about their actions. De La Warr informed Bishop Wand of London that he had 'heard from the Secretary of State for Scotland that the Church of Scotland is still far from happy about the terms of the Bill as they affect religious broadcasting' (BCC/7/1/9/2/2). In turn, Wand sent the letter to Say, on the proviso he kept its contents confidential and returned it to the bishop and Say responded with his private musings on the problems that could arise if the Council's stance, so far united under the leadership of the bishops of London and Bristol, was disrupted. He advised on strategy, for 'We shall run into difficulties if they now go to the Postmaster General on their own, albeit at this invitation, and I think it would be very much better if we were to ask to see him again with a Scottish representative included in the delegation as before' (BCC/7/1/9/2/2). Bishop Wand also wanted further information 'so that we know exactly what the Church of Scotland people are doing' (BCC/7/1/9/2/2).

Say monitored parliamentary proceedings carefully, noting in May 1954 with displeasure that the deputy postmaster general 'ran into difficulties on the very point which he laid so much stress, and on which he sought to reassure us—i.e. that no religious body should be allowed to "buy time" or advertise. It would seem the wording of the Bill does not cover the assurance given us', and he advised a further meeting with the Postmaster General (BCC/7/1/9/2/2).

Elsewhere in his private correspondence Say showed his awareness of key players and his channels of communication for what was taking place in Parliament. He contacted the Baptist minister Hugh Martin in January 1954, drawing in a BCC member who already had contacts at the Post Office. Say reported to Martin about 'an interesting hour at the Post Office yesterday, and got the impression that they were very much in need of all the help they can get' (CERC BCC/7/1/9/2/1). In return, Martin replied on February 22 and provided private insights that 'Govt. disposed to be cooperative. BCC representative kept their end up effectively. Govt. still at sea about a good deal' (CERC BCC/7/1/9/2/1).

Cumulatively, Say's correspondence leaves a trail of the interface between the Government, especially the postmaster general, and the Church, including the extent to which the Government reached out to Cockin and Wand and sought their input. Say informed Martin on January 22 of further plans for meeting with the postmaster general, including that 'The Post Office have now made it clear that the matter is too urgent to wait until March. The Bishop of London has agreed to lead a deputation to discuss the matter with the Postmaster General'. Say's private notes to Martin also reconstruct the degree to which Say, on behalf of Wand and Cockin, was setting the parameters for the discussion the government was seeking. 'Some of the Civil Servants concerned have asked me to go along and see them informally early next week, which I have agreed to on the clear understanding that is to help prepare the way for the more formal deputation and in no sense a substitute for it' (CERC BCC/7/1/9/2/1). Say wrote to the Broadcasting Department at the GPO with a briskly worded request that 'For reasons which I do not think I need explain, it would be a great help to us if a straightforward announcement about the fact and purpose of our discussion with the Postmaster General could be released to the Press immediately after we have seen Lord De La Warr tomorrow night' (CERC BCC/7/1/9/2/2). In addition, he sent a draft of proposed wording for the GPO to use.

During these internal and often private developments, Archbishop Garbett had been publicly expressing his fears about a second and commercial channel. With hindsight, a second (and third, fourth and fifth) terrestrial channel was a *fait accompli*, but the consultative and legislative processes leading to it involved bishops. Some like Garbett feared it, even though he admitted he did not own a television set (*The Times* February 19, 1954, 4). Others saw more television channels as more opportunity to reach large numbers. Debate on the floor of the Church Assembly in Spring 1954 included a discussion of the Government's ongoing proposals for a second channel, including uncertainty as to whether the BBC would run it or not, if it would permit advertising, and if it would feature sponsored programmes. Two currents ran through the debate, one being a culturally snobbish disdain of American examples and the other a degree of annoyance that the Government had, by February 1954, moved on and already decided that the second channel would not belong to the BBC.

The Church Assembly's perspectives were not monolithic however. Garbett wanted broadcasting to stay a monopoly and by extension to avoid American influences. However a motion welcomed the possibility of independent channels on the grounds of it being 'undesirable' that 'a means of communication of human thought which promises to become the most powerful of all instruments in the formation of opinion and national character should remain in the exclusive control of a State-sponsored monopoly' (*The Times* February 19, 1954, 4). The government reached the same conclusion (Sendell 1983, 149), but not because of the Church Assembly's opinion.

This chapter has shown the clergy as active behind the scenes. In forums including the House of Lords and through networks of correspondence and contacts, the clergy engaged in shaping the medium as the monopoly ended and a new channel that was also commercial came into existence. The reconstruction of these manoeuvres through correspondence, reports of speeches and the Hansards can create a fragmentary impression of who did what and how much they achieved. However the bigger picture of the creation of ITV has been well told; what is revealed from these more impressionistic sources is the expectations of clergy in guiding the medium and their main areas of concern. These concerns of the 1950s are preludes to the next decade, when another new channel required shaping and guidance.

References

Newspapers, Periodicals and Trade Papers

Birmingham Gazette
Coventry Evening Telegraph
Daily Mirror
Hartlepool Northern Daily Mail
Mercury and Herald
The Scotsman
The Times
Yorkshire Post and Leeds Mercury

Government Sources

UK Parliament. 1953. *House of Commons Hansard*, vol. 522, col. 113
———. 1953. *House of Lords Hansard*, vol. 184, col. 590
———. 1954. *House of Lords Hansard*, vol. 188, col. 346

Archives

Church of England Record Centre (CERC)

CERC CIO/RTV/1
CERC BCC/7/1/9/2/1
CERC BCC/7/1/9/2/2

Printed Secondary Sources

Harrison, Jackie. 2000. A Review of Religious Broadcasting on British Television. *Liberal Theology in the Contemporary World* 41 (4): 3–15.
Holmes, Su. 2005. *British TV and Film Culture in the 1950s: Coming to a TV Near You*. Intellect Books.
Sendell, Bernard. 1983. *Independent Television in Britain*. London: Palgrave Macmillan.

CHAPTER 5

Policy and Possibilities Part Two: The Third Channel and Beyond

Social changes in the 1960s seem inexorably liberal advances as the Church simultaneously diminished in influence and size; however, the Church should be seen as part of these impulses, even if they were secular. We have already considered in the introduction that seemingly signature acts of a more secular and less religious world such as the 1967 Wolfenden Report and the 1969 changes to divorce law involved the Church. Important intellectual and theoretical aspects of these changes included clergy demarcating between crime and sin, in ways that enabled legislative, if not doctrinal, change. Religious input also provided some intellectual framing of commercial television, not just in the pressure to 'insulate' religious programming from commercials but at a deeper level to understand in a theological way policy changes as first the second commercial and the third BBC channel came into existence.

The contribution of bishops to House of Lords debates on commercial television, the interactions between the Radio and Television Council and the postmaster general and even the occasionally individual pronouncements by newsworthy clergy were products of an era when the Church's approach to television was outward looking. Their points were marked by a degree of confidence that clergy, especially senior clergy, had the ear of the government and a right to shape legislation and policy. This chapter will move to later years that suggest a more inward focus, marked by an anxiety that television was a medium outstripping the Church in influence and where two things were no longer axiomatic: that broadcasting was

© The Author(s) 2020

M. Harmes et al., *The Church on British Television*,

https://doi.org/10.1007/978-3-030-38113-4_5

Christian broadcasting to a Christian nation; and that the Church could shape government and industry actions on television. Initially the development of the third channel, and then more widely debates on blasphemy and on the role of religious advisors illuminate the changes that took place around the Church.

A Third Channel

The BBC's 405 line transmission Television Service continued to be the Corporation's sole television channel until 1962. The launch of the 625 line BBC2 (and the designation of the original solo Service as BBC1) followed similar levels of deliberation that had preceded the creation of a second channel. The Church took a keen interest in the creation of this 'third channel' and the recommendations provided by the Pilkington Committee, which began meeting in 1960. Following the passage of the Television Act in 1954 and the subsequent creation of a second channel, the Government's Pilkington Committee looked back in 1962 and noted some of the successes of independent broadcasting. The three unlikely bedfellows of 'light theatre, news and religious broadcasting' were the stand out successes of independent broadcasting. Here in these fields, reported the committee in a 1962 Cabinet briefing paper, the independent channel was doing better than the BBC and attracting better audiences (*Spectator* July 6, 1962, 4). Religious broadcasting was an especial success of independent television, intersecting with efforts made through the charm school to produce polished performers and to experiment with religious broadcasting.

Expansion: Church Reactions

A number of the episcopate actively debated the findings of the Pilkington Committee in the Lords, in some cases revealing themselves as diffident or unclear about the medium and its impact as the notion of a third terrestrial channel gained momentum. Speaking in 1969, the bishop of Bristol (who was also the chairman of Central Religious Advisory Committee or CRAC) expressed approval of how Pilkington's strong definition had ensured hundreds of hours of religious content. The bishop also restated the speculations of churchmen several decades earlier that broadcasting religion would compete with actual physical attendance in a parish church. Noting that the ratings of *Songs of Praise* were typically ten million and those of

Meeting Point were three and a half million, 'there are, in fact, more people watching a programme of that sort than are likely to be in church on any given Sunday' (*House of Lords Hansard* May 21, 1969, vol. 302, col. 369). In the next decade, the CRAC was advising the Annan Committee that the religious traditions that ought to be broadcast were 'mainly' Christian (Potter 2016, 272).

Further episcopal input came from Roger Wilson, the bishop of Chichester, who described himself in the Upper House as a 'very infrequent viewer myself' and unfamiliar with the programmes other peers had described, but proceeded to offer a number of sensitively informed comments on the current state of British broadcasting. He revealed a keenly observant eye of differences in approach between the BBC and the independent companies and especially the 'freshness, independence and originality' of religious broadcasting on the independent companies compared to the 'rather more stilted approach of the B.B.C.' (*House of Lords Hansard* July 18, 1962, vol. 242, col. 637). Having listened to previous speakers that day in the Lords, the bishop also grappled with the possibility that it was television and not the Church of England, which was 'the main factor in influencing the standards and morals of our society' (*House of Lords Hansard* July 18, 1962, vol. 242, col. 639).

While pulling back from endorsing that view, the bishop of Chichester knew enough about television to pinpoint its unique impact in that unlike cinema, the theatre or the music hall, to which people have to go, 'television brings things to us in an intimate and off-hand way' (*Hansard* July 18, 1962, vol. 242, col. 639). His observations were a contribution to a debate that, although spoken in the civilised environment of the House of Lords, was critical of Pilkington's apparent bias against independent broadcasting and sense it was dumbing down television (Cooke 2003, 59). In the Lords, a number of peers, ecclesiastical and temporal, were anxious to see a third channel develop on what Viscount Hailsham recognised as 'technical necessity and practical politics' (see Sendell 1983, 148).

Lobbying: The Council

The Church's intervention in both the second and third channels was marked by several significant factors. As we saw in the previous chapter, the Church's input into debates about the second channel were more haphazard, and had been a series of speeches and proposals made without overarching coordination. Yet Fisher had realised the social power of television and by the time the third channel became a proposition, the Church of England was better organised to speak on the matter. The archbishops of Canterbury and York acted in 1960 to establish the Church of England Radio and Television Council, a now defunct body but one that acted swiftly and immediately in 1960 to begin lobbying the Government about broadcasting, especially the planned third channel.

Geoffrey Fisher's influence is notable. A letter from Fisher to Cockin on July 14, 1959, outlined plans for a Council of some sort to deal with broadcasting, and seeking (successfully as it turned out) to persuade Cockin to be the first chairman (CERC CIO/RTV/1). Headquarters were at Church House in Westminster and was soon equipped with a corporate identity including its own letterhead, secretarial support and an energetic executive officer. It was however timely, as confidential correspondence between Fisher, his staff at Lambeth Palace and Cockin shows the Church caught off guard by recent broadcasting developments. From Lambeth Palace, it suddenly seemed more important and more urgent to have a Church of England body able to advice on broadcasting as Geoffrey Fisher suddenly discovered the Churches' Television Centre had come into existence. On August 7, 1959, he told Cockin: 'I know nothing of the Revd. C.J. Thomas and his Centre. Clearly we ought to be in touch with it' (CERC CIO/RTV/1). On October 17 that year Fisher's secretary informed Cockin that advice was now needed about who should attend the Centre's opening; more broadly Fisher now found himself in need of a body with a chairman who could advise him about television matters in general.

The first chair, Cockin, formerly the bishop of Bristol, had some broadcasting experience such as speaking for the epilogue, as well as writing accessible texts on topics like sexuality and education (*The Times* January 17, 1969, 10). The Church knew his reputation for expertise and confidence in dealing with television. As early as 1958, the bishop of Manchester sought Cockin's advice for the membership of the embryonic council, in the expectation that it was Cockin who would know 'if there is any obvious person I have left out' (CERC CIO/RTV/1). The remainder of the council comprised a mixture of clerical and lay Anglican members. One notable lay member was the academic Dr Katherine Bliss, but the name of most significance is the Reverend David Skinner, appointed as the executive officer (*The Times* June 3, 1960, 9).

This trio, Cockin, Bliss and Skinner, stand apart from the other members as public lobbyists for the Council and the Church, especially as momentum gathered for the third terrestrial channel. Skinner had a particular range of responsibilities. The Council existed not only to advise but also to watch, and one of Skinner's roles was to watch television, and to train clergy to appear on it (CERC CIO/RTV/1).

When Cockin and Skinner appeared before the Pilkington Committee, their answers to the committee show both provided informed answers about production and content, based on their television literacy. Cockin discussed in depth the impact (positive in his view) of the independent competition on the BBC and the importance of including lay personnel in making religious broadcasting, for it was the laity who were 'bringing a new kind of mind to the programmes by trying to answer the questions in which they themselves were interested' (CERC CIO/RTV/1). These dual functions of watching what has already broadcast and preparing others to make broadcasts were two practical steps leading to the deeper purpose of the Council, which was to 'awaken clergy and Church people to a greater concern and sense of responsibility for the effective use of this medium, whether as contributors to actual programmes, or as informed and critical groups of listeners and viewers' (CERC CIO/RTV/1).

A private discussion among churchmen in Sheffield in January 1962 contributed harsh criticisms of the Church's failings with television. The clergy present learnt the 'C.of E. is publicity shy, inarticulate on the national level and possesses no overall television strategy' (CERC CIO/ RTV/1). The meeting notes record an overall push for the continued organisation of the Church around broadcasters, including the need for specialist advisors and for a nationally overarching strategy rather than planning taking place at a diocesan level and therefore piece-meal.

The notes of this meeting are in a collection compiled by Cockin for his successors at the council. One of them annotated the notes by hand and remarked 'heaven forbid!' at the suggestion of television strategy taking place at the diocesan level. Cockin himself felt that at its formation the membership of the Council had been haphazardly chosen with amateurs on board (CERC CIO/RTV/1). From the outset, the Council allowed the Church to enter debates, contribute to parliamentary inquiries and influence the emerging third channel. The Council had particular responsibility for training clergy to appear on television but from the outset, the Church intended its Council would be more impactful than just the God Slot programmes, but would enable the Church to have polished, convincing presenters in any programme involving discussion of matters of public concern (*The Times* June 3, 1960, 9). In October 1959 Cockin sent a list of points to Lambeth Palace on the Council's possible role, which included religious broadcasting but ranged far wider, including reporting on 'the religious significance of the big opinion-forming programmes such as Panorama etc.' (CERC CIO/RTV/1). From its outset the Council looked further than just religious content.

We can follow the emergence of the Council and its first and rather faltering interactions with the expanding broadcasting world through the archives of both the Church and the television industry. Bishop Cockin devoted much thought to establishing firm foundations for it, including a coherent succession plan, its financial stability after its initial financial provision ended in 1965 and its relationship with other Church bodies such as the Information Office (CERC CIO/RTV/1). Above all else, the Council was a timely creation as the Pilkington Committee began its sessions in July 1960.

Papers in the National Archives, unsealed in 1993, contain the Council's detailed recommendations to the Pilkington Committee on the third channel, and suggest the impact of the Council in requesting the Committee to think carefully about the nature of competition in broadcasting and the competing demands between quality and quantity that a third channel would create (NA HO244/443). By May 1961, Skinner was organising for a delegation to give oral evidence to the Pilkington Committee. His correspondence reveals a degree of assertiveness in providing the Committee, unasked, with 20 copies of a full draft schedule and Skinner seized the initiative in asking the Committee for an opportunity for the Council to give evidence (NA HO244/443).

The Church's suggestion that the third channel be educational received full development in its draft schedule. Sunday broadcasting was almost exclusively religious. In the hypothetical schedule, Sunday began with a brief news report, followed by a famous actor discussing her faith, a documentary about the Church in the slums, then a televised church service, and the day ended with a bishop conducting prayers. The only non-religious content was some classical music and an item about antique clocks (NA HO244/443). During the week, more classical music sat alongside informative documentaries on the stock exchange, medicine and the law, more news, and advisory programmes for young parents.

It is worth noting that the Church's appearance before the Pilkington Committee is one small fragment of a wider history. The implication of a detailed study such as this on one topic the Church on television can run the risk of magnifying the Church's involvement to a greater extent than is warranted. The wider history of the Pilkington Committee is well told in general broadcasting histories, which provide a broader perspective to put the Church's role into context, and from the perspective of narrower topics of interest such as left wing politics or the making of drama (Briggs 1995, 655; Çoban 2014, 94; Cooke 2003, 59). By the same token, in this wider history, the Church's input should not be underestimated. Cockin and his colleagues made their impact; the Committee's response to the Council's submission was by Sir Harry Pilkington himself, who read the schedule and took it seriously. Pilkington was a successful industrialist and part of his reaction to the Church's efforts was fiscal, noting in a letter from June 13, 1961, to a committee member that 'they have chosen those whom by almost any standard must be regarded as expensive artists, especially if they are only to interest minority audiences' (NA HO244/443). Indeed they had, with the Church envisaging the likes of Sir John Mills, Yehudi Menuhin, Myra Hess and Larry Adler among the guests. Pilkington was sufficiently interested to ask 'I wonder whether it would be worth submitting it to the BBC and asking them give some estimate, however rough, of the cost of mounting such a programme?' (NA HO244/443). The next year, the Committee was still interested in the Church's submission and wrote back to Skinner with the advice 'it seems likely that the Committee will wish to publish your Council's submission of 20th December 1960, in full' (NA HO244/443).

The Council's input sheds light on the different possibilities that had settled around the third channel, including that it was not always a guarantee that it would belong to the BBC, although the Church of England's representatives to the Pilkington Committee argued for it to be free of commercials. The Church's Council also seized the opportunity to suggest not only what should be broadcast, but the demographic the third channel should target and the types of issues the channel would best concentrate on. Fisher's concerns in 1953 that a balanced and responsible set of persons should run the second channel reappear in a new guise in 1961, when the Council proposed that the third channel be the joint responsibility of the BBC and the Independent Television Authority (ITA) with a firmly independent chairman in overall charge (*Daily Mirror* December 30, 1960, 6). Further, to marshal television's social power in a positive rather than a dangerous direction, the Church urged that the third channel should have a distinctive identity as the 'educational channel'. Its programmes should be especially relevant for people aged from 18 to 30 on content such as hire purchase, childcare and home building (*Stage and Television Today* January 5, 1961, 21).

David Skinner wrote to David Paton on July 29, 1962, passing on a memorandum from Cockin that was partly gloomy and partly strategic about how the still-new Council was going to bridge a communications gap between the Church and television professionals (CACEC/SEC/10). The memorandum was Cockin's effort to set out his thoughts after he had been part of the Television Training in June that year, and the occasion left him dispirited about the Church's engagement with television. 'It may well have seemed to be a rather inconclusive if not negative session' was his discouraging opening to the memo, but nonetheless 'it may at least have served the purpose giving us a rather realistic idea of the difficulties involved in convincing those concerned at the professional end of the possible ways in which our material could be used for their purposes'.

The Church had received a sobering reality check that the industry professionals who had participated in their training day were still at a loss as to how to broadcast the Church and what to broadcast. Cockin therefore proposed shrewd advice to attempt to open doors and bypass the polite refusals of what he termed 'official answers'. To that end, 'personal contact' [underline original] was essential and Cockin realised that two years into its existence, the Church's Council was still a relative outsider in the television industry, whereby 'there is a need for a great deal of preparatory work of this kind' still to do, and the Bishop had come to realise that the Council's official approaches 'are apt to be written off as "pressure" tactics'.

Other realisations had dawned on him about both causes of resistance from the industry and ways to seek entrée to this world. There was a 'need to think out a good deal further the distinction which was drawn more than once, (Douglas Stewart and Gordon Reece, I think) between material which can be classed as "Church propaganda" selling ourselves, and material which can properly claim to be the presentation of situations, work being done, challenges to be met, which ought [original underline] to be known and reckoned with by an informed public'.

Cockin also realised that the Church was competing against many other voices and content types for precious air time as it was at the sessions of the Pilkington Committee, a realisation that again made the third channel seem an exciting possibility providing more time and space for broadcasting and 'different modes of broadcasting' including 'snippets' like 'magazine programmes'. As part of his duties as chairman, he oversaw conferences at Lambeth Palace on broadcasting which were intended to provide brief-ings on the latest developments and in June 1963 the conference included 'New Ideas in Religious Broadcasting' (CERC CIO/RTV/1). In the mid-1960s, Cockin reiterated these points. The original funding provision for the Council ended in 1965, prompting Cockin to advance wide-ranging proposals for re-ordering the Council. A constant amongst changes was that the Council should 'continue to foster the valuable per-sonal links established over the past four years with B.B.C. religious broad-casting and I.T.V. Anglican advisors' (CERC CIO/RTV/1).

Following Cockin's memorandum, his colleague at Church House the Reverend David Paton got specific and pitched a set of detailed and elabo-rate ideas for television content. He thought it could be called 'The Unity Movement: Fact or Falsehood' for a programme about the British ecu-menical movement. Like Cockin's memorandum, Paton's ideas show a maturing awareness of the implications of working with and being on television and what the figurative bright lights could expose. Although an enthusiastic exponent of ecumenism, Paton wished for television to take a 'no holds barred' approach, for when 'the acids have burned away the falsities, magnalia Dei [mighty acts of God] will be visible' [original under-line] (CACEC/SEC/10). His statement on television verges on the eschatological, and he melded the clinical gaze of the television camera with the refiners' fire in the Bible.

The Council's ability to present a coherent and authoritative set of per-spectives received affronts from within the Church itself. One articulate and unusually personal contribution to the debate about not just a new channel but also the possibility of there being advertising came from the bishop of Worcester, Mervyn Charles Edwards. Unlike other prelates in the Lords, Edwards declared himself not just a television viewer but a television addict, being 'one who is devoted to Westerns, adventure and crime stories'. Because he was an enthusiastic viewer and upheld the qual-ity and importance of both independent and BBC television, Edwards dismissed and even lightly mocked the concerns of the Council.

At this juncture, the intersection between television and the Church had focused on thinking through the moral and theological implications of what was appearing on the screen. Independent television meant adver-tising, and before it became a *fait accompli* that the third channel would be controlled by the BBC, the possibility of a further outlet for television advertising had been before the Church. The question that transfixed some clergy was that of juxtaposition: would religious programming include advertising, and if it did, would it be tonally appropriate to the content of the programmes? By the early 1960s, religious content on the independent networks remained 'insulated' from advertising, but the proposal to experiment with including advertising in the usual religious spots such as the epilogue raised no objection from the postmaster general or the CRAC. The Church of England's Radio and Television Council, by contrast, found the development disturbing, even though it was initially only to be a six month trial.

At that point, the bishop of Worcester, Edwards, rose in the House of Lords, framing his concern as being 'perturbed by the thought that (shall we say?) a sermon on purity might be followed at once by an advertisement for a soap powder which washes whiter' (*House of Lords Hansard* January 20, 1965, vol. 262, col. 961). Worcester though declared 'I cannot reflect this view. Programmes, I believe, should reflect life, and far from wanting the Church to be insulated from life, I want it to be more and more involved in life. Nor am I particularly desirous, as I have said before, that the Church should have any special privileges in this field' (*House of Lords Hansard* January 20, 1965, vol. 262, col. 961). His comments cut across the Council's own advocacy, and they came from a bishop with significant broadcasting experience including not merely watching television but also appearing on it, and noting trends and developments in the medium including the demands of the licence fee and the occasions when the channels experimented with more controversial and exciting religious broadcasting.

Further, the formation of the Council did not preclude individual clergy acting as self-appointed guardians of public morality and offering public criticism of television. Some also showed they had carefully followed the development of television policy at Westminster. One instance is the Reverend Donald Plumley of Tunbridge Wells, who objected to the BBC's drama presentation *Stanboul Train* as 'distasteful' and 'disgusting'. Plumley made these observations in his own parish magazine, but they became newsworthy after the BBC's Controller of Television Stuart Hood apologised and agreed the television play had been off-colour for a family audience (*Telegraph* October 9, 1962, 17). Plumley not only received a response from the higher echelons of the BBC, he also showed he had been observing developments shaping the future of television. Plumley noted that the Pilkington Committee seemed to have been unnaturally biased against independent television and blindly in favour of the BBC. The distasteful broadcast of *Stanboul Train* gave Plumley a national press platform to wonder if 'those on the committee ever watched the BBC programmes' (*Telegraph* October 9, 1962, 17).

The expectation that religious broadcasting was the special responsibility of Anglican clergy was contestable. The CRAC was technically ecumenical but in actuality appeared to some to be an 'Anglican ghetto'. That impression seemed especially strong owing to the grip that the Anglican episcopate had on its leadership. In 1923 Garbett of York was the first chairman. Cockin served as chair later in the twentieth century. In the 1960s the bishop of Bristol was chairman. When bishop of St Alban's in the 1970s, Robert Runcie chaired the Committee. In 1989, Bishop David Sheppard took charge, in immediate succession to another Anglican, Bishop Graham Leonard of London (*Stage and Television Today* May 18, 1989, 15). The bishops leading CRAC therefore took responsibility not just on advising about religious broadcasting, but also protecting it. Sheppard stated that his intention in leading CRAC would be to set about 'improving and safeguarding religious programmes on the box' (*Liverpool Echo* May 9, 1989, 12). The episcopal involvement in CRAC also meant other members of the Church looked to particular members as the designated 'experts' on television broadcasting. The bishop of Wakefield, then Richard Hare, took the lead in a Synod debate on blasphemy, based on his experience as chairman of CRAC and of the Church's own Information Committee (Runcie/STA/CRAC/2).

Insider Perspectives

The CRAC and the Council were advisory bodies extrinsic to the BBC and IBA. Anglican clergy were intrinsic to the organisations and part of the BBC from its inception and held particular responsibility for religious broadcasting. In the decades from the period of the Reverend Iremonger in the 1930s to the 1950s and then into the apparently more sharply secular decades which followed, the involvement of clergy in religious broadcasting was constant. Their presence though and what they did and what they signified became more complex and emerged as points of contention. These were not just broadly religious but were specifically Anglican issues. The BBC being a Christian organisation broadcasting to a Christian nation ceased to be axiomatic, but the decline was long and complicated. In 1959, disgruntled clergy launched complaints to Canon Roy McKay, the head of Religious Broadcasting. In their view, he had failed on several fronts. One was allowing agnostic or even atheistic views to be heard. That objection though has to be interpreted with precision, as clergy did not object to such people being given air time but rather to how McKay organised retaliation to what was allegedly a 'disproportionate opportunity' for atheists to be seen and heard on television discussion programmes. A discussion programme meant a debate among guests, moderating different points of view.

In this way, the participation of clergy in religious broadcasting, not merely as guests or advisors, but as intrinsic and insider participants as the number of channels expanded, became a point of theological debate. McKay maintained that expecting a Christian panellist to 'win' a debate with an atheist was a theologically dubious approach to understanding both Christianity and television, as 'the argument is based on the idea that Christian truth can be proved by argument, which is not so'. That said, McKay was far from understanding his producer role as secular but instead being to 'encourage evangelism over great wide spheres of people'. McKay would prefer it if atheist views could be countered, but sometimes the Christian point of view was let down by the guests, when 'very eminent Christians' failed to carry their point. Where he, and the BBC, fell down in the eyes of other clergy was in letting the Anglican side down. McKay privileged non-denominational broadcasting when his fellow clergy had expected a more explicit Anglican emphasis. There was even objection (without examples given) to how the BBC portrayed Catholic priests compared to Anglican clergymen and why it was that 'Roman Catholic priests in BBC plays were always shown as wonderful fellows, full of wisdom, understanding and sympathy, while Anglican priests were always shown as fools, knaves, and apologies for men' (*Birmingham Post* May 28, 1959, 7).

The same concerns remained in place in the next few years. A private meeting of clergy in Sheffield in 1962 had to consider if 'the C. of E. [is] too gentlemanly in its relations to the other Churches. What of criticism of bad religion? The Anglican participant in joint discussions always comes off worst' (CERC CIO/RTV/1).

Those concerns were about the BBC but the independent companies also attracted displeasure. Again, these show the complex interaction between the Church, television and a viewing public who could now longer be considered broadly Christian. The Church of England's Radio and Television Council complained about the absence of religious content from the Granada Company. Granada's franchise gave it the weekdays to broadcast whereas the God Slot was traditionally on Sunday. That was not good enough for the Radio and Television Council, which wished Granada would provide weekday religious content, for it 'denies to Northerners during the week any formal religious recognition' (*Daily Mirror* December 30, 1960, 6). Candid and forthright opinions that passed between bishops, their domestic clergy and industry professionals showed the Church groping to understand the franchises and the regional opportunities. A memo marked 'confidential' in red ink came to the Reverend David Wyatt in January 1967, about efforts to find out more about 'a complete renewal of their system of allocations for religious programmes—and this, within a far wider re-assessment of their responsibilities'. Information had been sought from the Reverend Stephan Hopkinson, an effervescent clergyman who was a religious advisor for independent television (*Telegraph* August 26, 2004) but the letter writer felt he had not been doing enough to provide updates. However 'I have had a long talk with Stephan Hopkinson about the TV situation. He has not been as neglectful as I thought in my worst moments!' The letter indicates the interest of particular bishops and dioceses in particular franchises, such as the bishop of Manchester's anxiety to learn about what Granada would do. As such, the letter writer asked 'Could you please explain to the Bishop this irritating hiatus... I will then hold a pistol to Stephan Hopkinson's cranium and see which way he jumps' (CERC ACCM/VP/SEC/9). The exchange is revealing, showing not only regional bishops wanting to know about the regional franchises but also the expectation that 'insiders', such as religious advisors, ought to be able to provide updates on the negotiations about the franchises.

There was also the possibility that individual clergy would go rogue and pursue their own interactions with broadcasters. In 1970, the vicar of St Martin-in-the-Fields, Austen Williams, attacked the ITA for refusing to broadcast a series of commercials for *The Bible Today*. Williams's complaint was not just that the Christian commercials would not be shown but that independent television was showing commercials for the 'demonic' supernatural magazine *Man, Myth and Magic* (*Telegraph* January 27, 1970, 17). Williams already had a high profile as the vicar of one of London's most famous churches, which included Buckingham Palace in its parish, and he was an accomplished broadcaster on the World Service and public campaigner. His record of causes shows he was not necessarily a reactionary although a number of his causes perturbed the Church hierarchy (*Guardian* December 20, 2001). On this occasion, he intended his ire to suggest that the Church of England was being placed at a disadvantage not just by television but also by parliament. The Bible advertisements were not shown because of the Television Advertising Bill's ban on religious advertising.

The presence of advertisements on television at all had vexed churchmen before, during and after the introduction of the second and third channels in the 1950s and 1960s, as discussed above. On these occasions, the concern had been that inappropriate commercials would juxtapose against religious content. By 1970, the implication of advertisements had undergone a shift in emphasis, from a concern they would pollute religious content to a fear broadcasters were actively suppressing Christian content.

A further intersection between the Church and commercial television in 1970 provides a counterpoise to the Reverend Williams's fears that television would promote the demonic but not the biblical and opens a window onto individual churchmen finding more subversive ways to appear on television. In November 1970 press photographers paid a visit to the vicarage in Stanstead Abbotts in Hertfordshire, quickly followed by pictures of the Reverend Ronald Stephens. Meanwhile a film unit had set up equipment in his study for a day's filming. He was suddenly newsworthy because of the unlikely conjunction of the Church with margarine, as the vicar was one of several people who had agreed to appear on London Weekend Television and Southern Television advertising Blue Band margarine. A 45-second commercial is a tiny fragment of television but by 1970, it also opens a window onto the Church's evolving interactions with television, especially commercial television, beyond official channels such as the CRAC, the Council, or as a producer in a religious broadcasting department. A vicar could not appear on television to advertise his Church; however the margarine company had permitted the Reverend Stephens to script his own 45 seconds of fame, and included his discreet plug that 'the body needs fat like the soul needs God' (*Telegraph* November 19, 1970, 15). His suffragan bishop not only supported his television appearance but saw the margarine commercial as imbued with a deeper significance, seeing that the conjunction of the commercial product and the vicar could between them produce a moment of television with religious integrity. 'I see no reason why a sincere comment on margarine should not be coupled with sincere words about God' (*Telegraph* November 19, 1970, 15). For Blue Brand, a vicar sitting in a country vicarage sold a product by virtue of his sincerity and reliability. For the Church, 45 seconds selling margarine was a quiet way to get a commercial about God onto television and by 1970 was the best that could be achieved.

Singing the Lord's Song No Longer? The God Slot in Crisis

Anglican clergy monopolised positions of responsibility in the religious department of the BBC and Anglican bishops ghettoised the CRAC. Neither of these hegemonies, even while they lasted, could assuage a growing sense that broadcasting was becoming unsympathetic to the Church nor willing to accept its influence. That sense extended more widely than seeking the development of new channels. The tone and emphasis some churchmen detected in programmes made about the Church of England relate to a complex series of challenges, including declining congregations, struggles to build and maintain ministry in the inner cities, and the proper use of the Church's considerable resources.

The BBC's current affairs show *Panorama* became one flashpoint of controversy. An edition of May 24, 1971, reported on the Church of England's inner city ministries, questioned the use of financial resources and reported the numerical decline of urban congregations. The broadcast provoked a frenzied response from Edward Henderson, the bishop of Bath and Wells. Among his criticisms were that *Panorama* contained 'hostility, ignorance and contempt' and amounted to a 'travesty of the truth'. Henderson's attack contained a further note of shock, as he made explicit that the BBC had attacked 'the established church' in the worst manner possible (*Telegraph* June 11, 1971, 12). Bath and Wells is a largely rural diocese; Robert Stopford, the bishop of London and therefore the head of a diocese with actual inner-city parishes also joined the attack. Compared to Henderson's splenetic reaction, Stopford was more televisually literate or at least appreciated that television involved more than pointing a camera at something, instead realising that the careful selections and juxtapositions made by the editor could powerfully create impressions. He told a congregation at St Paul's Cathedral that 'the material you select' could slant viewers' impressions. In this case, he held that *Panorama*'s slant was to show the Church of England as 'dead or dying' (*Telegraph* June 7, 1971, 13).

Reactions to the *Panorama* broadcast brought a body of disunited bishops into view. Also joining in the attack was the bishop of Leicester Ronald Williams. The reactions to the BBC from Henderson, Stopford and Williams all carried slightly different emphases. Williams' particular concern was that all the Church of England had been tarred with the same brush of one diocese, as *Panorama*'s focus was on Mervyn Stockwood's diocese of Southwark, a 'centre of disillusion and defeatism in the Church of England', according to bishop Williams (*Telegraph* May 26, 1971, 6). Gerald Ellison, bishop of Chester, was likewise appalled that Southwark appeared to represent the entire Church in the documentary (*The Times* June 7, 1971, 3). One decade earlier, Archbishop Fisher had been the authoritative commentator on Church and State, embodying both in a logical and coherent manner. In the 1970s, the national broadcaster appeared to attack the national Church and Archbishop Ramsey openly discussed disestablishment in television interviews.

The 1970s marked further changes in the relationship between the national broadcaster and the established Church. The 1977 meeting of the General Synod noted the BBC's explicitness in saying 'the acceptance of Christian values is no longer one its aims' (*Telegraph* February 17, 1977, 19). The Synod objected to what some churchmen regarded as a clear swing in the other direction with programme makers taking all possible opportunities to broadcast blasphemy. The Reverend Gordon Dobson found to his distaste that broadcasters were taking 'a downward plunge into a sea of coarseness and vulgarity' in general, and specifically the 'repeated and calculated insult to the name of our Lord Jesus Christ' (*Telegraph* February 17,1977, 19). The Synod itself though remained an object of broadcasting interest. The February 1983 General Synod appeared as a live broadcast on BBC2 owing to public interest in a debate about nuclear deterrence (Grimley 2004, 162).

Underneath objections to tastelessness and blasphemy are more profound objections to changes to broadcasting and to ontological shifts in what television makers thought they ought to be delivering. A shift in understanding was apparent, from television being what people ought to have to what people wanted. This change is most significant in relation to the BBC but did not exclude other channels. The number of channels available to British viewers expanded from one, to two, three and then four when Channel 4 commenced broadcasting in 1982. If broadcasting on both the BBC and the independent channels was not intended to proselytise, churchmen expected that it would at least not seek to undermine the Church. As such, clergy and laity reacted with fury to the broadcast of *Jesus: The Evidence* on Channel 4 in 1984. The controversy about the programme is told by Richard Wallis, including the leaking of scripts, the mobilisation of an evangelical Christian campaign and Channel 4's ultimate agreement to broadcast a right of reply from theologians concerned with the show's academic errors (Wallis 2016, 678). A programme that raised provocative questions about Jesus became more than simply an

Anglican concern and raised alarm across a wide-spectrum of Christian churches and communities. The Church of England however found itself negotiating a distinctive set of concerns with the new channel. The fourth channel came into existence precisely to be beyond the mainstream. For religious broadcasting, according to its executive John Ranelagh, that included avoiding 'worship or *Songs of Praise*-type programmes' in favour of 'the depiction of religions not in the mainstream in Britain' (quoted in Wallis 2016, 682). Clifford Longley, writing the religion column in *The Times*, got the point and identified the fourth channel as one not meeting the Church's hopes or expectations about broadcasting, instead being 'tendentious' and 'a channel for all sorts of points of view' (Wallis 682).

The CRAC upheld the importance of dedicated time for religious content, although the shape, tone and purpose of that contest became contestable as British society changed around the Church, the CRAC and the BBC's religious broadcasting department. A watershed moment came in 1980, when the BBC began planning large-scale changes to what it broadcast in its religious slot. The BBC's plans were significant in a number of ways, including what the national broadcaster thought comprised the religious mainstream of Britain by then, why religious broadcasting took place and how viewers could participate in a religious experience via a mediated vision of the Church. In the case of the mainstream, the BBC's religious department found itself making choices about what would interest the widest audience possible, essentially based on demographics.

In 1980, the BBC vetoed the broadcasting of a Spiritualist service, instead upholding the 'mainstream' of national religion as being the Church of England, the Roman Catholic Church, and the largest Protestant churches that belonged to the BCC. The working definition of religious broadcasting remained Christian and specifically mainstream Christian (Harrison 2000, 4). A suggestion to broadcast live from a Reform Synagogue was similarly problematic for the national broadcaster which, mindful of a remit to appeal to the nation, considered the Jewish service would fail to be 'comprehensible or interesting' to the millions of people viewing the God Slot. These decisions are significant for understanding the sociology of the religion of broadcasting and audiences, in that the BBC understood the religious literacy of its audiences: could they understand an Anglican service as well as Catholic, Methodist, Free Churches or Church of Scotland worship but not something from a smaller or more exotic denomination nor from the religious landscape beyond Christianity?

Even that question though was tested by the BBC reviewing whether it should even broadcast worship from a church building. Uncertainties about this were longstanding. As already discussed in Chap. 2, the appropriateness of broadcasting an act of worship had been an aspect of the debate between contending forces in the government, the Church and the media about broadcasting the 1953 Coronation. Apart from the spectacular one-off occasion of the Coronation, a host of lesser services had continued to provoke questions about broadcasting worship, and to raise concerns about potential slippage between a congregation and an audience. Far back in 1951, the provost of Leeds Parish Church had consented to be part of the broadcast of Evensong, but had been sure to remind the television audience that they were not really participating in worship. In 1980, answers to these questions and concerns were no further advanced.

The BBC itself seemed uncertain as to why it even broadcast church services. It rejected evangelical arguments that they should be a means of converting people but also rejected arguments that they were a service to people who were already believers but prevented by ill health from attending church physically. The CRAC's contribution was calling into question the technical approach taken to broadcasting a church service, one that had not changed for many decades. CRAC summed up these long-standing limitations with the question of 'where to point the camera' when broadcasting something sacred. In 1953, the BBC, senior clergy and the Queen concurred that some aspects of the Coronation were too sacred to be seen by a camera. By 1980 broadcasters found that the interaction between a camera and a service were still unsatisfactory. In 1957 the ITA, representing Associated Television and ABC Television, sought permission from the CRAC to try 'experimental' broadcasts of church services and over 20 years later the independent channels still appeared to be struggling with the experiment (*The Times* August 21, 1957, 4). The IBA's struggles with this intersection appear vividly in one especially impractical suggestion that 'viewers should be invited to place bread and wine near the television set in their own homes while a communion service is being broadcast, and to eat the bread and drink the wine at the appropriate moment in the service'. There are no indications of the idea catching on (*The Times* July 18, 1980, 4).

If not complete services, what then could be broadcast? The technical frustrations and sacerdotal absurdities of televising a complete service prompted imaginative responses from the producers responsible for religious content. The BBC's General Features Department rather than the religious department produced *A Passion for Churches* in 1974, in which the poet laureate John Betjeman led viewers around the diocese of Norwich. Reviewers acclaimed the work on its first broadcast and Betjeman's commentary in poetry and prose speaks in praise of the Church of England. The footage, including of choir practice, a wedding, a baptism, a Mothers Union garden party, a village fete, and bell ringing, is a snapshot of the rural Church as it was. The documentary captures Betjeman's vast affection for medieval churches and the Church of England and distils what he valued most, from the language of *The Book of Common Prayer* to eccentric vicars who liked steam engines. But the production is also elegiac. The murky and muddy 16-mm film suits the overcast East Anglian landscapes and Betjeman laments as much as he celebrates. He laments the redundant churches and their repurposing for secular purposes and *A Passion for Churches* is not blind to institutional decline.

A Passion for Churches was a critically successful one-off; in asking what could be broadcast other productions about religion were more regular but less critically successful. *Stars on Sunday* resembled more variety and light entertainment programmes than televised worship. *Highway* included hymn singing and other choral music but not from within the framework of a complete church service but instead in a magazine format of discussion and readings, including solos from Sir Harry Secombe. The format of *Songs of Praise* inexorably changed from the words and music of a service, to congregational hymn singing interspersed among a wider palette of features and voices, although the people making it still comprised the 'greatest concentration of practising Christians' at the BBC, according to Michael Wakelin, the BBC's former head of Religion and Ethics (Bailey 2010, 187). When the 1994 comedy series *The Vicar of Dibley* included an episode where *Songs of Praise* comes to the village to make an episode in the church, the format shown was already an anachronism. This episode, in which the cameras making *The Vicar of Dibley* are themselves pointing at a fictional outside broadcast crew making *Songs of Praise*, suggested that the instalment would feature the complete service, including the sermon and the readings from scripture. These however were long gone from the actual *Songs of Praise*, which no longer faithfully followed the format of the whole service.

Clergy could be sensitive and often highly critical observers of religion on television and its changes in format and tone, not only because they appeared on it so often but also because television had important impacts on their careers and profile. Archbishop Donald Coggan was a seasoned television performer, including multiple appearances on *Stars on Sunday* and *Seeing and Believing*. Coggan was glad enough to have *Stars on Sunday* as a vehicle and made more than a dozen appearances. But his private papers contain candid accounts of what he really thought of it. In December 1974 he received a letter from a press officer congratulating him 'for your splendid decision to appear for a number of weeks on the erroneously popular ITV feature "'Stars on Sunday"', and also noted 'I know in certain church circles this programme is not viewed with great favour (being regarded as too sweetly sentimental)'. Coggan agreed, but explained 'I did not feel that I could refuse the invitation to appear on a dozen Stars on Sunday programmes. It is not my favourite series... But what an opportunity to get something across which one believes is worthwhile and sorely needed'. Coggan's correspondence showed that he was aware of changes in tone, format and approach, as he realised 'the present series is less saccharin in flavour than when Jess Yates was in control' (LPL Coggan 6). Coggan was referring to the presenter and producer of *Stars on Sunday*, who had departed after a *News of the World* scandal (*Independent* April 12, 1993). Coggan's appearances were on a wildly successful programme, and placed him as one among many guest performers including Val Doonican, Gracie Fields, Roy Orbison and Bing Crosby.

For Coggan and for other bishops and archbishops, appearing on television in a chat or talking format meant drawing themselves to the attention of a wide and varied audience. Coggan felt, as did other clergy, that it was worth it to get Christian messages across to people who never came to church and where broadcasters no longer thought of themselves as axiomatically Christian. It also meant that bishops attracted the attention and displeasure of a wide audience. Their papers are full of correspondence from irate members of the public who disliked what they saw on television. In 1974 Coggan broadcast a message calling for help for the starving in the third world. In response came angry letters complaining that aid to the third world was impossible as Britain faced economic collapse (LPL Coggan 6). Other correspondents implored him to get the BBC to broadcast the full chime of Big Ben before the 9pm news, to ask him to get the BBC to change the times of religions broadcasts, or complained when he spoke sympathetically about 'coloured people' (LPL Coggan 6).

The style, tone and content of British religious broadcasting was therefore not static and it was not one-way, as viewers spoke back to participating clergy. In his autobiography, Bishop David Jenkins briefly sketched the broadcasting history of the God slot from the iron-clad intentions of

Reith, its weakened position in the 1950s onwards to a period of crisis by the 1980s, which is when Jenkins entered the scene. As a sought-after broadcaster, precisely because he was controversial if not always articulate, in the sense that his academic background made him less likely to be able to speak succinctly or accessibly, Jenkins saw first-hand what was happening to the God slot by the 1980s. He sensed that 'the God slot was under siege and, feeling the pressure to bolster declining ratings, religious producers were inclining towards more controversial and sensationalist presentations of religious topics' (Jenkins 2003, 24).

By the 1990s the position of the God slot was no less precarious. The BBC's attitude to their chartered obligation to broadcast religion received biting and telling representation in the 1998 drama series *In the Red*. The series is an example of biting the hand that fed it, as it was made by the BBC and film locations included the Television Centre and Broadcasting House. The satire however was scathing of the Corporation's addiction to bureaucracy, its abandonment of Reithian ideals, and its contempt for audiences. This satiric treatment of the senior management's decision-making centres on desperate attempts to re-energise the God slot and drive up BBC1 ratings. A tightly woven plot that dramatised power play among the different controllers (the executives in charge of the radio and television channels) centred on a scheme by the controllers of Radio 2 and Radio 4 to oust the controller of BBC1 by masterminding the creation of a new religious comedy to replace *Songs of Praise*. In comes *O Jesus!*, featuring an Iranian ayatollah as a giant phallus, nuns with Alsatians, and a pope molesting children.

This bizarre hodgepodge of content is a reminder that religious broadcasting lacks a stable definitional basis, being more than simply broadcasting a church service. This definitional uncertainty has, in actuality, allowed for striking experiments in content and approach. This period of experimentation provides the broadcast context for the scandalous religious broadcast in *In the Red*. New religious-themed quiz shows *Holy Smoke!* and *Heaven Knows* and the series *It's Your Funeral* were celebrity-laden and variety attempts to move past hymn singing (Harrison 2000, 8). Safe within the fictional world of *In the Red*, *O Jesus* pushed beyond all possible boundaries of good taste and beyond the BBC's guidelines that stress care should be taken not to cause offence (Harrison 2000, 7). The Church could expect that it would asked to moderate content and uphold standards.

SHAPING THE MEDIUM: MORALITY AND MRS WHITEHOUSE

The previous sections considered the Church as a participant in shaping a third terrestrial channel, and from there broadened to consider bodies that allowed the Church to interact with broadcasters and the development of the God slot and beyond up to the end of the twentieth century. The next section of this chapter steps back again in time to consider the Church's responsibilities in shaping broadcasting included the tone and content of broadcasting, especially anything religious and even more so anything about Jesus. The content within the God slot was of particular concern and interest but the attention of church leaders ranged beyond that and involved more than just ordained clergy. As is apparent also from the previous section, their impact, and their assurance that they were interacting with Christian broadcasters, became uncertain and contested.

Debates about the broadcast of blasphemous content or more broadly of 'filth', sex and violence received a sharper focus and more impact in the 1960s after Mary Whitehouse formally launched the Clean Up TV campaign. Individual clergy expected and attempted to shape the medium. These intentions are complicated by their responses to Clean Up TV. Some clergy were forthright about television's moral failings. In a 1976 outburst sent to his diocesan clergy, Bishop Victor Whitsey of Chester said television was 'a faithless hussy with as much morality as the proverbial tomcat'. As for the people making television, he pitied 'the facile cleverness of the trifling men and women to whom such power is given' (*Daily Mirror* December 23, 1976, 3). Whitsey's comments now come with an additional twist. In 2017, the Cheshire constabulary announced, and the current bishop of Chester and the archbishop of York accepted, the claims of several people that Whitsey was a sex offender, including in the later 1970s when he was condemning television as lubricious (*Guardian* October 17, 2017; *Church Times* October 17, 2017; Diocese of Chester October 17, 2017). While that knowledge casts Whitsey as a hypocrite and worse, his stridency was not typical of his fellow bishops. Contextually a greater ambivalence is apparent with other bishops reluctant to rush to judgement, especially over claims of blasphemy and filth.

Anglican ambivalence is apparent in *A Christian Approach to Television* (1968), which presented the current thinking of an Anglican body, the Archbishops' Advisors on Radio and Television. It stood apart from assessments such as the campaigns associated with Mary Whitehouse to 'clean up' TV, and did not suggest television needed cleaning up as such. It certainly did comment in alarm at the 'pornography and sadism' but held back from suggesting that television could have a negative influence such as encouraging crime, instead proposing that research would be needed.

Michael Ramsey became the archbishop of Canterbury in 1961 and in that year he had proposed a 'scientific inquiry' into how television affected a person's morality (*Belfast Telegraph* July 18, 1961, 8). Characteristic with his other temperate comments on television, Ramsey suggested he did not condemn the medium, and therefore called for the participation of science not dogmatism in understanding the impact of television, while also acknowledging that he had himself seen spiritually meaningful programmes on television (*Birmingham Post* July 19, 1961, 5).

That call for research is characteristic of Ramsey and his academic caution in gathering evidence before making statements. The publication also contained flashes of televisually literate thinking and an awareness of how the technology involved and the manner of making television could shape the moral and emotional impact of a programme. The report envisaged the television camera and the other apparatus as stolid, impersonal and 'imperturbable' instruments; looking with the same blankness at 'the trivial, the obscure, the profound, the courageous, the terrified and the perplexed', the camera 'never blushes or turns away until the producer says the word' (*Stage and Television Today* April 4, 1968, 12). It was here at this mediated gap between the action and the audience that the possibility arose for the programme makers to misjudge their audience. The pamphlet is the product of a milieu around Ramsey, cautious about judging, seeing much good in television and conscious of not merely the impact but also the realities of production.

Into the next decade, the Church at an institutional level continued to evolve in how it engaged with and sought to advise television. In 1970 the newly formed General Synod debated on broadcasting and passed a vote to establish a Broadcasting Commission, which Sir William Hart chaired (Saward 1999, 282). The Commission attracted criticism regarding expertise and relevance because it contained no actual broadcasters. The Commission's final report, *Broadcasting, Society and the Church*, appeared in 1973 and pointed to the Church's ineffective use of television. It urged a rethink of communication from the physical pulpit to understanding the impact of broadcast media. Recognising that television called for people to 'think visually' and to mobilise techniques for presentation and communication, the report ultimately called for more and better training (*Telegraph* October 22, 1973, 12). Its recommendations reiterated Church actions from more than a decade earlier, from the charm school training to Lord Rank's intervention and support. The report also unwittingly presented views on television in tension with each other. One was that Anglican clergy needed television but also needed to do better when they appeared on it. The other was the disparagement of television, including even successful religious broadcasting. *Stars on Sunday* attracted 15 million viewers to its religious content but that was not good enough, as these 15 million saw a facile and sentimental programme, showing a 'fantasy world' (*Telegraph* October 22, 1973, 12).

Mary Whitehouse's vigorous campaigns exposed uncertainty on several issues: was the BBC in particular still a Christian organisation, where should the Church direct its energies when scrutinising television, and what constituted religiously offensive television? When archbishop of York, Michael Ramsey, offered public thoughts to the York Convocation in 1959 that the Church was losing influence over the nation to television, perceiving that in the 'space age' the Church seemed stuffy whereas television offered sensation and novelty, which he described as a 'fresh tickle every few minutes'. Ramsey was as uneasy about television's capacity to stimulate and shock as he was about the Church criticising it, as 'the Church will seem to be a set of people keen on prohibitions and negative rules who want to stop this and stop that and "spoil the game"' (*The Journal* January 14, 1959, 5). Ramsey, a scholar and academic, proposed that in place of strident denunciation the Church should use informed and reasonable intellectual engagement. He used references from the sociologist Richard Hoggart. Ramsey's caution and his concern that television possibly was too full of sex and violence but that it was counterproductive to say so is a measured response far removed from the tone that would characterise religious commentary on television in the 1960s and 1970s, when most male clerical voices were largely drowned out by the louder tones of Mary Whitehouse.

Mary Whitehouse points to the Church of England's emerging uncertainty about its own relationship with television. There are two particular catalysts for the expression of this uncertainty. One was the broadcast of Dennis Potter's *The Son of Man*, a 1969 instalment of *The Wednesday Play* featuring Colin Blakely's interpretation of the title role showing Jesus as human rather than divine and afflicted by doubts (Cook 1995, 60). The other was a debate in the Church of England's Church House on November 5 that year on broadcasting. Whitehouse attended the debate, but could only watch silently from the public gallery. Records of what was said indicate a degree of agonised confusion not just about *The Son of Man* and Whitehouse's organisation but more broadly how the BBC and the Church of England now related to each other. Whitehouse denounced Potter's play as a blasphemy yet most Church of England clergyman were reluctant to fall into line behind her. Whitehouse enjoyed good relationships with some quarters of the Church, such as the Mothers' Union (*Coventry Evening Telegraph* September 7, 1972, 17). In the Church Assembly, though, she was silent. One member patronised her as the designated spokeswoman of the 'middle-class mums' who were an important but demeaned sector of Church of England membership. The clergyman expressing this view of the middle-class mums, the Reverend Hugh Bishop, had earlier been principal of the all-male College of the Resurrection in Mirfield and he disparaged the possibility that 'this assembly was content simply to act as a rubber stamp for the views expressed by Mrs Whitehouse and her association'. Other speakers followed suit. The bishop of Bristol, Oliver Tomkins, admitted that *The Son of Man* had made him uneasy but felt 'that despite many criticisms... the author had a vision of the character of Jesus'. The dean of St Paul's meanwhile had seen nothing offensive in *The Son of Man* (*Birmingham Evening Post* November 6, 1969, 8).

In general, the clergy speaking in the debate offered views that were more ambiguous than certain, and more willing to engage seriously with what Potter was saying than Whitehouse's more strident claims of blasphemy. Their voices though were little heard compared to Mrs Whitehouse's forceful impact, which brought in sacks of letters supporting her. Her campaigns also became part of the fabric of television drama when the BBC's *Everyman* dramatised the Gay News trial at the Old Bailey in 1977. The debate in Church House also leaves us with an impression of the Church anxiously attempting to recalibrate its relationship with the BBC. In fact, the Corporation was going out of its way to assure the clergy that it was still a Christian organisation and to deny the fear in some quarters of a 'humanist plot' within its ranks, exemplified by the decision to transmit *Son of Man*. Instead the Church's assembly was assured that director general was Christian and two of his managing directors were Anglican (*Birmingham Evening Post* November 6, 1969, 8).

Another BBC programme played further with the nature of the interactions between Whitehouse and the Church of England. In 1971 *The Goodies* episode *Gender Education* put the two together. In the episode, the character Mrs Desiree Carthorse is an analogue and parody of

Whitehouse. Carthorse's denunciation of the filth of the 'gender education' film *How to Make Babies by Doing Dirty Things* borrows from and
amplifies how the real Mrs Whitehouse bruited that *Son of Man* was blasphemy. At the end of the episode, a man deranged by too much sex and
violence on television blows up the BBC Television Centre, therefore
blacking out all the televisions in Britain (within this fictional world the
commercial network is forgotten) and the populace has nothing to watch.
As a result, people everywhere retire to their bedrooms to make love and
the episode ends with Mrs Carthorse running in horror from sex happening everywhere.

The ending pre-empted a comment by the BBC scriptwriter Johnny
Speight the next year when Whitehouse bombarded the BBC with complaints about *Till Death Us Do Part.* 'If Mrs Whitehouse had her way,
there would be nothing to watch at all', he said, precisely echoing what
happened at the end of *Gender Education*, but where the additional twist
was that without any television to watch sex, people made do with the real
thing. Whitehouse reappeared in *The Goodies* in *Wacky Wales* (1975), an
episode where the parody is even more obvious, as an actress plays Mary
Whitehouse herself rather than a character disguised via an analogue. The
episode culminates in an 'Ecclesiastical Seven a side', with 16 teams including soberly suited Methodists, a team of Derek Nimmos, Nasturcian
monks, Greek Orthodox Clergy and Church of England archbishops playing rugby in mitres and copes. There is also a team from the Festival of
Light for Mary Whitehouse plays hooker, takes on all other players, scores
a goal, then physically tackles and overcomes Lord Longford and a
Catholic monk. 'No opposition can stand up to her' is the commentator's
awestruck comment as she rampages through the field. In the meantime,
other characters in the episode who themselves belong to the 'Church of
the Seventh Day Repressionists' deride the Church of England as 'that
poncy lot' in comparison to the dynamic solo efforts made by Mrs
Whitehouse. Her dynamism on the rugby field compared to all other
ecclesiastical players was *The Goodies'* way to bring to life the fraught relationship between her and the Church of England.

Before the broadcast of *Wacky Wales*, one of Mrs Whitehouse's noisiest
campaigns against filth on television had been about Speight's *Till Death
Us Do Part*, particularly an episode in 1972 where the characters had a
vulgar conversation about the Virgin Mary's sex life. Alf Garnett, the central character in *Till Death Us Do Part*, belonged to the Church of England
(and hated Catholics) and the blasphemy shocked him. Garnett however

was an unsympathetic antihero and the episode placed the irreverence and blasphemy with the younger and more sympathetic characters. The series aligned Whitehouse with the antihero when Garnett read her book *Cleaning up TV*, which his daughter and son-in-law then burnt as an 'unclean' thing (Sandbrook 2011). Whitehouse complained to everyone from the BBC director general and the posts and telecommunications minister John Eden to the Cardinal Archbishop of Westminster and the archbishop of Canterbury (*Daily Mirror* September 22, 1972, 3). In each case, the men she appealed to let her down, in her estimation, and Whitehouse's voice was louder and more confident in defence of Church dogma, especially her outrage that the character Alf Garnett had made 'the inference that God and the Virgin Mary had intercourse to create Jesus' (*Daily Mirror* September 22, 1972, 3).

The blasphemous language used in *Till Death Us Do Part* indicated the willingness of scriptwriters to keep pushing boundaries. In response, the Church of England's broadcasting specialists deemed that tentativeness was the order of the day. To move briefly to the focus of the next chapter, the comedy *All Gas and Gaiters* used the clean-up TV campaign for comedy. The bishop of St Ogg's is a television addict. The episode *The Bishop Loses His Chaplain* (1971) showed the bishop receiving a new television that was not only in colour but gave him BBC1, BBC2 and ITV. The bishop swiftly becomes entranced by the variety of programmes, in a manner more than a little reminiscent of his real-world contemporary Mervyn Charles Edwards, who had told the House of Lords of his love of westerns and crime dramas. The grim cathedral dean forbids television in his deanery, and the comedy comes from his equally forbidding wife making transparent excuses to visit the bishop's residence to catch a glimpse of the banned medium. In an imitation of Mrs Mary Whitehouse as obvious as *The Goodies'* Mrs Carthorse, the dean's wife is evidently disappointed that neither BBC1 nor BBC2 are showing anything obscene but she has faith that ITV will be showing something appalling and looks forward with relish to being shocked. Her hope of finding TV appalling matches her eagerness to watch, and equally contrasts with the bishop's frank enjoyment of his television. In a microcosm, the episode sums up the tensions informing the Church's national responses to television, including Whitehouse's altogether more vigorous attacks on the small screen and her frustration at the tendency of clergy to either equivocate or ignore her altogether.

The uncertain and even dithering reactions of clergy to ever more confronting broadcasting in the 1970s can be followed through Robert Runcie's 1970s correspondence when chair of the CRAC and bishop of St Alban's. Correspondence between Runcie, the bishop of Wakefield and Sir Brian Young of the Independent Broadcasting Authority, shows the Church's quest for effective ways to look decisive when receiving complaints about blasphemy. He accepted with gratitude a pro-forma letter drafted by Lady Plowden, chairman of the IBA, to an irate viewer upset by use of the Lord's name in vain on television. Plowden offered a thoughtful but firm response to an unrealistic request to 'stop the use of God's name and also the name of Jesus Christ in television programmes' (Runcie/STA/CRAC/2). She said 'we know there are those in our audience, like yourself, who would regard the trivial use of the names of Christ, Jesus and God as sinful and therefore wrong in any circumstance', but questioned 'whether it is right that all programmes should be controlled by the views of [people like the irate viewer]' and the broadcaster's dilemma was 'Should he adopt or seek to impose a morality of any particular section of his large and varied audience'. Lady Plowden thought not.

Having been provided with a copy, the bishops involved with CRAC and the Information Committee found its moderate tone to their liking. At the time, bishops were seeking ways to manage and resolve a debate in the Synod about blasphemy on television. Bishop Colin James of Wakefield had even found the Church's debate and the ensuing communication with both the BBC and the IBA tasteless, for 'It does seem rather bald simply for Derek Pattinson to send a note to the B.B.C. and I.B.A. informing them of the resolution passed' (Runcie/STA/CRAC/2). Indeed, Bishop James thought that notwithstanding 'a head of steam in the Synod' about blasphemy, it may even be 'sensible to let the matter drop' (Runcie/STA/CRAC/2).

The appearance of *Till Death Us Do Part* and *All Gas and Gaiters* reflected real-world concerns about the tone and content of British broadcasting. These were programmes about the Church, but were not products made for the God slot. In section one, these chapters have examined several Christian institutions. One is the Church of England itself and its various organs such as the Council. But others were the BBC and more broadly the culture of British broadcasting, and how the BBC for decades thought of itself and was thought of as Christian. The chapters have looked at the big and small impressions, of the Church shaping broadcasting through intervention in the creation of the second and third channels, and in the engagement with the medium by clergy who wanted to be effective broadcasters. But there is also confusion, ambiguity and hesitation. No amount of charm school training could stop clergy appearing on television saying explosive things about doctrine, and even the longest and most talky show could be an appropriate way to explain theological subtleties. Church and broadcasters could work together; television producers of religious content were often in holy orders, and the notion that the BBC was Christian and broadcasting to Christians was still considered a point needing reiteration well into the post-war era. But the Church was less certain of its involvement in the creation and content of the fourth channel. Churchmen seemed unsure of what to say or do about blasphemy, compared to the forthright certainties of Mrs Mary Whitehouse. Moving from these realms of non-fiction broadcasting to fiction via *Till Death Us Do Part* and *All Gas and Gaiters* is significant, as the Church was far from thrilled about the latter. This gentle comedy seemed to presage an alarmingly disrespectful approach to the Church, as clergy sat down to watch actors playing them as the medium shaped perceptions of the Church.

References

Newspapers, Periodicals and Trade Papers

Belfast Telegraph
Birmingham Evening Post
Birmingham Post
Coventry Evening Telegraph
Daily Mirror
Guardian
The Journal
Liverpool Echo
Spectator
Stage and Television Today
Telegraph
The Times

Government Sources

UK Parliament. 1962. *House of Lords Hansard*, vol. 242, col. 637
———. 1965. *House of Lords Hansard*, vol. 262, col. 961
———. 1969. *House of Lords Hansard*, vol. 302, col. 369

ARCHIVES

CHURCH OF ENGLAND RECORD CENTRE (CERC)

ACCM/VP/SEC/9
CACEC/SEC/10
CIO/RTV/1

LAMBETH PALACE LIBRARY (LPL)

Runcie/STA/CRAC/2

NATIONAL ARCHIVES, KEW (NA)

NA HO244/443

PRINTED SECONDARY SOURCES

Bailey, Michael. 2010. Media, Religion and Culture: An Interview with Michael Wakelin. *Journal of Media Practice* 11 (2): 185–189.

Briggs, Asa. 1995. *The History of Broadcasting in the United Kingdom: Volume V Competition*. Oxford: Oxford University Press.

Çoban, Savaş. 2014. *Media and Left*. Brill.

Cook, John R. 1995. *Dennis Potter: A Life on Screen*. Manchester University Press.

Cooke, Lez. 2003. *British Television Drama: A History*. BFI Publishing.

Grimley, Matthew. 2004. *Citizenship, Community, and the Church of England: Liberal Anglican Theories of the State Between the Wars*. Oxford: Clarendon Press.

Harrison, Jackie. 2000. A Review of Religious Broadcasting on British Television. *Liberal Theology in the Contemporary World* 41 (4): 3–15.

Jenkins, David. 2003. *The Calling of a Cuckoo: Not Quite an Autobiography*. A&C Black.

Potter, Jeremy. 2016. *Independent Television in Britain: Volume 4: Companies and Programmes, 1968–80*. Springer.

Sandbrook, Dominic. 2011. *State of Emergency: The Way We Were: Britain, 1970–1974*. Penguin.

Saward, Michael. 1999. *A Faint Streak of Humility*. Paternoster Press.

Sendell, Bernard. 1983. *Independent Television in Britain*. London: Palgrave Macmillan.

Wallis, Richard. 2016. Channel 4 and the Declining Influence of Organized Religion on UK Television. The Case of Jesus: The Evidence. *Historical Journal of Film, Radio and Television* 36 (4): 668–688.

Shaped by the Medium

In Part II, the Church is the object of broadcasters' attention rather than the active shaper of the medium. In Part I, the range of activities of clergy and broadcasters appeared largely through written evidence, archives and debates. In Part II, the focus shifts to visual evidence placed in its political and social contexts. Across this section, we will see a loss of balance in the ratio between activity and objectivity, when the Church remains a productive object of attention for writers, producers and executives, but loses its mainstream influence over broadcasting.

CHAPTER 6

Comedy and Blasphemy

In the first section, we saw real-life clergy appear on the small screen. Members of the Church of England appeared on television in broadcasts of services, documentaries about the Church, or increasingly, via interviews. This section in general and this chapter move from looking at the Church as a shaper of the medium to one being shaped by it. Why start with comedy? Fictional programmes about the Church cross genres and formats and the chapters, among others, encompass science fiction, sketch comedy and soap operas. But in the early to mid-1960s, comedy marks an important point of transition in the Church's interactions with television. This chapter treats the sitcoms *Our Man at St Mark's* and *All Gas and Gaiters* as landmarks. They appeared close in time to each other (starting in 1963 and 1966 respectively) and are the first occasions the Church began to appear in a sustained way on television in fiction. Yet the significant differences in approach and tone are important to understanding the discursive trajectories about the Church taken by television. This chapter then moves to subsequent decades, when affectionate portrayals eroded and a more stinging portrayal of the Church came to dominate. The medium presented increasing challenges as society became less respectful. Ecclesiastical comedies underwent a metamorphosis, with whimsy and affection replaced by grotesques like Dick Emery's Toothy Vicar, Spike Milligan's Sneezing Vicar and the Baby Eating Bishop of Bath and Wells in *Blackadder II*.

© The Author(s) 2020   109
M. Harmes et al., *The Church on British Television*,
https://doi.org/10.1007/978-3-030-38113-4_6

LAUGHING AT THE CHURCH

The clergy appearing on screen had often been exactly that: real-life clergy appearing in non-fiction broadcasts. The notion of an actor essaying the role of a clergyman only broke through gradually. From its earliest days, religious broadcasting contained notable diversity, including the transmission of medieval mystery plays in 1938, 1947 and 1949 (Wrigley 2015, 569–570). Plays set in more or less the present era (at time of broadcast) occasionally included a clergyman character. *A Comedy of Good and Evil*, a play by Richard Hughes shown on the Television Service on March 18, 1948, was set in the cottage of a poor Welsh rector. The Television Service presented the comedy *I Done a Murder* in July 1951, where the comedy was extracted from the situation of a murderer attempting to confess but finding that everyone he speaks to has a particular reason for not wanting to hear his confession. Among them is a vicar, who blocks his ears to confession because he will be in trouble with his bishop (an opponent of hanging) if the man is executed. Much of the Television Service's content relied on existing drama and the broadcast of A.A. Milne's 1930 play *Michael and Mary* in January 1952 was representative of that trend. It also included a clerical character, the Rev. Simon. The BBC's drama strand Sunday Night Theatre presented *The Wonderful Visit* in February 1952, based on the story by H.G. Wells. Starring Kenneth Williams as an angel, the cast also included Barry Morse as a vicar, the Reverend Hillyer.

These broadcasts are 'ghost' texts. No recordings of the live broadcasts exist. The texts survive and only a few scraps of information from their production paperwork and the *Radio Times* give any impression of what they comprised. They are however worth noting as early fictional appearances of the Church's clergy. Playing the angel in *The Wonderful Visit*, Kenneth Williams worried that he had been dressed and made up to look 'exactly like a tarty lesbian' (Williams 70), but that was a privately recorded opinion and the broadcast contained nothing to offend or shock the Church. Newspapers reviewers received it favourably.

Another 1952 broadcast, *The Cathedral*, was also a literary adaptation, this time of Hugh Walpole's novel of the same title. The novel, published in 1922, was a major critical success in its day. Its adapter, Nigel Kneale, thought that the 1952 adaptation was nothing special and merely part of what both Kneale and the BBC drama department focussed on at the time, which was seeking suitable novels to turn into television plays (Murray 2017).

Kneale's source novel for *The Cathedral* in 1952 had drawn comparisons with Anthony Trollope's Barchester novels in its delineation of life and politics in a cathedral close. Trollope's own novel *The Warden* became an instalment of the BBC Television Service's *Saturday Night Theatre* in 1951, with the entire novel condensed into one teleplay and comedy actors Arnold Ridley and Deryck Guyler playing the cathedral clergy. The clergy again appeared in a historical setting in *Prelude to Glory*, a 1954 television play about the accession of Queen Victoria, including the dramatic early morning arrival of the archbishop of Canterbury to tell the princess she has become queen.

THE SITCOMS

These are occasional 1950s productions. Then suddenly, programme makers found that clergy could be funny and in quick succession in the mid-1960s two ecclesiastical comedies appeared. Clergy had made occasional one-off appearances in drama but here is something new: television series based around the Church, lead characters in dog collars and television inviting the audience to laugh at the Church. Where did they come from? Initially, the answer is not the BBC. What the television historian Christine Davies calls 'rigorous' censorship had encased BBC comedy, and the Corporation's 'Green Book' strictly forbad jokes mocking religion (Davies 2016, 22). By the 1960s, the influence of the Green Book subsided but a comedy series about the Church was not a creative achievement of the BBC but of Associated Rediffusion. The comedy writer Edwin Apps thought: 'The BBC's early attempts at comedy about the Church came unstuck because the writers made the mistake of thinking that the Church is intrinsically funny, that it was enough to say someone was a vicar for everyone to fall about laughing. The scripts were tasteless and vulgar, they offended people and the BBC was criticized for it, something it does not enjoy' (pers.com.). In the face of criticism, the BBC temporarily left the field and Associated Rediffusion's *Our Man at St Mark's* (1963–1966) came from the pens of co-writers James Kelley and Peter Miller. Both were experienced writers, in particular having collaborated on *Bootsie and Snudge*. The ecclesiastical setting was however new for them, and for the series director Christopher Hodson and the veteran producer Eric Maschwitz. Almost nothing is left of their efforts; only 4 out of 46 episodes remain in the archives. *The Facts of Life* (1963) is the first. The character of the young vicar provides novel comedy situations for the writers. He has a young girlfriend who just wants to have fun and does not want him to attend a party wearing a dog collar. He also has a very young parishioner who believes that since a choirboy has kissed her she must be pregnant and he explains in direct terms that it can't be possible, as she and the choirboy have not made love.

The creation of *Our Man at St Mark's* shines a light on the tentative interactions between the creators and the Church, as Associated Rediffusion attempted something novel; making a situation comedy about a vicar. The tentativeness was on the part of the team at Associated Rediffusion, who worked with few precedents to guide them except a theatrical tradition of plays that 'have a vicar who is made to look like the biggest idiot ever' (*Stage and Television Today* July 29, 1965, 12). That tradition prompted concerns in the Church of England about what kind of lead character would reach a mass audience. Scripts went to the Church of England TV and Radio Council and the Reverend David Skinner for approval. The writers even made changes to ensure that an appropriately respectful tone defined the proceedings. One of the biggest changes was the title; originally it was to have been 'There was a young vicar', but ultimately that seemed too much like a limerick, which in turn could provoke obscene thoughts. The programme's producer Eric Maschwitz felt: 'It is a delicate subject and we don't want to offend anyone' (*Stage* September 5, 1963, 9). Far from it, after examining the scripts the Reverend Skinner was relieved to find no 'vulgarity, bad taste, or unreality'. The comments are suggestive. The TV and Television Council would not wish to have the Church featured alongside the profane or rude, but the Council did also commend the earnest attempt to portray the life of a parish priest. The producers were at pains to explain in their advance publicity that their vicar would not be a figure of fun but a well-grounded man (*Liverpool Echo and Evening Express* September 21, 1963, 2). Critics continued to appreciate a comedy that took pains to delineate a main character with 'dignity and a real understanding of his own frailties and those of his fellow men' (*Stage and Television Today* July 29, 1965, 12).

The makers of *Our Man at St Mark's* (which later changed its title to *Our Man from St Mark's*) therefore congratulated themselves on how positively the Church received their efforts. The producer Eric Maschwitz gave an interview when the programme was into its fourth year of production, expressing surprise that the show had become so popular, but also noting the ultimate accolade that the Dean and Chapter of Lincoln

Cathedral had permitted Associated Rediffusion to telerecord in the cathedral precincts.

The ongoing narratives in the series suggest that tentatively seeking approval remained the watchword for the scriptwriters. Their reluctance to write anything even remotely controversial ultimately made the series the butt of jokes rather than a source of comedy because of the writing and acting. Marjorie Norris, the television critic in *Stage and Television Today* found after one particularly insipid episode that the programme had 'delicious marrowbone jelly' instead of any creative backbone. The 'most controversial point to be discussed so far has been the [Leslie] Phillips moustache—a subject that can be happily argued over by all denominations without fear of religious schism'. Her reaction also pinpointed a possible cause of the writers' trepidation, that an outraged public would rush to send in letters of complaint if the Church of England were attacked, so therefore 'with all those tender toes just waiting to be stepped on, it's no wonder "Our Man at St Mark's" tiptoes around in stockinged feet' (*Stage and Television Today* October 24, 1963, 12). The writers' caution also resulted in what critics pinpointed as a tonal inconsistency to the scripts and production. Marjorie Norris continued to watch and review the programme as Leslie Phillips left and Donald Sinden replaced him. While she enjoyed the series, her review suggested it was popular for rather banal reasons: 'There is an immense audience longing to watch stories about nice people in happy situations' (*Stage and Television Today* May 27, 1964, 12). In seeking that 'niceness', Norris disapproved of some storylines and offered this unsolicited advice to the writers that 'funnies about unmarried mothers don't belong in the sunlit parish of St Mark's that they have created'. That said, the programme established and maintained its popularity with audiences and two years into its run was still in the TAM top 20 programmes for network television (*Stage and Television Today* July 22, 1965, 10).

The Bishop Rides Out

All Gas and Gaiters, the second ecclesiastical comedy of the 1960s, premiered as a one-off episode in the BBC *Comedy Playhouse* in May 1966. It was a stand-alone success, leading to a commissioned series. This development is not notable in itself and reflected a trend of the *Comedy Playhouse* strand that also bred *Steptoe and Son*, *Are You Being Served?* and *The Liver Birds*, among others. More distinctive in this stable of shows were the clerical characters and the ecclesiastical setting. The 1966 pilot episode, *The Bishop Rides Again*, set the tone for the next five seasons. An eccentric scholar has left a hefty bequest to ancient St Ogg's Cathedral but it is contingent on the bishop reviving a medieval tradition of riding a white horse around the city to distribute 40 pairs of stockings to 40 virgins.

Writing and directing an ecclesiastical comedy was new for the people behind the cameras and was a territory fraught with concern. One of the writers, Edwin Apps, was an experienced comedy performer in programmes such as *Whack-O!* (1958–1960), *Citizen James* (1961) and *Benny Hill* (1962). The producer (who was the director in contemporary BBC parlance) was the then inexperienced Stuart Allen. They had not previously used the precincts and personnel of a cathedral as a setting. Frank Muir, the assistant head of BBC Light Entertainment who oversaw the commissioning of the pilot script, remembered this milieu as 'a most unusual setting' (Muir 1997, 267). Apps was however fortunate in having a discreet contact at Church House, Westminster, and recollected that 'I had a reasonably good knowledge of the workings of the Church hierarchy, and when we needed specialist advice on arcane matters like the Court of Arches, Frank Muir, Head of Comedy at that time, put us in contact with a canon at Church House to whom we could turn whenever we needed to. He was very helpful' (pers.com.).

Our Man at St Mark's and *All Gas and Gaiters* often occupy a similar space in histories of British television comedy, and historians of British television and British post-war religion often place them together as the two mid-1960s ecclesiastical comedies. However lumping them together can obscure their important and revealing distinctions. Apps noted the distinctions, for 'I don't think we ever watched *Our Man at St Marks*. We came at the problem from a different angle; that of the cathedral clergy, a bishop and his *familia*. Our characters had very little contact with the man in the pew' (pers.com.). The comedy in the former was grounded in sometimes serious pastoral concerns, including the remarkably matter of fact discussion about making love in the first episode and *Our Man at St Mark's* did provide comedy based on the actual pastoral and personal concerns of a vicar. Eventually, it also moved the action to the inner city and to a more socially alert setting.

All Gas and Gaiters did not intersect with these more authentic flashes of pastoral concern. In that respect, the show is a dead end in the development of ecclesiastical comedies, with the exception of the subsequent comedies starring Derek Nimmo as a clergyman. Lucia Kramer places it in a longer trajectory, taking in *All in Good Faith* (1985–1988), *The Vicar of Dibley* (1994–2015) and *Rev* (2010–2014) (Kramer 2016). A more accurate view though would see that the high status characters, the focus on the hermetic and all-male bishop's palace and the farcical tone shows *All Gas and Gaiters* as a one-off leading nowhere, as later comedies take their place among the distinctively quotidian parish clergy and their authentic efforts to provide pastoral care. *Our Man at St Mark's* indicates both its own importance as the basis of a later trajectory of 'vicar sitcoms', and its divergence from a prevailing and largely negative appraisal of the Church associated especially with Dominic Sandbrook. According to Sandbrook the television vicars of the 1960s were 'comically naïve and incompetent' and 'inept in their attempts to appear modern'. Nigel Yates, citing Sandbrook, extends the vision to contemporary cinema and especially *Heavens Above!*, in which Peter Sellers played a comically well-meaning clergyman whose efforts at social reform end in financial catastrophe for the community (Yates 2011, 92). Television of the early 1960s has been characterised as showing the irrelevance of religion, especially the established Church, through the tendency to mock the clergy (Yates 2011). While the evidence is partial, owing to the archival disasters that have led to the loss of the programmes, the first episode of *Our Man at St Mark's* seems to stand apart from and in contrast to these assessments. By the end of the episode, the vicar has achieved a number of minor triumphs. An initially combative relationship with his housekeeper settles into a mutually respectful one. He compromises with his girlfriend and does not wear his clerical collar to the party, where he enjoys himself, and he tactfully settles the misunderstanding between the two young people about a pregnancy.

A lighter tone prevailed over *All Gas and Gaiters*; it was an instant success and suddenly large audiences were watching actors essaying roles of senior clergy lusting after women, hitting the sherry bottle and wandering around a palace in their pyjamas. The actor Jonathan Cecil, who took over the part played by Derek Nimmo when the BBC began a parallel radio version, recollected the Corporation's misgivings about *All Gas and Gaiters*. Equally, Cecil also found the robust scripts were 'without a trace of sentimentality', but were pure farce (*Telegraph* March 1, 1999, 19). *Our Man at St Mark's* showed the central character enacting pastoral concerns. *All Gas and Gaiters* takes place in a tightly contained world based on the structures and patterns of farce (Smith 1989, 12), and is a world where the antics push out any opportunity for pastoral depth or characterisation but where the ecclesiastical setting allows for some mild transgression (Apps 2013). Indeed the television critic Henry Raynor objected to *All Gas and Gaiters* not because it mocked the clergy, but because the characters were scarcely clergymen at all. He found it to be a programme that 'does not take the trouble to find out what exactly his [a clergyman's] job is' (*Telegraph* February 8, 1969, 19). The same critic objected to *Dad's Army* on the same grounds; that is, it did not actually show what the Home Guard had done.

Certainly the clergy in *All Gas and Gaiters* do not do anything especially clerical. They do not preach, officiate at services, administer the sacraments or offer pastoral comfort, and the avoidance of the religious seems a legacy of the strictly ingrained rules of the BBC's Green Book to not use the Bible, religious ceremonies or denominational identity in comedy (Davies 2016, 24). Looking back at the series from later years, it is striking however that the programme was steeped in contemporary ecclesiastical culture and expected a BBC1 audience to understand it, including the arcana such as the Court of Arches. In the pilot episode, after only one pair of the 40 stockings have been given away, the Archdeacon makes a joke likening the remaining pairs to the 39 Articles of Religion. The joke elicits a laugh from the live studio audience. In other episodes humour is extracted from the proposed but unsuccessful Anglican-Methodist reunion scheme that had been a point of controversy in in the later 1960s and especially in the primacy of Michael Ramsey, who argued for it up until its rejection in 1972 (Machin 1998, 139).

Brief Excursus: Ecclesiastical Details

A recent study of Anglicanism in *Dad's Army* has reiterated the impact of the actor Frank Williams, who played the vicar, on the depiction of Anglicanism within the series. As a member of the Church of England Synod in real life, Williams found himself in the position of the unofficial ecclesiastical advisor on matters such as which stole the vicar would wear, to the sermons and music used in services (Brydon 2018, 6). The detailed accuracy about the Church that prevailed in *Dad's Army* is the more apparent as the vicar, his church, his congregation and church rituals feature heavily and at times meaningfully. It is telling for instance that some humour in the programme is contingent on the audience having familiarity with Anglicanism. The 'spiv' character Private Walker at one point contemplates appropriating the chained Bible in the church, recognising that 'it's the Authorised Version, no rubbish!' The line elicits laughter from the studio audience and the response is indicative of an understanding of the culturally enshrined place that the King James Bible has in English history. Some jokes are even more arcane and based on quotes not merely from the Bible but from the Apocrypha. An insult is couched in the language of a canticle from Evensong, when the vicar none-too-nicely tells Captain Mainwaring to leave his office and recites the *Nunc Dimittis* canticle at him: 'Lord now letteth thou they servant depart in peace' (Brydon 2018, 7). David Croft's combination of verbal and visual humour found comedy in the frustrating of social ambitions and the absurdity of juxtaposing the dignified with the frantic, such as scenes of the vicar in full academicals frantically pumping a hand-powered railway cart, or as a harvest blessing descends into drunken chaos. The humour brought on to the screen involving the vicar, his verger and his church often transcends *All Gas and Gaiters* in its detail and the degree that an informed knowledge about the Church of England is needed to understand the jokes.

Ecclesiastical Comedy

The visual cues and style of *All Gas and Gaiters* reinforce its ecclesiastical tone even if the programme does not show the clergy being especially clerical. A pipe organ played deep organ chords in the opening music and the titles were in gothic typeface. As the title indicates, the actors wore the gaiters, aprons stocks and frock coats already seen on television whenever Archbishop Geoffrey Fisher graced a discussion or news programme with his presence.

Even if he would not have welcomed laughter at the expense of the Church, Fisher created and consolidated a space for the clergy on television. Although he had reservations about televising the Coronation, and placed limitations on which sacred mysteries the cameras could see, Fisher became an adept and enthusiastic television presence. The significance of Fisher in particular was his ability to pop up at all manner of times and in all types of programmes, not just the Sunday evening religious broadcasts. Fisher also appeared at key moments in the year, such as a broadcast from his study in his palace in Canterbury on New Year's Eve 1959. The authority accorded to him to comment on not just the Church but the state, on the monarchy, the Empire and on the medium of television itself, gave him a televisual versatility that transcended the God slot. He is a prelude to the emergence of a more sustained use of the Church in comedy and drama from the 1960s onwards. While television was inherently modern, Fisher and other clergy looked remarkable on screen in a modern television studio, with Fisher in particular rarely seen in anything other than the black gaiters, apron and frock coat once typical of English prelates.

The result is that from the standpoint of the twenty-first century, Archbishop Fisher can look like a stock figure from an Ealing film or a black and white BBC comedy, a turnaround in perception from the mid-1960s when an actor portraying a bishop on television was a novelty and emulated Fisher's well-known appearance. While doing research for the pilot episode, the series' co-writer Edwin Apps read a memoir by the archdeacon of Hastings and found inspiration for his plots in the fraught environment of the cathedral close at Canterbury. Fisher and Hewlett Johnson detested each other, and the unhappy relationship of prelate and dean struck Apps as the perfect farcical situation (Apps 2013).

Fisher retired from Canterbury early in 1961. As an archbishop he behaved like a headmaster (which he had been earlier in life) and strictly enforced the wearing of the 'uniform' of frock coat and gaiters by senior clergy, even publicly rebuking one for being a 'naughty man' for wearing normal trousers (*New York Times* May 20, 1970, 82). By 1966 when *All Gas and Gaiters* began production, English bishops had already celebrated their freedom from Fisher's stern authority by consigning gaiters to history and the attire of the *All Gas and Gaiters* television characters was, even just five years after Fisher's retirement, anachronistic. One up-to-date aspect of the programme is the casting of the imposing and white-haired William Mervyn as the bishop. Mervyn spent much of his career playing upper crust authority figures including a judge in *Crown Court*. He effectively captures and uses the fruity sing-song 'parsonical' voice once typical of clergy, but especially so Michael Ramsey, who by 1966 was appearing more frequently on television. There is a curious slippage between the actual and the fictional. The real bishop, Ramsey, came across on television to some as more like an actor playing the role of prelate. The perspective of one viewer was 'I can't believe in him as a real person' (Chadwick 1990, 122). Certainly, there was a very strong similarity between the tall, white haired and fruity voiced bishop in *All Gas and Gaiters* and Ramsey. As such, the central character in the gaiters of Fisher and the mannerisms of Ramsey occupied an unusual figurative space, both anachronistically emulating a former archbishop and channelling the demeanour of the current one.

Scenes of Clerical Life: The Characters

Reviewers noted that the programme presented an especially old-fashioned view of cathedral clergy, especially the younger character played by Derek Nimmo, which 'must be a particularly trying caricature of a young clergy-man for those who are trying to project the Church as the swinging holy city' (*Stage and Television Today* December 14, 1967, 12). It is further striking that the characters of bishop, archdeacon, chaplain and dean seemed to be 'stock' characters, when only five years earlier *Our Man at St Mark's* had seemed so fresh and clerical stereotypes were as yet unknown on television. The 'stock' element may be due to a longer theatrical tradition, not least because of to the links between the programme and the stage personified by the actor Robertson Hare (the archdeacon) and his long career in farce. Broadly written archetypes based around a person's job were also already the basis of television comedy. In 1961 in *The Lift*, an episode of his show, Tony Hancock trapped a host of archetypes in the lift, including the 'Producer', the 'Air Marshall', the 'Doctor', the 'House Wife', as well as the 'Vicar', each behaving broadly to type when a lift at the BBC breaks down. The Air Marshall takes charge in a crisis, the House Wife faints, the Vicar gives spiritual comfort, and so forth. It may also be because each episode of *All Gas and Gaiters* had largely the same plot of the bishop, archdeacon and chaplain conspiring to thwart the restrictive authority of the cathedral dean and fretting about ways to raise money for their crumbling cathedral. That does not diminish the semiotic importance of the clerical garb, but it does again distinguish the farce of *All Gas and Gaiters* from the more grounded social comedy in *Our Man from St Mark's* (as *Our Man at St Marks* became).

The World, the Flesh and the Devil

The action inside the bishop's palace in *All Gas and Gaiters* and the interactions with the general public reinforce the disjunction between the sheltered existence inside the palace and the people out on the streets. Edwin Apps recalled that by 1966, a cathedral close seemed the only remaining place to set a farce, as 'it was becoming almost impossible to write farce, because farce has to be about transgression. And in order to transgress, there needs to be a set of rules' (*Church Times* July 26, 2013). In the pilot episode, the contrast heightens because the bishop, the archdeacon and the chaplain are attempting to find 40 virgins to give the 40 pairs of stockings but find that thanks to the Pill, genuine virgins are rare. At one house, they are delighted to find a young unmarried woman and immediately assume a spinster is *ipso facto* a virgin. Then her *de facto* partner and bastard child appear in the doorway and the clergy flee in horror.

The comic potential of senior clergy bumbling around with women's underclothes and realising that there are no virgins anywhere in the 1960s is an on-screen reflection of the Church's engagement with sexuality and society. In the 1960s, the Church of England was actually less doctrinaire than the English Catholic Church on human sexuality. While the pilot episode script turned the fruitless quest for virgins around St Ogg's into farce, the association of the clergy with the sexually permissive suggests the writers were sensitive observers of the real-life Church in the years immediately prior to 1966. In 1958, the Lambeth Conference of Anglican bishops had produced a moderate response to the possibility of men and women using artificial contraception, contrasted to the outright ban ruled by Cardinal Heenan, the leader of the English Roman Catholic Church (Sumner Holmes 2016, 87).

The clergy in *The Bishop Rides Again* sought chaste young women. A couple of years before the episode aired, the actual as opposed to the fictional Church was fumbling towards an understanding of the connected issues of free love, contraception use and birth control clinics while clergy also worried about the Church seeming old fashioned. The journalist Wendy Cooper raised this point; she was a writer with the *Birmingham Daily Post* and later the *Evening News* and her career had a long-standing focus on women's sexual health. In 1964 she interviewed a Church of England moral welfare worker and the interview and its themes were anchored within this discourse of the old fashioned Church attempting to understand modern sexuality. As such, Cooper was at pains to point out that the moral welfare worker was not an old frump with 'tweeds, brogues and a worried expression' but was 'blond, attractive and elegant'. Stella Hunt, the welfare worker, described real-life equivalents of the permissive young women who caused the bishop of St Ogg's such trouble. These were young women lacking self-control, attempting to be modern, and seeking satisfaction in sexual intercourse. She concluded: 'Nowadays unfortunately anything smacking of religion is very often immediately labelled "old fashioned", and one hesitates to mention the word "chastity" to young people, yet, surely, this is the real answer [to avoiding illegitimate children]?' (*Birmingham Daily Post* June 24, 1964, 8). Other voices in the Church of England were part of a discussion about modern problems. The Venerable George Youell also worked with young people as chaplain at Keele University. He found himself at the eye of the storm in November 1964 when the student union began selling contraceptives on the university campus, along with providing family planning lectures and sex guidance counselling. Significantly, these decisions and actions were inscribed within a particular and determinedly 'modern' approach, exactly the same terminology used with anxiety by Stella Hunt. But, at Keele, the president of the student union declared 'we want to deal with modern problems in a modern way and we don't want to impose a morality ban' (*Birmingham Daily Post* November 12, 1964, 36). As for the chaplain, he was 'violently opposed' to the move. The comments are significant in considering the antics of the clergy in *All Gas and Gaiters*. At the time, the Church itself was attempting to modernise in some ways. The disappearance of the gaiters was a visual sign of change; the fruitless quest for virgins in St Ogg's was a comedic response to the Church's uncertainties with modern sexuality.

Get the Archdeacon a Glass of Sherry!

Our Man at St Mark's and *All Gas and Gaiters* presented distinctions between the Church hierarchies. St Mark's was a parish church and the lead character was a simple vicar. St Ogg's was a cathedral; the action takes place in the bishop's palace and all characters are from the upper ranks of the clergy. Significantly, there are almost no female lead roles in *All Gas and Gaiters*; the bishop, archdeacon and episcopal chaplain are all bachelors and the cathedral close is almost monastic. The pilot episode included some location filming in addition to the studio recordings, but as far as may be judged from production records and the surviving episodes, most later episodes eschewed the more expensive location filming and used standing sets: the study and hall of the bishop's palace, where a decanter of sherry was always on hand. In dramatic terms, the scope of the series shrank markedly to this interior world of the male senior clergy and highlighted a farcical hothouse of competing egos and ambitions. The only female lead role, the dean's wife, icily maintained her status as 'first lady of the close' and the male clergy bickered over status and resources.

Many episodes within this hermetic world revolved around money, as the Cathedral clergy rarely had enough to maintain the fabric of their ancient cathedral. In that respect, the writers of *All Gas and Gaiters* were sensitive to emerging trends not just generally within the Church of

England but specifically within England's cathedral closes. By the time the show began, real life bishops, deans and chapters were recognising that their ancient buildings were expensive to maintain and a means to make money, concerns that informed the plotlines of the programme (*Liverpool Echo* January 31, 1967, 2). In 1960, the dean and chapter of Lincoln Cathedral put on the first ever public display of historic treasures (*Coventry Evening Telegraph* May 16, 1960, 6). By 1963, Wells Cathedral opened a 'curio' shop' (*Illustrated London News* July 13, 1963, 53). In 1964, the clergy at Lichfield were seeking ways to raise cash to cover a major shortfall in their restoration funding (*Birmingham Post* August 3, 1964, 6). The *All Gas and Gaiters* episode *The Bishop Beats the System* toyed with these real-life priorities. The system in question was a new but very expensive security alarm system installed by the Dean to protect the Cathedral. The cost has been so high though that the bishop wishes to sell the cathedral treasure, the cloak of the blessed Ogg, to a rich American to raise much-needed money. As such, the system the bishop beats has a double meaning. He gets past the new security system to creep into the cathedral at night and steal the cloak, and he also defeats the Dean who had resisted the sale of the cloak. In the end, the medieval cloak is discovered to be a Victorian copy, but by then news of its threatened sale has galvanised a line of tourists to queue to see it, bringing money with them, and the clergy become complicit in keeping the fake secret.

By the later 1960s, cathedrals had become better organised at showcasing and promoting treasures and engaging whole heartedly with the tourist industry (Rowe 2011, 90). This aspect of the life in a cathedral close contained farcical potential but also distilled reality. The financial incentive also drove an abrupt turnaround in the Church hierarchy's attitude to television and Edwin Apps saw this shift first hand: 'When we wrote the pilot, the BBC had had several unsuccessful attempts at writing comedy about the C of E, so we were cautious and Stuart Allen, the director was careful to use French cathedrals rather than English ones. By the end of the series, Deans were begging him to use their Cathedral, as it would bring in visitors' (pers.com.).

All Gas and Gaiters also knowingly reflects the contemporary world in showing the medium of religious broadcasting commenting on itself. In *The Bishop Gets the Sack* from 1967 a BBC outside broadcast crew makes a documentary about the cathedral. The script takes the opportunity to find the humour in clerical fears of television, one worrying that the cathedral will become caught up in 'sex and satire'. There is also humour derived from the ineptness of clergy in front of the camera and the producer likens them to the puppets Pinky and Perky. The bishop is unable to take note of which camera he should look at, the dean is too frightening, the archdeacon loses his voice and the chaplain needs drugs to be relaxed enough to appear. However, the clergy also sense that a television documentary will be an opportunity to raise money by enticing tourists and the bishop has swiftly ordered a range of cheap and tacky merchandise. He laments his lowly profile and feels that, as a diocesan bishop in a remote cathedral city, publicity passes him by. His chaplain unkindly reminds him that he has only been mentioned in the press for asking for a window to be opened during a synod meeting.

Until the 1960s, the fictional appearances of the clergy on screen had been few and far between; the question arises of how the clergy reacted to seeing themselves portrayed in sustained television series. Accounts of the clergy's reactions have varied. Concerns that television was making fun of the Church are discernible from even before *All Gas and Gaiters* commenced. A voice from outside the Church of England, the Presbyterian minister Alan Macleod, suggested that television presented clergymen are only 'good for a laugh' (*Evening Chronicle* May 7, 1965, 6). His assessment was not however an outraged complaint but a sensitive appraisal of the impact of television and in his view, the medium served as a mirror to be held against the Church. No matter how critical the medium became, he found that 'criticism can be a salutary experience'. Macleod understood there to be different targets of television's scorn, with the institution of the Church rather than its faith receiving both scrutiny and ridicule. For Macleod, it was encouraging to see that the tangible institution rather than the metaphysical faith was the target, for those in the Church may have been laughing at themselves as well. 'Many churchmen are as unhappy about the present state of the church and the people's attitude towards us as the most violent of the critics outside' (*Evening Chronicle* May 7, 1965, 6).

The Saucy Church

The discovery that the Church and its clergy could be a source of humour should not be overstated. The clergy had provided laughs on stage since at least the nineteenth century, including Canon Chasuble in *The Importance of Being Earnest*, Mr Birchwood in *Pygmalion* and Dr Daly in Gilbert and Sullivan's *The Sorcerer*. *All Gas and Gaiters* remains notable along with

Our Man at St Mark's for opening a sustained space for the clergy to be amusing on television and this potential developed, especially in sketch comedy. Both *All Gas and Gaiters* and *Our Man at St Mark's* had been relatively 'clean' series. The development of clerical archetypes in comedy after *All Gas and Gaiters* ended in 1971 saw the increasing juxtaposition of the clergy with smuttier humour. *That Was the Week That Was* (1962–1963) took a disrespectful tone to religion in the sketch 'Consumer Report on Religion', which made religion seem a crass commercial property (Briggs 1995, 361; Davies 2016, 29). Then crassness gave way to smuttiness. For comedians, including the Two Ronnies, Spike Milligan and Dick Emery and their teams of sketch writers, Anglican vicars appeared as in a line-up of institutional and authority figures such as soldiers, traffic wardens, doctors, nurses and driving instructors getting involved in salacious situations.

A milder juxtaposition of the smutty and the clerical featured in *Two Ronnies* sketches. A vicar welcoming a congregation of cockneys to Evensong delivered a sermon about Cain and Abel in rhyming slang, of which the only truly suggestive instance was 'bottle and glass'. Their swear jar sketch supposed that men in a pub made a donation to church funds whenever they swore, as ever louder and more strident bleeps block out the bad language. The punchline of the sketch is the appearance of the meek and cardigan-wearing vicar himself, who ends the sketch having ordered an alcohol free drink but then uses his own bleeped-out expletive. Spike Milligan's *Q* toyed with Anglican vicars and the style and type of religious broadcasting that had prevailed until that point, such as a serious address from a cleric during the epilogue. Milligan performed sketches including a military chaplain delivering the Lord's Prayer as a series of shouted parade ground orders and a police chaplain telling the story of the Good Samaritan as though it was evidence of a robbery delivered in court. Milligan also pushed comedy to further extremes with an epilogue in which a quavering elderly vicar, having woken up in time to speak, asks himself 'how do I like women priests in the Church?'; 'With big tits' is the answer. Dick Emery's sketches about the toothy vicar kept the Church on the screen in the 1970s surrounded by risqué associations.

In these instances, the humour derived from the juxtaposition of the vicar with the mildly salacious. Beyond the obvious humour of vicars swearing or ogling at women, the comedy had a further implication in the models presented before audiences of millions. For the humour to be functional, the archetypal vicar needed to be mild, naïve and faintly incompetent, so that the contrast with the smuttier humour was strong. These comedians, at the height of their popularity throughout the 1970s, therefore kept on screen a particular iteration of a clerical character, before the 'trendier' type of vicar came into view in the next decade. The comedy was still presented couched in language that required, and spoke to, an audience familiar with the vocabulary and customs of the Church of England. Comedy based around Matins, Evensong and the Authorised Version of the Bible stories presupposed an audience who understood ecclesiastical language as well as the double entendre. An instance is Benny Hill's sketch about the Reverend Gray who, complaining about a piece of unappetising fish, says it is a 'Piece of Cod that passeth all understanding', humour requiring the audience to have read (or heard read in church) Paul's Epistles in the King James Bible.

In its time, the sketch comedy was daring and indicated the extent to which the attitudes of television executives and the wider viewing public had shifted. In the previous decade, the Church did not have to ask for script approval on *Our Man at St Marks*; it was axiomatic that the writers would seek it. By the next decade, there was no longer script approval but there were comedians playing vicars as lubricious old men. The change in the treatment of the Church is indicated from another source. In 1974 *Carry on Dick* featured Sidney James as the Reverend Flasher of Upper Denture, but the rector leads a double life and is also 'Big Dick Turpin' the highway man. The film was the 26th in the series and Talbot Rothwell's script was his 20th. By now his use of double entendre and smutty jokes was routine, summed up in this film by the tagline 'Dick Turpin carries on with his flintlock cocked!'. Perhaps because the patterns of script, scenario and dialogue were so familiar to the regular cast and crew for these films, the news that the Apartheid South African government intended to ban the film as 'anti-Christian' shocked the Carry On team (Merriman 2011). When he heard the news, the actor Kenneth Williams reflected that it was 'ironic that it takes a government like that about such appalling sacrilegiousness while *our* government pass it without a qualm' [original italics] (Williams 1993, 483–484). While there is a difference in medium, Williams's comment is a notable indicator of wider changes, in that an irreverence towards the Church, still considered unthinkable in more conservative countries, was becoming commonplace in Britain.

The Saucy Church Redux

Comedians such as Emery, Hill and the Two Ronnies disappeared from the small screen in the 1980s as tastes changed, although the association of the Church with the salacious re-emerged in the early twenty-first century in *Little Britain* (2003–2006), which repurposed the tone and targets of a number of earlier comedians. The programme attracted both large audiences and criticisms for the targets of its comedy and its sketch-based and catch-phrase dominated comedy. In both, critics found it to be a deliberately old fashioned reiteration of the likes of Hill and Emery in comedy attacking black people, gypsies, women, gay people and the disabled (Lockyer 2010, 12). Amongst the cavalcade of sketches, the vicar mixed with the smutty re-appeared. The comedy about the Church registers a debt to both the sketch comedians of the 1970s but also to the writers' awareness of the social and sexual issues affecting the Church of England in the twenty-first century; the smut now comes from the fact that the clergy are homosexual. In episodes from season two, a gay character expecting disapproval from the Anglican Church is confounded when he discovers the local vicar, verger, bishop and archdeacon are all homosexual. In addition, an elderly female parishioner advises that the young man needs 'a nice big cock up his arse'.

VERY NAUGHTY BOYS

Sketch comedy illuminates how comedy became more daring as attitudes became less respectful. The release of the *Life of Brian* into cinemas in 1979 caused an ecclesiastical and moral storm. A number of countries swiftly banned it, including Ireland and Norway, as did some British local authorities. Mary Whitehouse campaigned against it. Significantly, she did not find that it was blasphemous, as she had *Gay News* when she brought a prosecution for blasphemous libel about a poem (Cumper and Edge 2006, 614) and surprised many who had forgotten the blasphemy laws still existed, as she grasped the central narrative point that Brian and Jesus were separate characters. That same distinction bypassed the churchman Mervyn Stockwood and intellectual Malcolm Muggeridge who debated John Cleese and Michael Palin on television that year.

The Pythons successfully mobilised the shock and outrage in promoting the film and the Pythons themselves were open to intelligent debate. John Cleese and Michael Palin participated in a televised debate on the programme *Friday Night, Saturday Morning* in 1979 against Mervyn Stockwood, the bishop of Southwark and the satirist and public intellectual Malcolm Muggeridge. The debate has lived long in public memory but has also undergone notable shifts in meaning and emphasis as an example of the Church intersecting with comedy and seeking to uphold moral standards.

Life of Brian is set in the first century AD, too early for anything Anglican to appear. The Monty Python team had however earlier turned their attention to the Church in 'The Bishop' sketch in episode four of their second season (aired 1970). The sketch took the aesthetics and music of the *Peter Gunn* private eye show but inserted a gorgeously vested Church of England bishop and his clerical goons into a hard-boiled detective scenario. 'Da bishop' zooms around in a fast Pontiac but is never quite fast enough to stop a number of vicars meeting sticky ends (blown up baptising a bomb disguised as a baby, crushed by a 15 ton weight when officiating at a wedding, hanged by bell ropes, detonated in an exploding pulpit and so on). A flashing communications device hidden in the bishop's crozier signals each new mission. The sketch begins with a mock title sequence that again parodies hard-boiled American crime series, but with credits given an ecclesiastical twist. The credits are instructive in that they expect of their audience a far higher level of knowledge of institutional religion than would be possible now. In 1970, the Church of England's own Television Training Course for clergy was instructing 'Do at all costs avoid conventional theological and ecclesiastical terms. People who have no connection with the Church—and you are speaking chiefly to them—do not understand OUR terms' (CERC ACCM/VP/SEC/9). The advice, although needed, should be read with moderation as broadcasters of all types could make some assumptions that a wider audience would know something about the Church. In the same decade the Monty Python team could rely on audience laughter to mock credits such as special effects by the Moderator of the Church of Scotland, and the director is 'Prebendary "Chopper" Harris', terminology that would now be largely meaningless to an unchurched generation and where less than 2 per cent of the population of young adults identify as Anglican (*Guardian* September 7, 2018).

The Church's hierarchy made no recorded objection to the Monty Python sketch. In 1979, reactions to *Life of Brian* were strenuous. The Festival of Light denounced the film and so did the Church of England's Board of Social Responsibility. This latter body advised the Church on a range of social issues such as nuclear weapons, illegitimate children and abortion and in 1979 expressed concerns about the Python's film. Out of the many iterations of protest against *Life of Brian* around the world, Stockwood participated in a televised exchange with Malcolm Muggeridge about Jesus, blasphemy and comedy. Stockwood, at times waving around a large cross, spoke first; his comments set the tone for the remainder of what he and Muggeridge contributed. Having been the vicar of the University Church in Cambridge, Stockwood joked that he was used to undergraduate humour. Further, he was the governor of a home for the mentally deficient, and knew the type of humour liked by the boys in the lower fourth form. Muggeridge's contribution was to castigate the film as cheap, tenth rate, miserable and disgusting. To end his contribution, Stockwood suggested Cleese and Palin would receive their 30 pieces of silver.

The peculiarity of the broadcast was that the film should have caused more offence to trade unionists than to Christians, as it mocked the infighting and argumentative paralysis of the unions. Neither was Stockwood an immediately obvious choice to defend the Church against apparently blasphemous comedy. He was far from conventional and not even especially pious. He was a socialist and Labour supporter. As bishop of Southwark, he encouraged clergy who did trendy things such as wearing jeans. The archbishop of Canterbury rebuked him for attending the House of Lords in a lounge suit rather than the more traditional rochet and chimere and he had been one of the naughty bishops not wearing gaiters when Fisher was archbishop. He was a dabbler in mysticism and was gay (Ramsey 2018, 114; *Telegraph* October 19, 1996). He was also a seasoned television performer and had provided a number of unconventional and controversial moments on the small screen. During the 'marathon television coverage' of the 1964 general election, for some viewers the most notable moment was 'the spectacle of an Anglican bishop rejoicing without qualification in the swing towards Labour which marked the overnight election count' (*Belfast Telegraph* October 17, 1964, 6). His on-screen behaviour on that occasion prompted debate about whether the episcopate should have obvious political affiliations or if, as a socialist, Stockwood was an oddity among Tory-inclined bishops. These points suggested that the Church was the 'Tory party at prayer', a suggestion that continued as the Church was refracted through different broadcasts.

Ominously perhaps, Stockwood also rejoiced in a fight, all the better if in a television studio. In 1971, he launched frenetic attacks on the BBC's

Panorama programme, which had broadcast an edition critical of the Diocese of Southwark. Stockwood made robust counter claims, marshalling evidence point for point against what *Panorama* had said, complaining in writing to the director general Charles Curran, and gleefully accepting the opportunity to rebut the programme producer Julian Pettifer on screen (*Birmingham Post* October 30, 1971, 7). As for Muggeridge, he was a neophyte, as several decades of non-belief had given way to fervent Catholicism, involvement with the Festival of Light and admiration for Mother Theresa (Whipple 2010, 323).

In the debate about the film, Muggeridge and Stockwood, consciously or not chose, to treat Palin and Cleese as naughty schoolboys. Stockwood had been a schoolmaster and, as he pointed out, had preached at Clifton College when Cleese was a pupil there. Muggeridge and Stockwood were affronted by the possibility that the film mocked Christ and as the debate progressed, Michael Palin became sincerely upset and frustrated by the notion and attempted to explain the serious portrayal of Christ in the movie.

It is instructive to consider the journey that the interview has taken in popular consciousness. Cleese and Palin recalled they thought both Stockwood and Muggeridge 'stupid'. Enmity endured and Cleese later called Muggeridge the 'idol' of a 'snotty coterie' of public intellectuals (Cleese 2014, 265). During the debate, Rice remained a marginal presence despite being the moderator and Cleese and Palin were visibly frustrated at their difficulty in getting a word in edgeways over Muggeridge and Stockwood. It therefore fell to others to speak for them after the broadcast ended. Another team of British comedians including Rowan Atkinson and Mel Smith produced a sketch for their own shown *Not the Nine O'Clock News*. Smith played 'Alexander Walker', based on the film critic, and Atkinson played a bishop attired in a purple stock and frock coat but with a director's viewfinder around his neck rather than a pectoral cross. The film-making bishop is an early iteration of the inept and unpleasant clerics that recur in Atkinson's work, including *Keeping Mum, Four Weddings and a Funeral* and his sketch comedy (Sorensen 2014, 87). The sketch is a neat inversion of *Friday Night, Saturday Morning*. The bishop and his organisation, General Synod Films, come under attack for making a film *Life of Christ* as a thinly veiled parody of the life of the Monty Python team. As in the actual debate, discussion soon became bogged down on the extent to which the life of Christ was really about the lives of the Pythons.

In 2011, BBC4 brought Stockwood and Muggeridge back to life, convincingly played by the actors Roy Marden and Michael Cochrane in the drama *Holy Flying Circus*. Marsden was, according to Jack Seale's online *Radio Times* review, 'almost unwatchably creepy' playing Stockwood, and more like a witch finder than a guest in a television show. *Holy Flying Circus* placed the television debate in a wider context of battles over comedy and blasphemy in the 1970s as the Pythons fought protestors, religious fanatics and the tabloid media. Finally, the programme conveyed how the Pythons, Cleese especially, sensed that their controversies were of wider sociological significance in speaking to a country less inclined to care about blasphemy or to care what a bishop said on television.

What the dramatic recreation suggests is the significance of the debate as possibly the last time a senior churchman could appear on television and assume he was speaking to a Christian nation. That same impression is conveyed through inversion by the *Not the Nine O'Clock News* sketch, where 'Alexander Walker' angrily protested that the majority of people in the country were still 'Pythonists' who would be shocked and appalled by the General Synod's film.

Rowan Atkinson wore vestments again in the 1980s comedy *The Black Adder* and *Blackadder II*. The first was set in the late Middle Ages and the second in the Elizabethan era. Both however (like in fact *The Life of Brian* before them) extracted humour from placing modern attitudes expressed in modern language in historical settings. *The Archbishop* episode of *The Black Adder* (1982) concerns the murder of several archbishops of Canterbury in a row, leading to King Richard IV appointing his own son Edmund Blackadder the new primate. Edmund is reluctant, given that someone has violently murdered all his predecessors owing to a long-standing quarrel between the King and the Church about land and wealth. The comedy about the Church takes in multiple targets. The Reverend Mother of a convent is kinky. The clergy are lecherous and they are exploiting the credulous by selling false relics. The footage of Edmund's installation as archbishop lampoons the BBC's recent and reverential coverage of Robert Runcie's installation at Canterbury. The new archbishop's liturgical incompetence interrupts the sombre commentary when he accidentally knocks clergy over with too-wide swings of the thurible and blows his nose on his lavish vestments.

These sharper attacks need to be seen in the context of a greater willingness to attack other formerly respected institutions. *Spitting Image* lampooned the monarchy and politicians on a regular basis. The satire was reasonably kind to Elizabeth II but merciless towards other royals including Prince Andrew, and excoriated Margaret Thatcher. It also attacked the Churches; Pope John Paul II appeared as analogous to an Elvis Presley rock star and Robert Runcie's puppet was diminutive and shrill. The *Spitting Image* satire about the Church of England was itself the product of how the Church of England's clergy behaved on television. Bishop David Jenkins' efforts to discuss theological abstractions about the Virgin Birth misfired, as the medium proved the wrong place to attempt a subtle argument. For *Spitting Image*, the resulting furore from Jenkins' television appearances fuelled how Runcie appeared. In one sketch, the shrivelled primate discussed the 'true meaning of Christmas' with Bishop Jenkins, who suggests Christmas was 'an ancient pagan celebration to get rid of all the satsumas'. His patient but misinterpreted efforts to explain to Runcie that there is no Santa Claus mirror his ill-fated efforts to discuss the incarnation to a television audience.

There is a compelling irony that a Church originally affronted by the gentle comedy of *All Gas and Gaiters* had far worse to come as comedy continued to find the Church a fruitful source of jokes. The debate between Bishop Stockwood and the Pythons is an important turning point. In retrospect, Stockwood's demeanour and arguments suggests he was expecting to speak authoritatively, as bishops had been in earlier years. The reactions then and since do not match that expectation, and the comedy and reality merge when *Not the Nine O'Clock News* turned the debate and Stockwood into a comedy sketch. The next chapter narrows the comedy vision to the Church's established status and to the comedy found in the making and unmaking of its bishops.

References

Newspapers, Periodicals and Trade Papers

Belfast Telegraph
Birmingham Daily Post
Birmingham Post
Church Times
Coventry Evening Telegraph
Evening Chronicle
Guardian
Illustrated London News
Liverpool Echo

Liverpool Echo and Evening Express
New York Times
Radio Times
Stage
Stage and Television Today
Telegraph

ARCHIVES

CHURCH OF ENGLAND RECORD CENTRE (CERC)

CERC ACCM/VP/SEC/9

PRINTED SECONDARY SOURCES

Apps, Edwin. 2013. *Pursued by Bishops—The Memoirs of Edwin Apps*. Durand-Peyroles (Patrick).

Briggs, Asa. 1995. *The History of Broadcasting in the United Kingdom: Volume V Competition*. Oxford: Oxford University Press.

Brydon, Michael. 2018. The Prayer Book in Walmington-on-Sea. *The Magazine of the Prayer Book Society*, no. 9, 6–9.

Chadwick, Owen. 1990. *Michael Ramsey: A Life*. Oxford: Oxford University Press.

Cleese, John. 2014. *So, Anyway*. London: Random House.

Cumper, Peter, and Peter Edge. 2006. First Among Equals: The English State and the Anglican Church in the 21st Century. *University of Detroit Mercy Law Review* 83: 601–623.

Davies, Christie. 2016. The Rise and Fall of Taboo Comedy in the BBC. In *Taboo Comedy*, ed. C. Bucaria and L. Barra, 21–40. Palgrave Macmillan.

Kramer, L. 2016. Comic Strategies of Inclusion and "Normalisation" in *The Vicar of Dibley*. In *British TV Comedies: Cultural Concepts, Contexts and Controversies*, ed. J. Kamm and B. Neumann, 212–224. Palgrave Macmillan.

Lockyer, Sharon. 2010. Introduction: Britain, Britain, *Little Britain*. In *Reading Little Britain: Comedy Matters on Contemporary Television*, ed. Sharon Lockyer. I.B. Tauris.

Machin, G.I.T. 1998. *Churches and Social Issues in Twentieth-Century Britain*. Oxford: Clarendon Press.

Merriman, Andy. 2011. *Hattie: The Authorised Biography of Hattie Jacques*. Aurum Press.

Muir, Frank. 1997. *A Kentish Lad*. Corgi Books.

Murray, Andy. 2017. *Into the Unknown: The Fantastic Life of Nigel Kneale (Revised & Updated)*. SCB Distributors.

Ramsey, Laura Monica. 2018. The Church of England, Homosexual Law Reform, and the Shaping of the Permissive Society, 1957–1979. *Journal of British Studies* 57 (1): 108–137.

Smith, Leslie. 1989. *Modern British Farce: A Selective Study of British Farce from Pinero to the Present Day.* Rowman & Littlefield.

Sorensen, Sue. 2014. *The Collar: Reading Christian Ministry in Fiction, Television and Film.* Eugene, OR: Cascade Books.

Sumner Holmes, Ann. 2016. *The Church of England and Divorce in the Twentieth Century: Legalism and Grace.* London: Taylor & Francis.

Whipple, Amy C. 2010. Speaking for Whom? The 1971 Festival of Light and the Search for the "Silent Majority". *Contemporary British History* 24 (3): 319–339.

Williams, Kenneth. 1993. *The Kenneth Williams Diaries.* Edited by Russell Davies. London: HarperCollins.

Wrigley, Amnada. 2015. The Spaces of Medieval Plays on British Television. *Shakespeare Bulletin* 33 (4): 569–593.

Yates, Nigel. 2011. *Love Now, Pay Later?: Sex and Religion in the Fifties and Sixties.* SPCK.

DISSERTATIONS

Rowe, Peter A. 2011. The Roles of the Cathedral in the Modern English Church. PhD diss., University of St Andrews.

'Cricket, Steam Engines and a Complete Ignorance of Theology': The Comedy of Bishops' Appointments

This chapter continues to consider comedy iterations of the Church and focuses on the appearance of the high politics of the church, including two contrasting approaches to portraying the appointment of bishops. It traverses several decades of television, set against the real-life politics of appointments as politicians decided who would and would not lead the Church.

The appointment of Church of England diocesan bishops happens at Number 10 Downing Street. An appointments secretary provides two names to the Prime Minister. Theoretically, the Prime Minister could choose either name for the vacant bishopric but in recent years it has become the firm practice for the Prime Minister to choose the first name on the list. Choosing, those who are appointed and those who miss out, is a discreet process. The decision making takes place behind doors with the thought processes of the key stakeholders only hinted at. As a result, the process has made for effective television. In the absence of a visible and closely documented process, programme makers are free to introduce their own visions.

The manner of appointment of English bishops mirrors the Roman Catholic approach of a conclave deliberating out of sight. It deviates from the former as there are no clouds of white or black smoke, no crowds and no balcony appearance. Appointing the pope is a visual feast. *The Borgias* (2011) and *The Young Pope* (2016) exploited the sumptuousness of the papal trappings. The more subdued Anglican process centres on intrigue

© The Author(s) 2020
M. Harmes et al., *The Church on British Television*,
https://doi.org/10.1007/978-3-030-38113-4_7

and talk. Despite the absence of visible drama, the process of making a bishop has become the subject matter of not only television programmes but of comedies in particular. A dry administrative process, which few would know about and fewer see happening, is the basis of plots in two political comedies, *Yes, Prime Minister* and *Absolute Power*. The first takes viewers deep inside Number 10 Downing Street to the PM's private office and a decision-making process including his civil service advisors, his wife, the Crown Appointments Commission and dons at Oxford University. Tellingly, no clergy actually appear in the episode. They are talked about as allusive presences on the fringes of decision making. *Absolute Power* shows the decision-making process as remotely manipulated from a public relations firm, a tabloid newspaper and the set of a reality television programme but on this occasion the competing clergy have a voice and are active participants in the outcome.

The constitutional arrangements that provide the background for *Yes, Prime Minister* stemmed from an understanding reached in the late 1970s between the Church of England and the prime minister James Callaghan, a non-Anglican, to be guided by the research undertaken by the appointments secretary and provided to the Crown Appointments Commission (Lee et al. 1998, 50; Cranmer 2001, 114). The prime ministers' part in the decision-making process and their very real power to make or veto appointments has gained them the title 'Heaven's talent scouts', although the real work in talent scouting is done by a civil servant (Flinders 2012, 792). In practice, Callaghan's successor Margaret Thatcher (and the same applies to her successors) was still at liberty to reject both names if she so wished, which left her at the heart of a patronage network (Chapman 2016, 201; Buchanan 2006, 238; Flinders 2012, 793). Also in practice, the appointment of an archbishop of Canterbury was a one-off as the incumbent Prime Minister had an even more direct part in proceedings through making the choice of chairman for the Crown Appointments Commission (Lee et al. 1998, 50), who could exercise impactful leadership. Traditionally also, the Prime Minister has been at liberty to disregard the wishes of the outgoing archbishop of Canterbury. Geoffrey Fisher vigorously pushed then Prime Minister Harold Macmillan *not* to appoint Michael Ramsey (the archbishop of York), as Fisher's successor. Macmillan famously spoke to his own view that the Church of England 'had had enough of Martha and it was time for some Mary'. In other words, he was after a theologian rather than a busy administrator (Hein 2008, 100).

Further, he rebuked Fisher's efforts to persuade him and rejected Fisher's headmasterly advice.

Macmillan is a case where the selection of the archbishop of Canterbury made both religious and personal sense. Macmillan was Anglican, he found time to read one of Michael Ramsey's books before appointing him, and was a fan of both Anthony Trollope's novels and the ecclesiastical patronage they evoked (Palmer 1992, 253). His comment about Martha and Mary was subtly apposite and showed his scriptural literacy. In other instances the process lost clarity and appropriateness. Some prime ministers including James Callaghan were not Anglican, leaving the Church of England in the remarkable state where the final say on its leaders rested with a non-Anglican. In Thatcher's case, there was a prime minster who was entirely willing to make up her own mind, as was Macmillan, but unlike Macmillan, was unlikely to be interested in the theological scholarship of the men on her list.

Yes, Prime Minister and then *Absolute Power* are comedies with ecclesiastical elements as was *Our Man at St Marks* but without affection. Instead, their contribution to broadcasting about the Church is a clinically astute interpretation of how bishops are made and unmade. The programmes distil anxieties about social welfare, war and single mothers as all intersecting with the problem of choosing the right sort of person to be a bishop. The murkiness and cynicism of the Crown Appointments Commission provide gifts to comedy. *Prime Minister* and *Absolute Power* dramatise respectively the intervention of the 1980s Thatcher Government and the turn-of-the-century Blair administration in the choice of bishops, especially the refusal of Margaret Thatcher to appoint a left-leaning clergyman to Birmingham and her growing rift with Archbishop Robert Runcie. A wider implication is how they both shape particular perceptions of the Church of England: as a denomination which believed in everything and nothing; as a body led by social climbing bishops; and as too close to the upper classes.

A longer historical perspective comes from period drama. The BBC's 1982 mini-series *Barchester Chronicles* (based on the novels *The Warden* and *Barchester Towers*) included the drama ensuing when the elderly incumbent bishop of Barchester died. In both the Victorian source novels and the BBC adaptation, the choice of a new bishop is explicitly political. The old bishop takes a long time to die, too long in fact and even a new-fangled electric telegram is too late to get his son Dr Grantly into the bishopric. In the interval, a government sympathetic to Dr Grantly falls and the new administration instead chooses Dr Proudie to be the new bishop. Both Trollope's novels and the television adaptation subvert even this Erastian decision-making process. While the new administration has chosen Dr Proudie, it soon becomes clear that the real power in the bishopric of Barchester is the odious Mrs Proudie, the bishop's wife. Her power is not absolute, and when the BBC miniseries ends, a family alliance is firmly in place in the cathedral close. A father-in-law and two of his sons-in-law are respectively the precentor, dean and archdeacon of Barchester.

The BBC's adaptation evoked the ecclesiastical controversies over appointments, sinecures and nepotism that had animated Trollope's novels and many nineteenth-century critics of the Church. Owen Chadwick's authoritative study of the Victorian Church points out that not all administrations were explicitly political in choosing bishops, and Queen Victoria resisted political appointments (Chadwick 1972, 332). The other side of the life and activity of the Church was the clear willingness of both bishops and patrons to offer choice appointments to friends and relatives (Schlossberg 2000, 278).

The BBC brought Trollope's world of ecclesiastical scandal onto the screen in the early 1980s, including the dramatisation of the entirely non-religious reasons for choosing a bishop. These intrigues were dressed in period costume but were by no means historically remote from what was current practice. Winston Churchill's choice of a new archbishop after William Temple died in 1944 rested with Geoffrey Fisher. Church historians generally concur that Churchill's dislike of George Bell for condemning the obliteration bombing of German civilians cost Bell Canterbury, even though Bell was the most high-profile bishop in the Church with a vast international profile (Edwards 1971, 338; Hein 2008, 41; Chandler 2016, 126). Even if Churchill disapproved of Bell's wartime speeches, he has left behind a fuller impression of a prime minister choosing a bishop based not just on personal prejudices against one cleric but the active investigation of another. Before choosing Fisher, Churchill met him and sought his views on the controversial nineteenth-century French theological text *Vie de Jesus*. Ironically, Churchill had read it whereas Fisher had not, and proved reluctant to discuss theology (Hein 2008, 42). The incident is small, but it is suggestive of a prime minister's personal involvement in choosing the new archbishop and the decision-making processes taking place in Downing Street.

The appointments lay within the gift of the prime minister; the potential for comedy and drama lay in where the choices could rest on political preference as Trollopian as the scramble for Barchester. Margaret Thatcher had strong views on the Church and on the sort of men whom she wished to make bishops. In public, Thatcher's comments on religion were cast as personal thoughts rather than interference in the Church, yet some churchmen found it disquieting that they may have held to contrary ecclesial or doctrinal views and therefore missed the chance of a bishopric. One such possibility was the ordination of women, not achieved in the 1980s but much discussed. Thatcher herself was in favour (*Economist* August 6, 1988, 24), leading more conservative priests to fear 'they may have spoiled their chances of advancement by opposing the ordination of women' (*Evening Chronicle* August 1, 1988, 8).

Yet a safe choice could backfire. Thatcher's premiership was almost coterminous with the primacy of Robert Runcie (1979 to 1990 and 1980 to 1991 respectively) (Medhurst 1991, 240). Runcie had known Thatcher decades earlier in Oxford University Conservative circles; however, he became a thorn in her side (Williamson 2012, 170). Explicitly identified in the press as an anti-Thatcherite and a Social Democrat, Runcie opposed Thatcherite social and economic policies on a number of levels. He revealed he voted in the 1983 General Election but did not say for whom, provoking suspicions that he had voted Labour and prompting searching constitutional debate about whether the Lords Spiritual were permitted to vote, when the remainder of the peers in the House of Lords did not (*House of Lords Hansard* June 13, 2007, vol. 692, col. 1697). The perceived antagonism between Runcie and Thatcher resonated in other ways. The government's contingency planning for a nuclear strike, the Wintex Cimex exercises, included a draft scenario where both opposition leader Michael Foot and Runcie were arrested in civil disturbances immediately before the bombs fell (*Guardian* April 3, 2019).

Thatcher's closest religious relationship in the 1980s was with the Chief Rabbi Immanuel Jakobovitis, whom Thatcher placed in the House of Lords and whose belief in self-improvement and disdain for welfare proved far more congenial than Anglican anxiety about inner city deprivation (*Economist* April 13, 2013, 28; *Irish Independent* October 7, 1989, 10). Other bishops proved similarly uncongenial on issues including South Africa, the Bomb, health and social security, and race (Medhurst 1991, 240). The bishop of Durham, David Jenkins found his diocese was the eye of the storm during the mining closures and strikes of the Thatcher era and he used the media to challenge not only theology but politics as well. He called Conservative social policy 'wicked' and Conservative ministers repaid him in kind by attacking him in the press. Thatcher also disliked the liberal-minded Hugh Montefiore, bishop of Birmingham. To his face, Thatcher told him he was 'always so controversial'. Behind his back, Thatcher called him 'dreadful' (*Independent* May 16, 2005).

Montefiore openly supported the Liberal Party, while Stanley Booth Clibborn, the bishop of Manchester, openly supported the Labour Party and in turn Thatcher's supporters openly detested him (Filby 2015; *Independent* March 8, 1996). These prelates had dioceses in areas scarred by social deprivation, whether mining closures or inner city decay. They were also appointees of the late 1970s, before Thatcher won the 1979 General Election. Once consecrated and enthroned, there was nothing Thatcher could do about difficult incumbent bishops, but their political turbulence made the choices she *could* make for vacant dioceses all the more important.

Civil servants in *Yes, Prime Minister* liken the process to 'a conjuring trick. Take any card, you always end up with the card the magician forced you to take'. By the end of *The Bishop's Gambit* Prime Minister Hacker has broken with tradition, refusing both original cards and demanding an alternative. That more iconoclastic approach is an informed interpretation of Thatcher's actions. It is believed that Runcie was the second of the two names which came from the Appointments Committee; Montefiore was first. It is further believed from confidential sources that in a break with custom Thatcher vetoed the first choice and selected Runcie (Campbell 2011, 389; Williamson 2012, 169). A decade later, Thatcher (according to a source also confidentially disclosed to Runcie's biographer Humphrey Carpenter) rejected Archbishop John Habgood, the first name, and chose George Carey, the second name on her list (Carpenter 1996, 370). After her keenly felt frustrations with Runcie and other diocesan bishops, it was sensed that 'only a saint' could have resisted strong involvement in the choice of Runcie's successor (*Economist* January 20, 1990, 34). These tensions, taking place behind closed doors but leaving behind suggestive traces of discord, are the stuff of literate, word-based drama.

The Bishop's Gambit

At no point in *Yes, Minister* had the identity or sex of the British prime minister been made clear, nor whether Jim Hacker belonged to a Labour or Conservative government. The setting of the Department of Administrative Affairs enabled the show to toy with absurd minutiae in

British government. In *Yes, Prime Minister* the show's canvas expanded markedly, with administrative detail and clerical occlusion giving way to Jim Hacker's stumbling attempts to run the entire country. Like other episodes in *Yes, Prime Minister*, *The Bishop's Gambit* allowed Anthony Jay and Jonathan Lynn to highlight a specific aspect of prime ministerial responsibility. Along with choosing a bishop, Prime Minister Hacker tried updating Britain's defence capabilities, dealt with a spy scandal, negotiated the balance of power between himself and the permanent secretary to the Cabinet, managed a diplomatic incident over the Channel Tunnel and attempted reform of the education system. In each case, Jay and Lynn possessed valuable insider information about tensions within Number 10 and the Cabinet Office, especially involving the cabinet secretary Sir John Hunt (Seldon 2016, 179). In *The Bishop's Gambit* the comedy emerges from an immaculate delineation of how the Crown Appointments Commission brought about an episcopal appointment, and the decision-making process within Number 10 that led to a choice of two names becoming one recommendation to the sovereign for a new bishop.

Almost every line in *Bishop's Gambit* is a bright and polished diamond, tying together a complex plot of machinations traversing Oxford University, the Church of England, Number 10, the Foreign Office and a remote Middle Eastern kingdom, together with an acutely observed portrait of the Church as it sat in popular consciousness by the middle of the Thatcher era. That included bishops appearing on television saying controversial things about faith, the impression that clergy gave of simultaneously believing in everything and nothing, the rise of the 'trendy' manifestation of Anglicanism alongside a treasured snobbish establishment status, and the whispers in some clerical circles of disestablishment of the state Church. The plot is set in motion when the bishopric of Bury St Edmunds becomes a *sede vacante*. There is an actual diocese of St Edmundsbury and Ipswich, and in 1986 the bishop was the Cambridge-educated John Dennis. The fictional diocese, according to Sir Humphrey, had the appeal of being an old bishopric, therefore entitling the incumbent to a seat in the House of Lords. The real diocese of St Edmundsbury is new, dating only from 1914 and the television version is not a direct analogue. It is, however, a productive fictional site as it encapsulates the status and perks that would provoke episcopal ambitions.

The episode is significant not simply for the way the appointment of a bishop becomes the substance of both drama and comedy, but the manner in which *The Bishop's Gambit* shows the appointment of bishops as embedded in a television culture. The complex scheme by two Oxford dons, the civil servant Sir Humphrey Appleby, and the Crown Appointments Commission to get their favoured candidate into the bishopric plays out largely through their use of televised images to 'sell' their candidate to the Prime Minister. The dean of Ballie College, the man they want to get out of Oxford and into Bury St Edmunds, is already a seasoned but controversial television performer. While the dean is never actually seen during the course of the episode (barring one still photograph in a television news story), the Dean has used television appearances to make controversial points about faith. Sir Humphrey notes that 'The Dean only believes in Islam, steam engines, and the MCC'. Further, 'some smart-aleck once asked him on television if he knew what The Bible was… He said it was some Christian version of The Koran'. The bursar of Sir Humphrey's old college adds that 'sucking up' to the aristocracy is the Dean's other hobby.

A senior Church of England clergyman primarily interested in cricket, Islam and socialising with the nobility was a recognisable archetype by the mid-1980s. Jim Thompson, bishop of Stepney and then Bath and Wells, was an enthusiastic cricketer and a campaigner for Islamic groups (*Guardian* September 22, 2003). The *Telegraph* obituarised Roger Wilson of Chichester as one of the Church of England's 'most elegant bishops', whose 'progress to high ecclesiastical office and to a place at Court had an air of inevitability about it'. He also loved cricket (March 2, 2002). Bishops more interested in Islam than Christianity existed among English prelates, such as the Right Reverend Kenneth Cragg, an academic bishop who devoted his scholarly life to Islamic theology (*Telegraph* November 14, 2012).

A senior clergyman making controversial theological comments on television was also timely and familiar by 1986. The descriptions of the fictional dean bear some resemblance to the theologically contentious Reverend Don Cupitt, the dean of Emmanuel College Cambridge and author of *Taking Leave of God* in 1980 and presenter of the controversial *Sea of Faith* in 1984. The episode also comes only two years after David Jenkins had apparently said on television that the Virgin Birth and the Resurrection had not actually happened. The controversy that had followed, including questions in the House of Commons, the lightning strike on York Minster, and the eruption of media commentary in the press, had fuelled protests against Jenkins' consecration and enthronement and fuelled a determined push by evangelical and conservative clergy to halt it. The controversy itself was also a creation of television in ways not always understood in modern scholarship. The transcript of what Jenkins said reveals the bishop-nominate did not actually deny the Virgin Birth or the Resurrection. The allegation he said the Resurrection was a 'conjuring trick with bones' omitted the all-important word 'not', as in 'not a conjuring trick with bones', therefore entirely changing what Jenkins said. This distortion emerges from Chinese Whispers or folk memory of what he seemed to have said. It is in subsequent reports of what people thought he said that the claim appears of a bishop denying core Christian dogma.

Yes, Prime Minister plays with, reflects, but also subverts this controversy as a product of the perceptions of a television audience. In actuality, Jenkins' television reputation as the 'doubting bishop' and the televisual dissemination of complex theological discussion in crude binaries to a mass audience led to strident calls for Jenkins not to be a bishop. In *The Bishop's Gambit*, it is the contrary, as the dean's television profile, his use of the medium to espouse unorthodoxy and his controversial reputation are all points in his favour. Indeed, according to Sir Humphrey, he has all the markings of a 'thoroughly proper British bishop' and it is his adroit use of television that makes him a bishop.

As the manoeuvres to get the dean into Bury St Edmunds play out, the television has a key role. Two parallel narrative threads converge when one of the Prime Minister's problems, a British nurse trapped in a Middle Eastern jail awaiting flogging for drinking alcohol, is resolved by another, the choice of who will be bishop of Bury St Edmunds. The dean, an Arabist and aficionado of all things Islamic, goes to Kumran (the fictional Middle Eastern country) and intercedes successfully for the nurse's release. All of these actions have been manipulated by Humphrey, including how the media portrays the controversial clergyman. As it transpires, the television reports of the Dean's 'mercy dash' give the clergyman just the national profile needed to be a contender for the bishopric. Then the media is informed that the Prime Minister had the idea to send him, then, finally another leak suggests it was the foreign office that gave the Prime Minister the idea to bypass diplomatic channels. The result, as Sir Humphrey sums it up, is 'Perfect. That way nobody gets the blame and everybody gets the credit'. The skilful use of television by the clergy and by their behind-the-scenes manipulators is worlds away from the controversy Jenkins created, but the actions draw inspiration from the 1980s' context where incoming bishops could be made or unmade in the public's mind by what television showed of them.

As neither *Yes, Minister* nor *Yes, Prime Minister* revealed if Jim Hacker belonged to Labour or the Tories, one key absence from the episode is the sharply political element that accompanied Thatcher's decision making about episcopal appointments, and her frustrating interactions with socialist Anglican bishops over social policy. *Yes, Prime Minister* does however still bring onto the screen the implications of the establishment on how the Church interacted with politics. The broader political landscape of 1980s' politics was remarkable for the Church of England in two ways. One was the dynamic and, in some eyes, intrusive action of members of both the House of Lords and House of Commons in initiating bills about Church government, defeating an ecclesiastical measure and calling into question the principle of synodical government. The other is the way this Conservative Party intervention paradoxically showed the traditional label of the Church as 'the Tory Party at prayer' as drained of meaning, as the actions of some MPs and Lords were profoundly at odds with the Church's leadership (Chapman 2016, 204).

Yes, Prime Minister showed the decision making about a bishopric taking place in Number 10. The programme thus reiterated a central but, by 1986, a fraught reality that the Church was Erastian. That is, the state actively and authoritatively intervenes in the government of the Church. By the 1980s, churchmen and some politicians spoke different languages on this aspect of the Church, in exchanges provoked by numerous flashpoints. The appointment of David Jenkins to Durham (discussed elsewhere in this study) and the reform of the liturgy into modern language and away from the 1662 prayer book provoked disharmony between bishops and politicians.

These tensions informed *Yes, Prime Minister*. Hacker, with the advice of his senior civil servants and the Commission, found himself responsible for choosing the new bishop, without having recourse to any advice from a churchman, not even the archbishops of Canterbury and York. Lynn and Jay's script shows Hacker moving from initial uncertainty about his role in this process, to undertaking diligent research into the proposed candidates and the Church of England in general (including his astonished discovery of its enormous property portfolio) and his eventually stubborn insistence on breaking protocol and rejecting both names on the initial list.

Behind the scenes, Hacker's Cabinet Secretary Sir Humphrey Appleby is adroitly manipulating the Prime Minister, the Church, Oxford University, the Foreign Office and the nurse trapped in a Middle Eastern jail, so that the eventual choice of the new bishop emerges from a self-serving expediency that satisfied multiple people all at the same time. As such, the current of the episode still all runs in one direction, in that ecclesiastical decision making is Erastian, even svengalian. Significantly, for an episode entirely about the Church of England and its hierarchy, there are no clerical characters and a clergyman does not appear on screen. They are instead silent, passive parts of the decision-making process, discussed, picked over, evaluated and in some cases rejected by the politicians and civil servants.

The Candidates

Counterpoised against this cool and cynical manipulation are the two possible candidates who at the start of episode are both front runners for Bury St Edmunds and who must be put out of the way to clear the Dean's path. One is the radical clergymen Dr Harvey, who 'tends towards disestablishmentarianism', meaning he wishes to see the Church of England lose its established status and be freed from state control. Harvey's characterisation aligns with some actual and prominent clergy of the period. The unsuccessful proposals for Anglican and Methodist reunion in the 1960s prompted a series of reports that noted the complexity of the establishment in mediating the roles and relationships between different churches in England, but the failure of the reunion scheme meant these reflections met a dead end. In the 1970s, Archbishop Ramsey speculated openly on television about disestablishment, and took a number of decisive actions in creating the Synod in 1970 and promoting the Church of England (Worship and Doctrine) Measure of 1974, therefore giving his Church a legislative responsibility for what it taught and how it worshipped (Grimley 2011, 50–51). During Coggan's tenure, the Crown Appointments Commission retained the Prime Minister's control over the appointment of the diocesan bishops but allowed some clerical participation (Grimley 50–51). In the 1980s and into the 1990s, clergy from within the Church of England spoke forthrightly on disestablishing their own Church. Archbishop Runcie, preoccupied with achieving reunion with the Church of Rome by the year 2000, downplayed the importance of the Royal Supremacy and the Queen's headship. Other flashpoints of controversy about establishment appeared during the 1980s, including when the House of Commons rejected an ecclesiastical measure to allow divorced men to be ordained (*Economist* March 31, 1990, 38). The scholar and churchman Colin Buchanan derided establishment, seeing it at odds with a nation that was no longer formally or universally Christian. In 1986, the year Hacker was making his choice for Bury St Edmunds, Buchanan published a topical reflection on establishment, calling for disestablishment of a Church now situated in a world of 'pagandom', and in which the political arm of establishment obscured the religious (see Atherstone 2011, 95). He instead called for a national church, not an officially established one.

Dr Harvey's disestablishmentarianism was at least a positive belief. Hacker is presented with a second choice, Canon Mike Stanford, whose socially aware initiatives included being 'the diocesan advisor on ethnic communities and social responsibility. He organised conferences on interfaith interface and between Christians and Marxists, and between Christians and the women of Greenham Common'. The last was those groups of female protesters who in 1981 set up a permanent camp and protest movement outside an American airbase (Shepherd 2014). *The Bishop's Gambit* is embedded deeply in the ecclesiastical politics of the 1980s and engages with how these high politics were themselves rooted in the television culture of the period. Canon Mike Stanford is a 'modernist', a euphemism for an atheist. According to his file, 'He designed a new church in South London with places for dispensing orange juice, family planning and organising demos—But no place for Holy Communion'. The terminology of 'modernist' harks back to the radical 'South Bank' theology of the 1960s, including Bishop John Robinson, but more immediately to the appearance of Jenkins the 'doubting bishop' in current television culture.

The Civil Servants advising Hacker deride theology as 'a device for enabling agnostics to stay within the Church'. Yet Canon Stanford, for all his theological heresy, is the diametric opposite of Dr Harvey; the latter's article of faith was disestablishing the Church of England, including removing the royal supremacy from the Queen. Stanford is theologically radical but socially acceptable and certainly imbricated with the establishment. According to the Commissioner, his wife is 'eminently suitable', meaning not that she is devout or charitable woman but is the daughter of the earl of Chichester. That statement is a fictional analogue to actual bishops who had made well-connected marriages. Bishop Cyril Easthaugh for example had married Lady Laura Palmer, the daughter of the third Earl of Selborne. A clergyman such as Canon Stanford therefore held in balance in his person what would otherwise have been competing influences of the radical and the establishment. 'So, the ideal candidate from the Church of England's point of view would be a cross between a socialite, and a socialist' is Hacker's summation of how he feels the Commission would wish him to act. In actuality, these apparent contradictions had been effortlessly embodied in Mervyn Stockwood, who had only retired from Southward in 1980 and whose episcopal ministry mixed socialist concerns with high living including partying with romance novelist Barbara Cartland and the actresses Wendy Craig and Barbara Shelley. Stockwood's vibrant social life presented a model for the type of bishop discussed in *Yes, Prime Minister*. Sir Humphrey agrees with Hacker, brushing off concerns that Canon Stanford's atheism makes his consecration as a bishop impossible, for 'the Church of England is primarily a social organisation, not a religious one'. In addition, the Church is 'part of the rich social fabric of this country. So bishops need to be the sorts of chaps who speak properly and know which knife and fork to use' says Humphrey. In that characterisation Lynn and Jay drew on a recent tradition of 'well-bred bishops', such as Gerald Ellison, Bishop of London until 1981 and who was obituarised with reference to his good breeding and social graces (*Independent* October 20, 1992).

Canon Stanford is the first name of the list of two, above Dr Harvey, and the name the Church Commissioners want Hacker to pick. Unlike Dr Harvey, Stanford has no objection to the establishment and the Queen's royal supremacy. He therefore aligns with Humphrey's assessment of the Church's core identity and theology that 'the Queen is inseparable from the Church of England', whereas God is merely 'an optional extra'. In this way, Canon Stanford, who never appears on screen in the episode but is discussed in absentia, therefore had the potential to be a radical *and* a pillar of the establishment.

These characterisations in *Yes, Prime Minister* are both a part of but also distinct from the actual episcopate of the period. Mervyn Stockwood was a socialist who mingled easily with high society. David Jenkins was a live wire of theological controversy, but also an affront to the establishment through his explicit support of non-Conservative politics. In choosing Robert Runcie, a familiar face from Conservative circles in Oxford, Thatcher is believed to have felt she had found an archbishop who would meet a certain set of needs, but found that his lukewarm but obvious support of *Faith in the City*, a 1985 report on Urban Priority areas, made him the patron of explicit criticisms of Conservative social and welfare policies (Moore 2015). Runcie also became an effective fundraiser for the Church Urban Fund, again placing his weight behind a scheme antithetical to

Conservative policy and that Conservatives derided as 'pure' Marxism (Carpenter 1996, 173, 276).

Perhaps the clearest real-life analogue to the unseen Canon Stanford was Bishop John Baker, the bishop of Salisbury from 1982 to 1993. Baker had impeccable establishment credentials, including education at Marlborough College and Oxford, serving as chaplain to the Speaker of the House of Commons and voting Tory. As a bishop though he went rogue, including promoting the report *The Church and the Bomb* calling for unilateral British nuclear disarmament and therefore promoting an ideal entirely at odds with Thatcher's defence policy. He also criticised British policy towards Ireland, attacked the British police and condemned foxhunting, all actions to get him off side with gentry in Wiltshire. Where the fictional Canon Stanford pursued interfaith dialogue with the Women of Greenham Common, the actual Bishop Baker met with IRA prisoners in Maze prison (*Belfast Telegraph* January 15, 1983, 4).

The character sketches of the various clergy appraised but not seen in *The Bishop's Gambit* intersect with social and theological developments in the Church in the mid-1980s. The candidate Canon Stanford is theologically radical and socially alert. Actual bishops, as well as members of the lower clergy, attracted this criticism. Bishop David Sheppard of Liverpool exercised his episcopate in a large and socially deprived city. Key events such as the 1982 visit of Pope John Paul II were occasions that showed Sheppard's liberal social attitudes as he expressed concern about meeting a pope whose views on contraception and family planning were at odds with his own (O'Connor 2008, 269).

Yes, Prime Minister was also a televisual vehicle to show a large audience an iteration of one interpretation of the English episcopate: that it was a body of clergy believing everything and nothing. Jenkins is one part of that perception, but so is the longer history of the Southbank Theology. Prime Minister Hacker's amazement that an atheist can be a bishop was only partly assuaged by Sir Humphrey's reassurance that bishops need only fit in at up market dinner parties or the Buckingham Palace garden parties. On Easter Day 1985, after Bishop David Jenkins' controversial comments about doctrine appeared in the media, Robert Runcie's sermon at Canterbury Cathedral 'made a personal declaration of his faith in the Gospel', said the *Daily Telegraph*, pointing to Runcie's implicit but obvious reaction to Jenkins. *Private Eye* made the same point but with more irreverence: 'I believe in God: Archbishop's shock claim' (Carpenter 1996, 274). The *Daily Express* portrayed Runcie in a cartoon with a speech bubble saying 'we don't know anything about God any more' (Carpenter 1996, 275). Members of the 1987 General Synod of the Church of England engaged with this perception, providing a real-life echo of the insistence in *Yes, Prime Minister* that the next bishop be someone who actually believed in God, rather than viewing him as an option.

The immediate ecclesiastical context to *Bishop's Gambit* was one shaped by renewed concern that the Church of England seemed to believe in everything and nothing. A plan by the government to end compulsory religious instruction in schools had placed a focus on what, if anything, local churches did to instruct young people. The 1987 General Synod debated a report 'We Believe in God', a title inciting mock surprise at what it declared, with the report and a planned catechism also encountering resistance for being too prescriptive (*Economist* July 11, 1987, 33). Jointly written by a team of senior clergy and theologians, the report 'addressed challenges to believing in God', as one of the authors recalled (Thiselton 2014, 51). For some readers, the report merely reinforced that the Church of England was doctrinally out of control. One statement in it for instance was 'If the Church is to become fully itself, it will not do so by attempting to achieve a doctrinal definition to which all can assent, for some would always be unable to assent and would then risk being "unchurched"' (Doctrine Commission 1987, 32). Critical responses to the report modulated further to be critical responses of the whole Church. The scholar and clergyman Gerald Bray responded sarcastically, feigning surprise at any Anglicans who 'have a tendency to believe in God in spite of the social trends of our age' and wondering 'Does the Church of England worship a God substantially different from that of the rest of Christendom, which would make a peculiarly Anglican statement valuable and necessary?' (Bray 1989, 120–121).

BLAIR'S BISHOPS

From time to time, the Anglican episcopate is largely uniform in composition. Eliza Filby's landmark study of Margaret Thatcher and English religion points to one of these occasions, characterising most 1980s' bishops as 'Anglo-Catholic liberals, ecumenical in outlook and centrist in politics'. That uniformity is not due entirely to the whims of the prime minister, as some of these pre-dated Thatcher's 1979 victory. At other times, the episcopate takes on a more varied character as bishops seek to shift and adjust to changing political circumstances and the attendant changes to social policy and social life.

A significant change facing bishops was the 1997 election of the 'New Labour' government, as this government explicitly identified itself as 'We don't do God'. The irony of that stance was the new prime minister, Tony Blair, who was religious, initially High Church Anglican and latterly Roman Catholic. A further irony of the position 'We don't do God' was New Labour's suite of policies and initiatives that highlighted religion and faith (Allen 2011, 260). These tensions between a religious prime minister and a revamped Labour Party of the 'Third Way' that, at least in its early years in office, eschewed publicly identifying with religion, bore fruit for television comedy. Blair's earnest manner of speaking as well as his own faith, suggested the comic possibility of making Blair into a trendy Anglican vicar and allowed the transplanting of Tony Blair's image into an Anglican frame of reference. By the time Blair became prime minister, the 'trendy vicar' was an established trope with long antecedents. Experiments with liturgy and church design, jeans and informality were hallmarks of the clerical archetype from the 1960s onwards, especially in urban parishes (Sandbrook 2007/2015, 459). *The Verger*, 1988 episode of *Tales of the Unexpected*, updated Somerset Maugham's original story and reflected current awareness of a trendy vicar with a story about the 'old guard' verger and his wife being displaced by a new vicar who thinks of the church building as a social and community centre rather than a place of worship. By the 1980s, a tendency to play the guitar in worship and use the modern language liturgy became part of the archetype (Jasper 1984, 179). Then in 1998, the comedian Harry Enfield starred in *Sermon from St Albion's*, playing the Reverend Tony Blair. The series derived from a long-running parody of both Blair and the typical Church of England newsletter in *Private Eye*.

Two creative threads combine in *Sermon from St Albion's*. One is the inherent tension of a religious leader of a political party ambivalent about religion (Graham 2009, 1). The other is the televisual potential of the Church of England's own efforts to seem modern in the period of a consciously reforming and modernising 'Third Way' Labour government. When viewing the series, the *Guardian*'s Nick Cohen described Enfield's characterisation of the Reverend Blair as 'meretricious, priggish, bossy, vacuous, simpering, dogmatic, vainglorious, saccharine, platitudinous and phoney', who 'speaks English as if he learned it in an evangelical summer camp in Finland' (*Guardian* September 2, 2001). The means to convey this vision of Blair came from the trendy vicar trope but Enfield's comedy was sharper about Blair than it was about the Church of England.

Tony Blair lent himself to religious parody precisely because of his earnest manner, his intense personal religiosity and his inability to understand jokes about himself. *Private Eye's* editor Ian Hislop despaired during the 2001 General Election campaign when 'a casually jacketless Blair' posed 'in front of a stained glass window and lead hundreds of ecstatic schoolgirls into the hymn "We are all the Children of the Future"' (*Guardian* September 2, 2001). Hislop's frustration was that *Sermon from St Albion's* had come to life for real, making parody unnecessary. Blair was himself embodying the stock character of the trendy vicar, without the need for Enfield to mediate the role on television. The intersection between Blair and Church remained prominent, irrespective of the 'don't do God' insistence of his spin doctors. In particular, the appointment of diocesan bishops retained controversial potential during Blair's premiership. The actual Church of England found Blair was as capable as Thatcher of decisively influencing appointments.

The deliberations of the 12 members of the Crown Appointments Commission remained obscure, down to where and when they meet, with leaks and hints often adding little in the way of clarity. In 1998 several papers suggested an unusual degree of prime ministerial intervention in the appointment of the new bishop of Southwark. The strongest suggestion was in the *Independent*, which claimed the 'Church bends knee to Blair' in offering the usual two names, but without any order of preference (*Independent* February 1, 1998). Rumour, which is inevitable in episcopal appointments as the Commission works behind closed doors, also suggested that Blair had been attempting to bring the bishop of Monmouth, Rowan Williams, into Southwark (Goddard 2013, 32). The year before, similar controversy arose about the new bishop of Liverpool, when again the *Independent* (although the article was by the editor of the *Church Times*) led reports of Blair rejecting the two offered names. Further complexity surrounded the issue as the Labour Government was then engaged in large-scale reform of the upper house.

Absolute Power shows that much has moved on since *Yes, Prime Minister* in the tone of both British politics and national religion. There had been a change of personnel at the top of the Church of England. Runcie retired in 1991, and Downing Street course announced George Carey of Bath and Wells as the new Primate of All England. Carey's appointment surprised a number of people. He had only been a bishop for a short period of time (since 1987) and was a lesser known and less experienced bishop than many of his contemporaries who had been spoken of as likely successors to Runcie, including the bishops of London, Chichester, Wakefield and St Albans (*Economist* December 12, 1987, 29). His sudden accession out of a crowded field of brought into public view a level of unease that had been present throughout the 1980s about Downing Street's intervention in the appointment of bishops and Thatcher's firm decisions about who would not make it to Canterbury. For instance, David Sheppard, already a figure of national prominence because of his Test Cricket career was equally notable as a socially interventionist bishop of Liverpool, whose criticisms of Conservative social policy may have ensured he did not replace Runcie (Beeson 2007, 189). That impression though is not absolute and many viewed Thatcher as not having insisted on 'one of us' making it to the finishing post (Lee et al. 1998, 50).

Nonetheless Thatcher's choice of chairman for the Appointments Commission was an opportunity for decisive if indirect influence on the type of man who would become archbishop. Her choice fell on the engineer Viscount Caldecote, an evangelical Anglican in sympathy with Carey's churchmanship (Baker 1991, 90; *Independent* September 23, 1999). The race for Canterbury also brought into public view the sometimes unseemly jockeying of bishops for the top place. This competitive streak registered in public discourse, not least when Ladbrokes called the race the 'Cantuar Stakes', after the Latin abbreviation for Canterbury. The notion appealed particularly to Clifford Longley, the religious affairs writer for *The Times* who deemed first prize would be 'two palaces and 10 years or so in purgatory' (*The Times* March 31, 1990, 10). Longley was further inspired to 'call a race' between the contenders with the names of their 'horses' encapsulating what could either help or hinder their selection. The bishop of Oxford rode 'Ethical Dilemmas', the archbishop of York 'Public Faith' and so forth, and some had no horse at all (*The Times* March 31, 1990, 10).

Pope Idol

The bishops who appear in *Absolute Power* as possible choices for the vacant archbishopric of Canterbury appear as comedic distillations of the 'decade of evangelism' (1991–2001) associated with George Carey's archiepiscopate. One of the actual outputs of this endeavour was the video 'Yours Faithfully, the Church of England'. The video launch in February 1993 to industry professionals was met with surprise at the scenes of Carey wearing a paper hat and talking to young people at a 'Christian rave', and elderly parishioners dancing in the aisles of Christ Church Brixton. 'It tries a little too hard' said one commentator when the Church launched their video (*Telegraph* February 11, 1993, 4). According to the Church's then director of communications, the Reverend Eric Shegog, the point of the 28-minute video was to show the Church as 'alive and kicking'. However it was the possibility that dancing, raving middle-aged bishops were 'trying too hard' that is the chief characteristic milked for comedy potential in *Absolute Power*, including bishops attempting to sing music by the American rock group the Doors or using painfully stretched sporting analogies. The Church of England provided further inadvertent comedy material in 1997 in commercials broadcast on the Central Television franchise. The commercial showed footage of a male model driving a sports car, a basketball player, girls in a laundrette and a disc jockey in a Ministry of Sound night club, all revealed to be Christian as well as young and trendy and all overlaid with Hip Hop music. Like the 'Yours Faithfully' video, the intention was to encourage not just higher church attendance but higher attendance by young people (*Telegraph* March 20, 1997, 1). The impact of the commercial may have diminished when Archbishop Carey admitted to *The Times's* religion correspondent Ruth Gledhill that he was weary and ready to move onto retirement, and the appearance of the exhausted archbishop undercut the youthful zest of the commercial (*The Times* March 20, 1997, 2).

Absolute Power takes place not in Whitehall but in the offices of a commercial PR company. The setting was, by 2003, one where it had become possible to dramatise the campaign for the archbishopric of Canterbury, because of the Church's own 'decade of evangelism' and the steps taken by the Church to use advertising to seem relevant and reverse declining attendances. During Carey's 'Decade of Evangelism', the Church's communications officers carried out the task of making the Church seem young and relevant rather than 'old fashioned and staid'. The Church also corporatised, including its own corporate logo (*Telegraph* March 20, 1997, 1). During the Decade for Evangelism, the broadcasting context also changed. The rules regarding religious advertising had kept commercials about God off the screen. In 1990, the Broadcasting Act made a greater degree of religious advertising possible, although the Church of England did not act immediately. In 1993, the Lichfield diocese bought screen time on the Central Television franchise and viewers saw a striking juxtaposition: the Iraqi dictator Saddam Hussein and other disturbing and unsettling images appeared, followed by the text 'The Church of England. This Sunday' (*The Times* January 20, 1993, 6).

For the writers of *Absolute Power*, the Church's own actions provided the means to bring the selection of bishops into a fictional corporate world but one with a strong anchorage in reality. Much has changed since *Yes, Prime Minister* and scheming but gentlemanly civil servants are eclipsed by public relations gurus. Into this world comes the archbishop of York, who believes he is likely to succeed to Canterbury but who unctuously declares that 'Running is thought vulgar'. To be certain though of getting Canterbury, the archbishop of York feels some public relations will not hurt. Thereafter the innate competitiveness of the Prentiss McCabe public relations company drives the plot. Half of the firm is overseeing York's campaign. In retaliation, the other half of the company seeks a competitive rival from among the current crop of bishops. Although the working environment and personnel have changed from the power dynamics shown in *Yes, Prime Minister*, the two programmes concur in showing television as intrinsic to the selection of bishops. In *Absolute Power* Downing Street is worried about the politics of the new primate, concerns echoing the criticisms of the Iraq War made by the new Archbishop Rowan Williams in 2003 (Anderson 2014, 1–2), making the right choice of archbishop not someone interested in steam engines and cricket but someone who can say the right thing in a television interview.

Although amateurish in comparison to Prentiss McCabe, Sir Humphrey had grasped that the dean needed a major public relations success to get him into Bury St Edmunds. Far more slick and professional are the efforts made in *Absolute Power* and the episode culminates in both archiepiscopal campaigns harnessing reality television. The episode is from 2003, and *Big Brother* had debuted in 2000 and *Pop Idol* in 2001, underlining the timeliness of the archiepiscopal engagement with the genre. The episode revels in showing churchmen attempting to engage with an unchurched society through banal television. One of the partners at Prentiss McCabe tells the archbishop 'I'm a bit of an Easter and Christmas Anglican. I give Good Friday a miss when ITV have got one of the better Bonds on' and the receptionist confuses denominations and announces the arrival of the Cardinal of Yorkshire. A tabloid proprietor's sudden interest in the race for Canterbury is only because after a heart attack: 'He's worried that St Peter will give him a hard time for printing pictures of women's tits each day', explains the editor. The *News*, a fictional version of the *Sun*, appoints a religion editor who is actually a sports writer and the race for Canterbury is demeaned by a crass campaign calibrated to the limited reading age of the tabloid readership. A three-word headline 'You play God' is deemed like *War and Peace* for the readers and replaced by the inaccurate but shorter 'Pope Idol', as the two candidates take part in a live televised debate. The debate is make or break for the candidates, who learn double speaking slogans and glib answers to questions posed by a tabloid journalist, a rabbi, a secular humanist and the Anglican Archbishop of Nigeria. The break moment for York is an awkward question that suggests he may be gay. The Nigerian archbishop asks 'are there any heterosexuals in the Church of England?' *Yes, Prime Minister* had toyed with the same possibility, but its 1980s' context was before clerical homosexuality had become a crisis in Anglicanism and the issue is only alluded to in the droll comment 'With the Church, you usually get the choice of a knave or a queen'.

The contribution to the debate by the archbishop of Nigeria shows the media image of the Church of England folding back on itself. The brief moment is an observant comment by the programme makers on the current state of the Anglican Communion and the energetic actions by many African Anglican bishops to stem what they viewed as the immorality of the western Church, which was condoning homosexuality (Shortt 2009). The script is aware of the impact of the Nigerian Anglican Church on the larger Anglican Communion, ongoing in 2003 and culminating in 2005 in a new Nigerian Church constitution that omitted reference to the See of Canterbury. The African bishop in *Absolute Power* is particularly analogous to Bishop Emmanuel Chukwuma of Nigeria, and more particularly to the spectacular footage from the 1998 Lambeth Conference of the bishop attempting to exorcise the gay rights activist Richard Kirker of his homosexuality. The footage made the evening news bulletins (Bates 2004, 137).

The process of choosing an Anglican diocesan bishop has been and remains largely unseen and unknown and takes place behind closed doors. It has rarely featured in drama or comedy, but has taken its place in a roll call of other prime ministerial activities in *Yes, Prime Minister* and was brought into the twenty-first century in *Absolute Power*. The Church's secure but challenging establishment, its clergy relationship with television, and national and internal controversies are clinically delineated in comedy. This chapter has brought together many of the themes of this book, in considering how the Church is shaped by the medium. In Part I, we studied how actual clergy coped with appearing on television, the sort of things they said, and the impact of their appearances. *Yes, Prime Minister* and *Absolute Power* present fictional follow-ups to that and show how being on television could make or break episcopal ambitions. But they also show the Church as something believing in everything and nothing and as a creature of the establishment.

Disputes within the Church of England about human sexuality, alluded to briefly in *Yes, Prime Minister* and more fully in *Absolute Power*, provided the basis of comedy, but in reality have also posed existential threats to the Church and the unity of the Anglican Communion. The next chapter though examines the Church in peril from more direct but also more fantastic sources of threat, exploring it as it interacts with the imaginations of science fiction writers.

References

Newspapers, Periodicals and Trade Papers

Belfast Telegraph
Church Times
Economist
Evening Chronicle
Guardian
Independent
Irish Independent
Telegraph

Government Sources

UK Parliament. 2007. *House of Lords Hansard*, vol. 692, col. 1697

Printed Secondary Sources

Allen, Chris. 2011. "We Don't Do God": A Critical Retrospective of New Labour's Approaches to "Religion or Belief" and "Faith". *Culture and Religion* 12 (3): 259–275.
Anderson, John. 2014. "On Very Slippery Ground": The British Churches, Archbishop Fisher and the Suez Crisis. *Contemporary British History* 29: 1–18.
Atherstone, Andrew. 2011. Gospel Opportunity or Ungodly Relic? The Established Church Through Anglican Evangelical Eyes. In *The Established Church: Past, Present and Future*, ed. Mark Chapman, Judith Maltby, and William Whyte, 75–97. London: Bloomsbury.
Baker, D.L. 1991. Turbulent Priests: Christian Opposition to the Conservative Government since 1979. *The Political Quarterly* 62 (1): 90–105.

Bates, Stephen. 2004. *A Church at War: Anglicans and Homosexuality*. London: I.B. Tauris.

Beeson, Trevor. 2007. *Round the Church in 50 Years: A Personal Journey*. Hymns Ancient and Modern.

Bray, Gerald. 1989. *We Believe in God*: A Critique of the Report of the Doctrine Commission of the Church of England. *Churchman* 103 (2): 120–128.

Buchanan, Colin. 2006. *Taking the Long View: Three and a Half Decades of General Synod*. Church House Publishing.

Campbell, John. 2011. *Margaret Thatcher Volume Two: The Iron Lady*. Random House.

Carpenter, Humphrey. 1996. *Robert Runcie: The Reluctant Archbishop*. Sceptre.

Chadwick, Owen. 1972. *The Victorian Church Part 2*. Black.

Chandler, Andrew. 2016. *George Bell, Bishop of Chichester: Church, State, and Resistance in the Age of Dictatorship*. Wm. B. Eerdmans Publishing.

Chapman, Mark D. 2016. Church and State in England: A Fragile Establishment. In *Religion, Authority, and the State*, ed. L.D. Lefebure. Palgrave Macmillan.

Cranmer, Frank. 2001. Church-State Relations in the United Kingdom: A Westminster View. *Ecclesiastical Law Journal* 6: 111–121.

Doctrine Commission. 1987. *We Believe in God*. London: Church House Publishing.

Edwards, David L. 1971. *Leaders of the Church of England 1828–1944*. London: Oxford University Press.

Filby, Eliza. 2015. *God and Mrs Thatcher: The Battle for Britain's Soul*. Biteback Books.

Flinders, Matthew. 2012. Heaven's Talent Scout: Prime Ministerial Power, Ecclesiastical Patronage and the Governance of Britain. *The Political Quarterly* 83 (4): 792–805.

Goddard, Andrew. 2013. *Rowan Williams: His Legacy*. Lion Books.

Graham, Elaine L. 2009. Doing God? Public Theology Under Blair. In *Remoralizing Britain?: Political, Ethical and Theological Perspectives on New Labour*, ed. Peter Manley Scott, Christopher R. Baker, and Elaine L. Graham, 1–19. A & C Black.

Grimley, Matthew. 2011. The Dog That Didn't Bark: The Failure of Disestablishment Since 1927. In *The Established Church: Past, Present and Future*, ed. Mark Chapman, Judith Maltby, and William Whyte, 39–55. Bloomsbury.

Hein, David. 2008. *Geoffrey Fisher: Archbishop of Canterbury, 1945–1961*. Wipf and Stock Publishers.

Jasper, Tony. 1984. *Jesus and the Christian in a Pop Culture*. R. Royce.

Lee, J.M., G.W. Jones, and June Burnham. 1998. *At the Centre of Whitehall*. Springer.

Medhurst, Kenneth. 1991. Reflections on Church of England and Politics at a Moment of Transition. *Parliamentary Affairs* 44 (2): 240–261.

158 M. HARMES ET AL.

Moore, Campbell. 2015. *Margaret Thatcher: The Authorized Biography, Volume Two: Everything She Wants*. Penguin.

O'Connor, Garry. 2008. *Universal Father: A Life of John Paul II*. Bloomsbury Publishing.

Palmer, Bernard. 1992. *High and Mitred: A Study of Prime Ministers as Bishop-Makers 1837–1977*. SPCK.

Sandbrook, Dominic. 2007/2015. *White Heat: A History of Britain in the Swinging Sixties* (2 vols). Hatchette.

Schlossberg, Herbert. 2000. *The Silent Revolution and the Making of Victorian England*. Ohio State University Press.

Seldon, Anthony. 2016. *The Cabinet Office, 1916–2016*. London: Biteback Publishing.

Shepherd, Laura J. 2014. Sex or Gender?: Bodies in Global Politics and Why Gender Matters. In *Gender Matters in Global Politics: A Feminist Introduction to International Relations*, ed. Laura J. Shepherd. London: Routledge.

Shortt, Rupert. 2009. *Rowan's Rule*. Hachette.

Thiselton, Anthony C. 2014. *A Lifetime in the Church and in the University*. Wipf and Stock Publishers.

Williamson, Cliff. 2012. The Church of England and the Falklands War. In *God and War: The Church of England and Armed Conflict in the Twentieth Century*, ed. Stephen G. Parker and Tom Lawson, 165–185. Ashgate.

CHAPTER 8

The World in Peril: The Church and Science Fiction

Apocalypse is a religious term. As one of the names given to the final book in the New Testament, it means something revealed. However, the dramatic and eschatological language of the Bible has meant apocalypse has gained a narrower meaning. As religious terminology, it is a good place to consider how the makers of science fiction television have done two things: envisaged the world in peril; and made the Church part of this peril.

This chapter moves from comedy to the bleakest drama. Actual science, especially nuclear research and the development of first the Atom Bomb and then the Hydrogen Bomb (from 1955) lent itself to religious discourse because it 'evoked traditional repertoires of eschatology and millenarianism' (Grimley 2012, 148). Science fiction that involves the Church of England complicates key Church teachings on hope, judgement and God's goodness to his people. Science fiction threats can take two forms. One is man-made, where humanity's science such as the Bomb or virological warfare destroys the world. The other is extra-terrestrial, where the menace comes from outer space.

This latter type is responsible for an early and successful juxtaposition of the ecclesiastical and the otherworldly. Among the millions of people watching the Coronation on television was Nigel Kneale, a writer at the BBC. When drafting the climax of his 1953 television serial *The Quatermass Experiment,* he realised that Westminster Abbey had suddenly become a familiar sight to millions of people and accordingly the climax of his story took place in Poet's Corner. The visual effects were crude. A few

© The Author(s) 2020
M. Harmes et al., *The Church on British Television,*
https://doi.org/10.1007/978-3-030-38113-4_8

polystyrene pillars, a blown-up photo of the Abbey's Poet's Corner from a guidebook, and Kneale's own fingers manipulating the puppet monster realised the effects. The moment though is the start of several decades of television that presented sharply felt and equally sharply observed concerns about the end of the world. Science fictions, telefantasies and imaginative dramas made the Church part of the end of the world.

This chapter's initial focus is the vastly controversial and Oscar-winning 1965 docu-drama *The War Game*, and the intersection between the programme, the Church, and actual anxieties about threats from science and war. The docu-drama depicted a cogently researched vision of the impact of nuclear war, which later influenced the equally distressing *Threads* in 1983. The science is technically and dryly explained but participates in a *mise en scène* that eventually resembles a hellish nightmare reminiscent of a painting by Hieronymus Bosch, as the world burns, people writhe and distort in agony and the physical environment shatters. There are also religious resonances in the script. The narrator describes the sound of nuclear detonation as 'an enormous door slamming in the depths of Hell'. Three characters in *The War Game* are a bishop and two vicars. The bishop believes in a just war, whereas a vicar tries in vain to provide spiritual support after tactical nuclear strikes hit Britain and sweep civilisation away. The bishop is a fictional extension of Geoffrey Fisher, the archbishop of Canterbury who made the now-notorious statement that 'The very worst the Bomb can do is to sweep a vast number of people from this world into the next into which they must all go anyway'. While the BBC could countenance comedy vicars and bishops, it cancelled the broadcast of *The War Game*. The docu-drama was too shocking for the BBC to broadcast for nearly 20 years. Part of that shock was the suggestion that clergy could be so insouciant about the end of the world. It also showed remorselessly that the Bomb would not merely sweep people into the next world but marshalled evidence from physics, psychiatry and physiology to show how survivors would be in hell on Earth and explicitly showed the pastoral ministrations of Anglican clergy as worse than useless. *The War Game* was a closely observed study of not just the science but also the politics and religion of a nuclear threat. Besides Archbishop Fisher's blithe unconcern about the destruction of the world, the Church of England's hostility to the Campaign for Nuclear Disarmament and the Aldermaston Marches are actualities that shape the impression of the Church in this delineation of the end of the world. From there, the chapter will broaden to the later history of programming that united the Church with scientific fantasy and the challenges to priestly authority and church dogma through the 1960s, the mystical but also perturbing meditation on the end of existence in *Survivors* and *Penda's Fen* in the 1970s, the alien intrusions in *Doctor Who* to the depiction of the Church confronted by a zombie apocalypse in *In the Flesh* (2014).

SCIENCE FICTION IMAGINES THE CHURCH

Science fiction has imagined a number of futures of not just religion in general but of Anglicanism in particular. For example, *Doctor Who* has offered creative and challenging future visions of the Church and religion. These have included the Church as a de-sacralised but still recognisably Anglican institution with bishops, deacons and vergers in the far future (Harmes 2013, 226). The juxtaposition of religious trappings with a futuristic setting has long proved a source of creative inspiration. The science fiction anthology series *Out of the Unknown* contributed a 1967 episode *The Prophet*, based on an Isaac Asimov story 'Reason' about a robot who develops a form of religious conviction and works out a complete robot theology. Among the production crew for the episode was the electronic music pioneer Delia Derbyshire who wrote a special composition for the episode, *Ziwzih OO-OO-OO*, a religious chant performed by robots. However as well as reading mathematics at university and being an electronic innovator with the BBC Radiophonic Workshop, Derbyshire had also studied medieval music and her avant garde composition is like medieval organum music given an electronic twist. Her efforts here are a captivating instance of the ecclesiastical and the electronic, or the traditionally religious and the futuristically weird in dialogue with each other. That combination encapsulates television when the Church of England encounters science fiction, an encounter with a dramatic focus about fears the world could very well be on the verge of destroying itself.

THE ATOMIC ARCHBISHOP

Britain began testing atomic weapons in 1952, becoming the third nation after the United States and the USSR to do so. In succession, France and China also weaponised nuclear technology. For many decades, the argument for nuclear weapons was that they exist to deter precisely because no one will launch them, but the hideous potential of either tactical or strategic nuclear war entered both public consciousness and religious discourse.

As the film historian Matthew Jones points out, the possibility of a nuclear strike had particular force in the British popular consciousness. The United States' vastly greater land mass prompted different expectations of the results of a nuclear war; a strike on the west coast for example did not necessarily mean the whole country would be destroyed, but the small scale of the British Isles meant a nuclear war could end life as it was known everywhere. The whole country could be 'choked by radioactive fallout'. On the other hand, politically, post-imperial Britain could become even more a global irrelevance without weapons (Jones 2017, 72). Organised opposition was prompted by concerns that nuclear war was actually going to happen. At an organisational level, the Campaign for Nuclear Disarmament (CND) grew in numbers across the 1950s, recruiting Christopher Tynan, Christopher Logue and Lord Bertrand Russell, among others.

Its membership did not include Geoffrey Fisher, the archbishop of Canterbury. The poet Christopher Logue has a number of strong memories about the Archbishop and the CND at the time of the first Aldermaston March in 1958. This march, a protest moving from Trafalgar Square to the Atomic Weapons Research Establishment in Berkshire, reached its destination on Good Friday and some marchers had participated in religious services along the way. Programmes about the Church of England intruded fiction into the history of Aldermaston and British nuclear anxiety. In *Call the Midwife* the Anglican sisters of Nonnatus House received civil defence advice in case of nuclear war and their handyman formed a civil defence corps. Likewise in ITV's 1986 miniseries *Paradise Postponed* the 'raving red' socialist rector Simeon Simcox participated in the march, with the marchers themselves described in the series as a 'collection of vicars' sons carrying sandwiches'. Simcox preaches outside the Aldermaston research establishment against achieving peach through fear, dialogue that offered a retort to comments made by actual bishops. In real life, the Church's connections to the march were ambiguous. Clergy like the fictional Simcox did participate. Marchers initially thought that the vicar of St Mary's Church in Reading rang his church bells to welcome them, but later discovered he was trying to drown out the march (Vähäsalo 2016, 42). Logue remembered the writer Christopher Tynan catching up to him on the march and showing him the report of what Fisher had said about the CND and the Bomb: 'The very worst the Bomb can do is to sweep a vast number of People from this world into the next into which they must all go anyway' (*Guardian* August 28, 1999). Fisher also argued 'for all I know it is within the providence of God that the human race should destroy itself in this manner'.

Fisher's comments attracted criticism then from members of his Church who had expected him to be the 'keeper of the national conscience' (Kirby 1993, 252). They have not lost their questionable implications in succeeding years. Some of his own bishops held strongly contrasting views. During the Second World War, George Bell of Chichester had condemned the carpet-bombing of German civilians and later expressed horror at the even greater destructive potential of hydrogen bombs (Besier 2015, 590). Based on other contextual comments, including private remarks to bishops, it is clear that Fisher was not exaggerating in any way in his horribly appropriate choice of language of the Bomb 'sweeping' people away. He confided in the bishop of Winchester an impression that the 'world was in jeopardy', and recognised that people were expecting the Church to offer moral leadership opposing nuclear weapons.

Why did Fisher make that comment about the Bomb? It is important to remember his 1950s context, one where people could approach atomic research with optimism rather than fear (Jones 2017, 1). Fisher's comments also require interpretation with attention to theology. While aware that international relations in post-war Europe were complex and that it was not the role of the Church to complicate the British government's interactions with the Soviet Union, Fisher was personally in no doubt that Communism was pestilential and antithetical to England and Englishness (Kirby 2012, 129). He belonged to a generation who remembered the implications of Appeasement and invoked that failure to argue against a ban on nuclear weapons (Kirby 2012, 139). One of Fisher's most recent biographers has offered significant intellectual, political and theological grounds for understanding Fisher's comments about the Bomb, which otherwise seem startlingly blasé about the possibilities of mass slaughter. For a churchman, the Bomb had theological implications as it was in the hands of the Soviet government that 'openly proclaims that it does not believe in God or in spiritual laws', as Fisher said (Hein 2008). His biographer David Hein notes Fisher's stance that the value of the bomb was to deter rather than destroy. He also notes that Fisher's stance on nuclear war tends to be reconstructed from that single quote, whereas over time Fisher became more fearful about the possibility of nuclear war while also encompassing the Bomb in a worldview dominated by the protection of religion from atheist Soviets (Hein 2008, 90). In Fisher's lifetime, he and other churchmen had seen Soviets destroy churches and persecute the clergy and the Bomb in British hands became inextricably entwined with opposition to an atheist regime.

What churchmen said about the Bomb was more coherent because of the connection of the Church with the state. Gerald Ellison, the bishop of Chester from 1955 to 1973, blessed the fleet of Polaris submarines, including their nuclear missiles. His action attracted controversy similar in tone and scale to the reactions about Fisher's comments (*Living Church* March 26, 1967, 7). Ellison's actions though were those of a bishop of the established Church praying for an instrument of the state. As the historian Peter Webster points out, churchmen, politicians and army officers were often 'drawn from the same stock', and shared similar instincts as each other to the defence of the realm (Webster 2014, 129).

It is useful to consider the cultural and theological crucible from which Fisher's comments emerged to reveal his expectations of the impact of a nuclear war, and that in turn explains key characteristics of the Church of England's portrayal in science fiction. Some bishops disagreed with Fisher and some had condemned nuclear warfare since the bombing of Hiroshima in 1945, including Henry Wilson the bishop of Chelmsford (Willis 1997, 428). George Bell called the H Bomb a 'sin' (Kirby 2012, 143). Yet others were even more strident in making the same points as Fisher. Robert Stopford the Bishop of Peterborough urged 'better dead than red' (Grimley 2012, 151). Archbishop Garbett of York looked prophetically to a post-nuclear world. When he visited Australia in 1951, Garbett reflected that the Australian people, safe from Northern Hemisphere bombs in a Third World War, would have to take up 'the English speaking world's heritage' if England was destroyed (Kirby 1993, 272). An archbishop envisaging the end of civilisation in England and speaking in such apocalyptic terms is startling and evokes works such as *The Lord of the Flies* but was not unusual in this era. Dr Christopher Chavasse, the bishop of Rochester, who was also a decorated war hero, went even further. In July 1958, he told a congregation in his cathedral that H-bombs raining down from the sky would be 'better than serfdom'. The precise type of serfdom he had in mind was atheist Soviet communism (*Daily Mirror* July 14, 1958, 7). In his sermon he also made clear his contempt of pacifists as he described the result of war in excruciating detail: 'in the event of a third world war total destruction and possibly lingering death for survivors would be a lesser evil than serfdom under a totalitarian domination' (*Daily Mirror* July 14, 1958, 7). Chavasse had chaired the Commission on Evangelism that in 1945 issued *Towards the Conversion of England*, a document that shocked some in the Church for its aggressive insistence on judgement, annihilation and destruction, and its confidence that all things will pass (Manwaring 2002, 63). Although Fisher had not been one of the bishops on the Committee, he echoed its claims in preaching that 'there is no evidence that the human race is to last for ever, and plenty in Scripture to the contrary effect' (*Daily Mirror* July 14, 1958, 7). Thus it was that English bishops could, from within a thoroughly worked out theological position, calmly envisage the end of the world, as well as the appalling human suffering that would be part of that process.

'This Is a Tactical Nuclear Missile'

Chavasse was the bishop of Rochester and in 1965 a thermo-nuclear blast destroyed Rochester. Or rather, in the drama-documentary *The War Game*, a team of largely non-professional actors enacted the outcomes of a nuclear war around Rochester and Chatham. In this fictionalised but plausible account of nuclear war, the missiles come after the USSR supports a Chinese invasion of Vietnam and then the USSR enters West Berlin, escalating conflict until world leaders press the nuclear button. Few in 1965 saw *The War Game*. The reasons for suppression by the BBC remain unclear, including the extent to which the Director General, Sir Hugh Greene, succumbed to government pressure to block transmission (Murphy 2003, 27). The internal politics at the BBC as well as pressure from ministers, civil servants and the military have been analysed by historians, although the focus here remains on what appeared in the docu-drama, regardless of its broadcast history.

The docu-drama follows two parallel strands. In one of these strands, characters outside the diegesis provide commentary on what could happen if there was a nuclear war and comment, like a Greek chorus, on what may be unfolding. The other is a portrayal of an actual nuclear strike with characters caught up in that drama. In both strands, there are clergy. A bishop and vicar commentate; another vicar ministers to a shattered flock in irradiated and bomb-ravaged Kent. Peter Watkins and his team scrupulously researched what would happen if the bombs fell, including lessons learned from the firebombing in Dresden and Hamburg, the atomic blasts in Hiroshima and Nagasaki, and from psychiatrists for what the effect would be on the mental health of anyone unlucky enough to survive a nuclear blast. But they also observed what combative Anglican bishops had said from their pulpits and in the press. Watkins' film, despite or because of its suppression, has attracted a large body of admirers and interpreters, but the way the Church of England is woven into critical moments is largely overlooked.

The docu-drama begins with an authoritative voice-over explaining that the Russians have aimed their bombs at major population areas in the UK and explains how efforts to evacuate even some of the population would likely cause massive social disruption. From the outset the tone is controversial, suggesting the social and racial disharmony that will follow an evacuation from the inner city. Further it reinforces the futility of these actions by noting that some population areas would still be neutralised by radiation. The documentary style is dry but remorseless and both sober and harrowing, as the voice-over provides analysis of geopolitical pressure that could lead to tactical nuclear war and the physics that explain the force of a firestorm. At one point the camera rests on a warhead and the narrator's voice solemnly instructs 'this is a tactical nuclear warhead' and explains what a liquid fuelled missile will do if fired at millions of people. Key facts include that 'the heatwave is sufficient to cause melting of the upturned eyeball'.

Watkins constructs the sequence of events so that the first missile strike on England, including the hideous noise of the blast, burning skin, blinding and fires, is immediately associated with the Church. Footage of the initial strike is followed by this statement: 'An English and an American bishop expressed the view that "the Church must tell the faithful that they should learn to live with, though need not love, the nuclear bomb, provided that it is clean and of a good family"'. The action then cuts immediately to a small boy, blinded by the bomb flash, on fire, and screaming. A firestorm consumes Rochester, and then the voice-over returns attention to the Church and declaims 'a bishop told the press that he was sure "our nuclear weapons will be used with wisdom"'. Then the bishop himself appears, preceded by a caption card explaining that the views expressed by the actor playing him are 'based on the recorded statements of an Anglican bishop'. There is no escaping the association of the Church of England and the possibility of nuclear holocaust, and no escaping the moral questionability of Anglican bishops who believe in 'the war of the just' and the theological rightness of a tactical nuclear war. As soon as the bishop stops speaking, the voice-over begins again, tonelessly stating, 'within this car a family are burning alive'.

PEOPLE LIVING IN THEIR OWN FILTH

Approximately the first half of *The War Game* is the nuclear strike; the second half is life in Britain after the nuclear attack. As the camera moves over the charred faces of a row of corpses, an earnest vicar explains that there is a moral responsibility: 'if I give the government the right or the means on my behalf to kill people of another country… then I must again myself accept the moral responsibility'.

The third clergyman appears at the end of the drama. Unlike the bishop and vicar who were detached from the drama and commentated on it, the third is trapped in the post-nuclear hell and first appears giving the last rites to two men about to shot by a police firing squad. As he recites the Lord's Prayer, the police cock their weapons and prepare to fire. The clergyman mutters 'God forgive them for they know not what they do' but the scene is written and directed so as to leave it unclear if he is referring to the thieves or the police. The possibility that the police would should English civilians in a major calamity was an eventuality forcefully denied by government authorities but here shown as an unavoidable action in a post-nuclear world, and the vicar casts doubt on the morality of the authorities. The majority of the cast in *The War Game* were local amateur performers with brief parts but the vicar's role is larger. Surrounded by children with scarred faces and dying of radioactive poisoning, he questions if there is any real hope to be found for them, recounting how one child's game abruptly ended when the child subsided into an introverted and depressed state. He also leads a forlorn Christmas Day service for them in the ruins of a Church. A final pathetic touch is that, without electricity, he has manually to turn the turntable of the record player to play them a carol. The children portrayed in *The War Game* are distressingly articulate and explain their existential horror at being 'nothing'. They gain no comfort from the clergyman, and have no future.

Archbishop Fisher's comments on nuclear weapons and nuclear war were shaped by the interplay of national and international factors. Internationally, Fisher thought British bombs formed a necessary deterrent against the Soviets. Nationally, Fisher's conservative instincts and the imperative to defend the realm pulled him back from condemning the bomb or supporting measures calling for disarmament. Beyond the simple fact of having clergy in the docu-drama parroting Fisher's words or succumbing to despair in the ruins of the civilisations, *The War Games* responds to Fisher on one deeper level related to the Church and its establishment. Critics of Fisher at the time he spoke about nuclear weapons positioned him as the leader of a 'state-tied Church', unable to 'transcend the expedience of State politics', in the assessment of the commentator C.E.M. Joad (in Kirby 1993, 255). Other critics saw Anglican responses to the Bomb as hamstrung by the establishment and being the 'Church of the nation' (Kirby 261). Tied to the establishment in reality, in *The War Game*, the state, its leaders, its infrastructure and its future are all swept away, taking the institution of the Church with it. The vicar's evident disapproval of shooting civilians and his horror at the actions of the last surviving vestiges of state power highlight the apocalyptic loss of both Church and State.

THE GLANCE OF GOD

The War Game was a scrupulously researched and informative film with detailed explanations of each action and outcome. In the next decade, similar themes including the possibility of the nuclear devastation of England and the inadequacy of efforts to prepare appeared in the one-off television play *Penda's Fen*. David Rudkin's 1974 drama is notably different to *The War Game*. It is diffuse rather than crisply informative and is a mixture of themes and influences including ancient British mysticism, the morality campaigns of Mary Whitehouse, nuclear war, William Blake's poetry, Edward Elgar's music for the *Dream of Gerontius* and heterodox Anglican theology. Where *The War Game* sincerely set out to instruct, *Penda's Fen* rejoices in ambiguity. It was set and filmed around Malvern and Worcester and as the title credits open, the camera tracks across the open countryside to a country rectory then the camera enters the bedroom of a teenage boy, Spencer, the rector's son, who is writing about Elgar's *Dream of Gerontius* while listening to his music. The audience soon learns more: the boy is preoccupied with Elgar, moral cleanliness and judgement and has been recently been outraged by a television documentary *Who Was Jesus*.

The outrage that could be caused by theological speculation is part of a richer narrative concerned with change and destruction. In a debate at his school, he derides the documentary for being spurious investigative theology and calls it 'atheist and subversive trash'. Stephen ardently admires a pair of moral campaigners, clearly modelled on Mary Whitehouse and Lord Longford, who have succeeded in gaining an injunction to ban the documentary about Jesus and whom he calls the 'mother and father of all

England'. The headmaster of his school and his form master meanwhile
are preoccupied with breeding the next generation of the 'sons of
England'. Boys sing Blake's 'Jerusalem', and Spencer listens to more Elgar
and wonders what will happen to his soul. Woven into the mystical reflections provoked by Blake, Elgar and theology is the revelation that Stephen
is homosexual and then he learns he is not in fact English at all, having
been adopted. The ideas in the script move over several levels, with secrets
of identity and sexuality presaged by the classical education Stephen is
receiving at the grammar school that allows him to translate a Delphic
Greek tag as 'discover thyself'.

On its first broadcast in 1974 *Penda's Fen* struck a chord with viewers,
even if the 'confused, yet enthralled' audiences on its two broadcasts
(1974, repeated in 1975) were not sure which chord exactly (*Stage and
Television Today* October 30, 1980, 12). The *Daily Mirror's* television columnist Mary Malone was impressed but bemused by Rudkin's imaginative
script: 'Given a free rein across the time zones, anything could happen and
most of it did. Pot-bellied devils squatted on his bed at nights. Angels with
jumbo-sized wings reared up over streams where he fished for tiddlers.
Moving from tiddly concerns to mighty ones, it wasn't long before he
came across Elgar himself complaining about a rotten stomach operation'
(*Daily Mirror* March 22, 1974, 18). The *Birmingham Post* was proud that
the BBC filmed it locally in the Midlands but also conceded that 'it was
one of those rare television moments where absolute concentration was
vital. Without it you lost a thread—and there were a fair number of threads
to keep hold of' (*Birmingham Post* March 23, 1974, 3).

Although ambiguous, with visuals that give *Last Year at Marienbad* a
run for their money in obscurity, Rudkin's drama withstands analysis as
expressing concerns about the ending of the world. Across multiple levels
of meaning, from the literal to the metaphysical and theological, the drama
is literally apocalyptic. One way or another, it is preoccupied with things
emerging from underground, from shadows, from mysteries, and in revelation. Stephen's parents are aware their son is gay, the father remarking
wryly that 'A late spring never lies'. Stephen is himself outraged that a
radical television writer has moved to the village. The writer character, to
some extent an analogue of Rudkin, later addresses a village meeting and
points to the sinister unreality of the beauty of the Malvern Hills.
Underneath the landscape, which inspired Elgar, something is being built
that is a response to the ugliness of atomic warfare. He says it is 'Farmland
and pasture now, an ancient fen, the earth beneath your feet feels solid

there', but 'the land is hollow'. 'Somewhere beneath is being constructed something we are not meant to know, a top secret', meaning an atomic air raid shelter. The camera then settles on a radio telescope dish as a signifier of the government's activities in watching the skies for missiles. The writer challenges the villager to realise the basis of government decision making about strategically expendable populations, with the government asking itself: 'How many millions of civilians can we afford to let get slaughtered before the remainder revolt and depose us'. The writer articulates a threat of 'a hideous angel of technocratic death' that will be launched in less than four minutes against a strategically expendable strategic population. Elsewhere in the diegesis, Stephen sees actual angels and demons, while also being able to hold a conversation with the long-dead Edward Elgar. When playing the organ in his father's church, large cracks begin to open in the floor. Revelations of all kinds abound, with words, images and metaphors insisting in various ways of things hidden under surfaces (an atomic bomb shelter, Manicheean resonances in the scriptures or Stephen's homosexuality) together with the suggestion of old orders passing.

The Home Counties in Peril

Other drama, more straightforward in both theme and narrative than *Penda's Fen*, brought otherworldly peril to the Home Counties. A subtle sense of the grotesque and the sinister could inhere in televised representations of the Church. Ghostly apparitions in Norwich Cathedral in *The Stalls of Barchester* (1971), lingering shots of grinning deaths heads on baronial monuments in an old church in *Father Brown: The Hammer of God* (1974) and preternatural menaces lurking in old churches in the *Doctor Who* serials *The Daemons* (1971) and *The Awakening* (1984) were ways the rural and ancient church buildings could seem unpleasantly weird. Sinister resonances also surround a charming country church in *Survivors*. Like *The War Game*, the end of the world in *Survivors* (1975 to 1977) was manmade (Bignell and O'Day 2004, 130). Rather than a nuclear bomb, the world-ending disaster was a plague leaked from a laboratory and spread around the whole world, killing about 99 per cent of the global population.

In *Survivors* the few who remained were either naturally immune or remote enough from population centres not to be exposed. The three seasons followed some of these survivors in rebuilding society and suggesting that a new type of society could be build out of the ruins of the old world. Characters move around the English countryside, establishing first a community in an empty country house and then on a farm called Whitecross. It is at this location in the programme's second season that a Church of England vicar appears, featuring in two episodes *By Bread Alone* and *Parasites* (1976).

By that point in its ongoing storylines, *Survivors* had made clear the toughness needed to survive and the community at the Whitecross farm needed everyone to be able to do everything. Lewis, a new arrival into this robust milieu, seems too effete and too useless to contribute to the community's survival. It seems he has never held a shovel before, and struggles to manage livestock and dig a drain. Soon, it becomes clear that before the plague Lewis had been an Anglican curate in Cheltenham.

The revelation prompts a change of pace; the episode's writer highlights the extended discussion of religious faith and practice after an apocalypse has taken place. That discussion arises owing to a series of contrasting reactions from the other survivors realising that they have a clergyman in their midst. Ironically, the person most pleased is the Roman Catholic cook, who hopes to be able to hear mass and have her confession taken again. The reaction raises the possibility that denominational differences will still matter in a post-apocalyptic world, as the curate refuses the Catholic form of address: 'father', and refuses to hear confession as it is not an Anglican sacrament.

The character is sensitively written with insights into a clergyman's pastoral responsibilities in the midst of a crisis, and it gradually becomes clear that, in scriptural terms, he has failed to be the good shepherd to a flock but instead was the hireling shepherd. Arriving without dog collar, Bible or vestments, it becomes apparent that when the plague first hit and society started to collapse, he ran and escaped rather than stayed and helped. The character has a television ancestor in the vicar in *The War Game*; that vicar however stayed put in the midst of the disaster.

Religion had already appeared as helpless in *Survivors* in the series' first episode *Fourth Horseman* (1975). Immediately after the plague had hit, a surviving character enters a village church and finds it full of corpses of plague victims who had sought but failed to find help there. The imagery is disconcerting, juxtaposing the solidity of the old Church with the grotesque impact of scientific drama. The two episodes featuring Lewis brought the subject back into consideration. For a time it seems Lewis may make a spiritual contribution to the community. Someone improvises a dog collar and surplice to replace those he abandoned, a local church provides hymn books and communion wine, and for the first time since the viral apocalypse, divine service is celebrated. The change however is short lived; in a succeeding episode, thugs murder the curate and the brief Anglican interlude among the survivors comes to an end. *Survivors* suggested other types of post-apocalyptic religious life including a monastic community and a party of survivors who interpret the plague as a divine judgement. The character of Lewis and the religious culture he briefly brings with him are though the only ways the series engaged directly with the Church of England making sense of life after a catastrophe.

The world ended again on the BBC in 1981 in a six-part mini-series adapted from John Wyndham's 1951 novel *The Day of the Triffids*. The catastrophe here combined the mass blinding of most of the world's population by mysterious flares in the sky, the rampaging of the killer plants the Triffids and a devastating plague (Heathcote 2014, 82). The science fiction writer Brian Aldiss calls Wyndham's works, especially this one, the 'cosy catastrophes' (see Ketterer 2008, 376). That means a disaster takes place in agreeable circumstances in the Home Counties. Aldiss disparaged Wyndham's works, but the notion of a cosy catastrophe opens up a narrative space for the Church to be part of the drama. The cosiness is that of the old world, before the disaster happened. A cosy catastrophe is also only possible with a relatively 'clean' disaster such the plague in *Survivors* and the blindings in *The Day of the Triffids*. In *The War Game* the bombs create a downmarket catastrophe, where the infrastructure essential for civilised living is swept away and the people end up scavenging for food and drinking filthy water. In a cosier environment, the Church can become part of the diegesis as an intact environment still exists where divine service can take place. Like *The Day of the Triffids*, his 1957 novel *The Midwich Cuckoos* (filmed in 1960 as *Village of the Damned*) took place in England's 'green and pleasant land', and in pastoral settings surrounding ancient village churches (Heathcote 2014, 82). Wyndham's creative achievement was to render these settings menacing and sinister. More than that, a cosy catastrophe, meaning that quite a lot of the infrastructure and trappings of the pre-disaster world have survived (as they would not in a nuclear war) opens up dramatic potential, as characters need to judge if they wish to attempt to revive and go back to life as it was, or create a wholly new society. The temptation to go back to things as they were and its tension with an impulse to start afresh is a dramatic potential made visible and effective when the place of the Church becomes part of the drama.

John Wyndham's 1952 novel, which was the source for the 1981 series, evoked the Church of England in different ways and to varying effect. After the various catastrophes that blind and kill people, the physical environment is largely unaffected and the still-standing church buildings induce nostalgia for the world that has passed away. This religious component carries over into the adaptation and come to the fore in the fifth episode. There the protagonists Bill Masen and Coker arrive at Tynsham Manor, a remote country house sheltering the community of blind people and cared for the still-sighted Miss Durrant. Durrant, as per the novel, is a deeply religious woman whose instincts are to preserve the world as it had been rather than forge a new type of existence after catastrophe. That choice became explicit earlier in the miniseries, when another sighted survivor who was also a sociologist had proposed an entirely new type of society based on the Isle of Wight, with the few sighted males breeding with multiple blinded women. Miss Durrant rejects these ideas, telling Coker and Masen that her establishment runs on Christian principles. When Coker and Masen arrive at Tynsham a blind vicar is leading prayer and the remainder of the people, all blind, desultorily sing a hymn. Later still, the community at Tynsham fails drastically. Durrant and the rest die of plague, having failed to take such constructive or practical actions as repairing an electricity generator.

It is the Church that catalyses failure and the narrative positions it holds as an unhelpful irrelevance in a new world. The blind vicar besets the community with impracticalities, directing people's energies to such useless ends as basket weaving, and encouraging Durrant to take in too many people so that the community becomes unsustainable. The less conventional community on the Isle of Wight survives. In showing these events, the miniseries faithfully adapts the 1951 novel. Wyndham thought of the novel as 'logical fantasy', and the science fiction disaster and the drastic sociological changes that come in their wake were carefully and remorselessly developed causal patterns (Stock 2015, 436). In both the book and the miniseries (that typical of its era of production includes a large number of static and wordy scenes recorded in a studio) characters have time to pause and reflect on change. Masen concludes that human civilisation as it was will not survive and the remorseless causality of blinding, killer plants and the collapse of civilisation sweeps away the world as it had been, taking the Church with it.

British television provided future visions of other types of catastrophe. The dystopian series *1990*, made in 1977 and set in the future, did not revolve around a nuclear or scientific catastrophe but suggested instead the gradual disintegration of British society following recession, national bankruptcy, and political upheaval. The dystopia drew inspiration from Orwell and Aldous Huxley as well as contemporary accounts of life in East Germany, as exit from the United Kingdom is restricted, food is in short supply and a socialist government with a secret police is in control via a Public Control Department (Worley 2017, 88). The Church of England still exists in this future nightmare but is effete. The one clergyman seen in the series is duped by government propaganda despite efforts from his friends to persuade him to see past official lies. Too late the clergyman realises the nature of the government when a friend is murdered by agents of the state. Efforts to hold a dignified funeral fail when government agents fly a helicopter at the graveside service, scattering the crowd and drowning out the cleric's voice. A final shot shows the prayer book blown and scattered.

The dramatic impact of a dystopia comes from the impression of normal life continuing, but in a disconcertingly unsettled manner where subtle distortions undercut everyday familiarities. In *1990* many aspects of normal life recognisable to a 1977 audience are still in place, including the commonplace of supermarkets and public transport and important institutions like parliament, the courts and the Church. St Paul's Cathedral is briefly glimpsed. Sinister differences undercut familiarity. There are few groceries in the supermarkets but many surveillance cameras and the courts are strangely unsympathetic to any causes that are not the government's. The Church contributes to this unsettling future vision, at once familiar but uncanny. Wilfred Greatorex's *1990* was part of a creative trajectory including Alan Moore's graphic novel *V for Vendetta*, which included a further debased image of a future Church of England complicit in state corruption, in thrall to a totalitarian government, and the victim of revenge killing (Booker 2007, 194).

THE QUICK AND THE DEAD

The Church continues to appear in science fiction on television in circumstances where communities are challenged by the preternatural. Anglican doctrine presupposes that the burial of the deceased is permanent and a faculty for exhumation is something ecclesiastical law will grant only under the most compelling circumstances (Welstead and Edwards 2013, 231). What therefore can the Church do when the dead rise *en masse* from the ground? A clergyman has been on hand to witness the appearance of zombies in a number of science fiction and horror productions, from Hammer's movie *Plague of the Zombies* (1966) to *Doctor Who*.

The Church confronting the undead provided the plot for the BBC's *In the Flesh* (2013–2014). The programme is set in a small Lancashire town, Roarton, where the local churchyard is denuded of cadavers after the local deceased erupted from their graves during 'the Rising'. The writing and the characters engage with some heavy handed allegorising in which the undead, like the gay, those who come from a minority or are marginalised in some way, all cohere. The series juxtaposes the banal with the sacerdotal. The British government has bureaucratised the zombie uprising, turning the living dead into a special medical category of the 'Partially Deceased Syndrome Sufferers' and creating a website for the community, together with information pamphlets and a help line. Early in the series, a slick government minister addresses the community, offering a series of clichéd statements about the living dead now returned to the community.

Set against the prosaic bureaucracy is a world more deeply steeped in religion. The Treatment Centre in Norfolk where the living dead receive treatment has a monastic ambience, including spartan rooms, crucifixes on the walls and a deep silence. In Roarton, the vicar is a figure of authority. The series gives a peculiar twist to the Church of England's actual tagline 'A Christian presence in every community', as it becomes clear the appearance of the living dead, while seemingly a major disruption to Christian teaching about death and the afterlife, has strengthened the faith of the local people and increased the vicar's prestige and stature. Most villagers are regular churchgoers and the ancient tradition of 'beating the bounds' now has additional force, as the villagers enforce the barriers around their village to protect themselves from the undead 'rotters'.

The rising undead seems to have been the best thing that could have happened to the Church of England. Frightened people have started re-attending church. Religious texts and religious teaching have received renewed energy and vigour. The local parish registers contain information vital to the central government and are highly sought after by a visiting member of parliament. The vicar uses bible verses, especially from the Book of Revelation, with force and impact in argument and debate. Even that most pastoral of Psalms, the 23rd ('the Lord is my shepherd') is used to exhort a local man to acts of violence against the undead. Yet the Church of England as presented in the series is a confused jumble. The vicar preaches barnstorming fire and brimstone sermons and runs services akin to evangelical revivals. But his meeting house (the actual church is sealed off because of the undead activity in the graveyard) and vicarage are filled with ritualistic iconography such as statues of the Blessed Virgin Mary. The Church of England therefore has an ambivalent presence in both the community and the series. The rising of the undead paradoxically re-energised the local church but in ways that lacked clarity.

THE CHURCH DYNAMIC

British science fiction imagined the end of the world through nuclear, viral or political catastrophes and where these involved the Church, the institution appeared doctrinally bankrupt and institutionally weak. Occasional alternatives presented on television science fiction suggested a more dynamic and constructive participation of the Church in a damaged future society. After *1990* dystopian future visions continued to appear on British television, although politically re-oriented away from fears of socialist domination to extrapolations of future right-wing rule. An iteration of this approach to dystopian story telling is *Knights of God*, a drama series made in 1985 by Television South, broadcast in 1987. The series' writer Richard Cooper blended science fiction with themes from Arthurian literature and Anglo Saxon history. By 2020, a long civil war has split the British Isles into Anglia and Northumbria and Winchester is the capital, as it was under Alfred the Great. The authorities, the titular Knights, govern with appropriated trappings of the Church including titles such as prior. The Knights however eschew belief in the Christian God. The actual Church of England also survives, confined to a civilised enclave in Canterbury led by the archbishop of Canterbury. The blending of a futuristic totalitarian state with aspects of medieval and early modern English history is especially reminiscent of John Christopher's novels *The Guardians* (1970) and *The Sword of the Spirit* series (1970–1972), including a repressive post-apocalyptic state, a suppressed Church, and the use of Winchester as a modern capital with ancient resonances.

The historic trappings in a futuristic setting also create a dramatic space for the Church of England to participate in the science fiction. Towards the end of the series (episode 11 of a 13 part series) the protagonists make a type of pilgrimage to Canterbury. Resolution of the narrative depends on finding the one surviving member of the British royal family, and the archbishop of Canterbury inside his Anglican enclave possesses vital information about where he is.

Knights of God is an instance of British science fiction that positions not merely Christianity but the Church of England as a forceful and even weaponised source of hope in a dystopian future. Life inside the Anglican enclave is civilised compared to the rather grubby and dilapidated Anglia seen elsewhere. An Anglican liturgical life also continues as normal and the visitors attend Matins that includes boy trebles, organ music by Bach, and vested clergy. The Church is described as being the 'most resolute enemy' of the fascist Knights and is key to ending their rule. *Knights of God* draws on a longer history of British dystopian fiction but is also a distinctive statement on organised religion in the future and a rare instance of the Church as a dynamic part of a solution rather than redundant and invalidated, running contrary to much science fiction that includes the Church of England.

The focus of this chapter has been the dramatic potential broadcasters have found in the genre of science fiction, and the tension that can underpin drama when scientific progress challenges Christian faith, in particular how science fiction has tested the role of the Church after a disaster of some type and ultimately has found it wanting. The Church of England has a longstanding presence in British science fiction, from the curate in H.G. Wells' *War of the Worlds* (1897) to the examples discussed in this chapter. Anglicanism in science fiction is one smaller part of wider story telling tradition that has placed religion in science fiction settings (McGrath 2012). The Anglicanism in science fiction suggests the Church and its clergy are confounded by the supernatural or sidelined, with only rare instances of a more dynamic impression. From the fantastic to the demotic, the next chapters bring the Church back down to Earth with the concerns of the Church in its communities, rural and inner city.

REFERENCES

NEWSPAPERS, PERIODICALS AND TRADE PAPERS

Birmingham Post
Daily Mirror
Guardian
Living Church
Stage and Television Today

PRINTED SECONDARY SOURCES

Besier, Gerhard. 2015. *'Intimately Associated for Many Years': George K. A. Bell's and Willem A. Visser 't Hooft's Common Life-Work in the Service of the Church Universal—Mirrored in Their Correspondence (Part Two 1950–1958)*. Newcastle: Cambridge Scholars Press.

Bignell, Jonathan, and Andrew O'Day. 2004. *Terry Nation*. Manchester: Manchester University Press.

Booker, M. Keith. 2007. *May Contain Graphic Material: Comic Books, Graphic Novels, and Film*. Praeger Publishers.

Grimley, Matthew. 2012. The Church and the Bomb: Anglicans and the Campaign for Nuclear Disarmament, c.1958–1984. In *God and War: The Church of England and Armed Conflict in the Twentieth Century*, ed. Stephen G. Parker and Tom Lawson, 147–164. Ashgate.

Harmes, Marcus. 2013. The Church Militant? The Church of England, Humanity and the Future in Doctor Who. In *Time and Relative Dimensions in Faith: Religion and Doctor Who*, ed. Andrew Crome, 221–234. London: Darton, Longman and Todd.

Heathcote, Christoher. 2014. Triffids, Daleks and the Fragility of Civilization. *Quadrant*: 80–88.

Hein, David. 2008. *Geoffrey Fisher: Archbishop of Canterbury, 1945–1961*. Wipf and Stock Publishers.

Jones, Matthew. 2017. *Science Fiction Cinema and 1950s Britain: Recontextualising Cultural Anxiety*. Bloomsbury.

Ketterer, David. 2008. John Wyndham: The Facts of Life Sextet. In *A Companion to Science Fiction*, ed. David Seed, 375–388. John Wiley and Sons.

Kirby, Dianne. 1993. The Church of England and the Cold War Nuclear Debate. *Twentieth Century British History* 4 (3): 250–283.

———. 2012. The Church of England and the Cold War. In *God and War: The Church of England and Armed Conflict in the Twentieth Century*, ed. Stephen G. Parker and Tom Lawson, 121–145. Ashgate.

Manwaring, Randle. 2002. *From Controversy to Co-Existence: Evangelicals in the Church of England 1914–1980*. Cambridge University Press.

McGrath, James F. 2012. *Religion and Science Fiction*. Casemate Publishers.

Murphy, Patrick. 2003. *The War Game*: The Controversy. *Film International* 503 (51): 25–28.

Stock, Adam. 2015. The Blind Logic of Plants: Enlightenment and Evolution in John Wyndham's *The Day of the Triffids*. *Science Fiction Studies* 42 (127): 433–457.

Webster, Peter. 2014. God and War: The Church of England and Armed Conflict in the Twentieth Century (Review). *Journal of Beliefs and Values* 35 (1): 129–130.

Welstead, Mary, and Susan Edwards. 2013. *Family Law*. Oxford University Press.
Willis, Kirk. 1997. "God and the Atom": British Churchmen and the Challenge of Nuclear Power 1945–1950. *Albion: A Quarterly Journal Concerned with British Studies* 29 (3): 422–457.
Worley, Matthew. 2017. *No Future: Punk, Politics and British Youth Culture, 1976–1984*. Cambridge: Cambridge University Press.

Dissertations

Vähäsalo, Minna. 2016. They've Got the Bomb, We've Got the Records!: Roles of Music in the Making of Social Movements: The Case of the British Nuclear Disarmament Movement, 1958–1963. Masters diss., University of Tampere.

CHAPTER 9

The Church and Its Communities: Upper, Middle and Lower Class

A 1966 sketch on *The Frost Report* performed by John Cleese, Ronnie Barker and Ronnie Corbett demonstrated the distinctions between the upper, middle and lower classes. The upper-class man had innate breeding, the middle-class man had money but no taste, and the lower class man knew his place. The sketch, widely remembered and much celebrated, sums up in miniature a wider ranging preoccupation with social class that runs through British television drama and comedy (Bacqué et al. 2015). This chapter examines the importance of dramatisations of the Church of England for understanding upper-, middle- and lower-class identities as a prevailing aspect of British television. The Church of England proclaims it is a 'Christian presence in every community', seeking to break bounds of denominationalism and be nationally relevant. How therefore has television drama shown the interactions between the Church and the different social groupings that surround it? On the small screen, is the Church really in every community? This chapter examines the church lives of the inner city and the country and its modulations across these communities, moving up and down social classes.

THE TORY PARTY AT PRAYER? THE CHURCH IN ITS SOCIAL WORLDS

Chapter 7 pointed to the uneasy relationship between Margaret Thatcher and Robert Runcie, even though Runcie was Thatcher's own choice for Canterbury. In 1985 when, following two years' work, the Church of

© The Author(s) 2020
M. Harmes et al., *The Church on British Television*,
https://doi.org/10.1007/978-3-030-38113-4_9

England produced *Faith in the City*, government responses sharply and dramatically illuminated these tensions. *Faith in the City* responded to several social tensions, including mass unemployment and inner city riots (Williamson 2012, 166). The criticisms of Conservative policy and welfare in the report and the strident response of Conservative ministers disrupted relations between the established Church and the Conservative Party. That party happened to be in government, but observers found that the level of conflict extended beyond the established Church and the elected government, to be disruptive of a deeper and older relationship of the Church with Toryism and the fabric of society.

The fallout from *Faith in the City* gave the Church a sharper and more partisan role, especially from bishops with inner city dioceses such as Manchester and Liverpool (Baker 1991, 92, 98; Wolffe 2013, 39). By the mid-1980s, Thatcher's supporters, if not Thatcher herself, criticised the 'pink bishops' and held Anglican leaders to account against a dichotomous 'one of us' or 'one of them' classification (Baker 1991, 101). Clerical reputations though could be deceptive. For instance, Thatcher rejected the first named candidate for Birmingham, Jim Thompson, allegedly for his left wing views (*Telegraph* September 20, 2003). Her choice of the second named candidate, Mark Canter, backfired when the new bishop joined the CND. Similarly, her choice of Graham Leonard as the bishop of London had seemed a conservative choice but the new bishop then opposed Conservative policy on local government and the abolition of the Greater London Council (Baker 1991, 101).

The implications of a vicar's actions in the ITV miniseries *Paradise Postponed* (1986) present these charged issues in a microcosm. The series' director Alvin Rakoff remembered John Mortimer as 'an ardent Labour supporter and it shows in his writing' (pers.com.), and Mortimer's scripts show his fascination with the slick but repulsive aspects of Conservative politics. John Mortimer's story spanned several decades in a small community, with the plot driven by the central thread of the mystery of why a socialist rector left his wealth to a Conservative member of parliament. The MP, Leslie Titmuss, pulls himself up from a working-class childhood to political success, tearing down old certainties as he does so. From a worker's cottage and a grammar school education, he displaces the old gentry, taking a constituency from an old landed MP, before also taking his country house.

Margaret Thatcher's biographer Charles Moore likens Titmuss to Norman Tebbitt. During the 1980s Mortimer's novel (the basis of the miniseries) became required reading for the Labour shadow cabinet owing to its uncanny distillation of the newer type of technocratic Conservative minister, engaged in property development and from lower middle class and working-class backgrounds, who were increasingly influencing the Conservative government (Moore 2015). Tebbit and other contemporary ministers like Cecil Parkinson (also a grammar school boy), could be embarrassed by reminders of their working-class origins (Strong 1997, 403). There was also still snobbishness to face. Harold Macmillan also remarked of Tebbit 'Heard a chap on the radio talking with a cockney accent. They tell me he's one of Her Majesty's ministers' (*Independent* October 26, 2003; Bale 2012, 247). In *Paradise Postponed* Titmuss systematically obliterates traces of his origins teaching himself to speak with a posh accent from listening to the BBC's cricket commentaries. The story deals with the complexities of Anglican and Conservative identities in the Home Counties. Ironically, the socialist rector comes from old money, lives comfortably because of a private income, and educates his sons at a public school, in fictional emulation of blue-blooded socialist clergy like Roden Noel, the 'red vicar' of Thaxted (Burns 2013, 101). A character, seeing the rector in a panama hat and smoking a pipe, remarks on seeing a personification of the 'Tory Party at Prayer'. But appearances are deceptive. It is the working-class Titmuss who insinuates and overtakes Conservative politics, whereas the rector is a conflicted but clearly socialist thorn in the side of the establishment.

The Church Under the Squire's Thumb

The concern the Church expressed about inner city life disrupted vestiges that remained of the 'Tory Party at Prayer' as being a Conservative identity. However, it is drama set in times and places far removed from inner city Brixton, Birmingham or Manchester that evokes that older relationship. Some drama delineates a social fabric in which the Church is an essential but class-bound element of the social fabric, especially in the lives of the upper classes, the gentry and aristocracy. However, drama that insists on the Church's establishment links to the state but may also subvert it. The archetype of the 'Tory Party at prayer' is now largely drained of meaning, but it articulates a relationship between social and ecclesiastical forces stemming from at least the 1830s (Williamson 2012, 167) that explains creative decision making about the association between the Church of England and its community milieu in television drama and comedy. The birth of the Church of England as shown in period drama portrays the emergence of an institution subject to the will and whims of an autocratic king. The Tudor archbishop Thomas Cranmer appeared as a character in the BBC's 1970 series *The Six Wives of Henry VIII*, and as the series moved through each wife and the English Reformation took place, the scripts asserted the subordinate place of the Church to the State and to the whims of the Tudor tyrant.

The BBC's adaptation of Trollope's *Barchester* novels was a period drama that again maintained on the Church's unequal relationship with political forces. That relationship shows on a larger political scale the type of aristocratic patronage apparent in period drama. *The Hammer of God* opened the 1974 series of *Father Brown*, based on G.K. Chesterton's detective fiction. It takes place in a pre-war setting of a small rural community in thrall to a tyrannous lord of the manor, who takes seriously his *droit de seigneur* to bed the local women. His younger brother is the local rector, bringing onto the screen a once-typical aristocratic arrangement whereby the younger son of the lord's or squire's household would take holy orders and hold the local benefice.

The relationship between a patron and the clergy in a local community provides the substance of both comedy and drama. Programmes made with a period setting including *Jeeves and Wooster* (1989–1993) and *Downton Abbey* (2010–2015) differ in tone and approach from comedy to drama respectively, but share a similar milieu of upper-class gentry and titled society between the World Wars and articulate a similar type of relationship between the Church of England and the social elites. The appearance of the Church takes its cue from the legal realities of the presentment rights of lords of the manor. The house and glebe land and therefore the parson's means of making a living came from the lord of the manor to the clerical incumbent of the benefice (often a brother or younger son). *Jeeves and Wooster* and *Downton Abbey* are both set during a period when these rights lost legal force, but neither programme dwells on that change, instead insisting on the power of lay patrons over their clergy. The ITV adaptation of P.G. Wodehouse's novels and short stories featuring Bertie Wooster and his manservant Jeeves brought the Church and its subordination to the gentry onto the screen. Additional concern comes from the way future personal happiness is woven into the ecclesiastical relationship between a patron and a benefice. The lord of the manor of Totleigh Towers, Sir Watkyn Bassett, has the power to grant the young curate H.P. Pinker a living and to consent to Pinker marrying his ward. One action becomes contingent on the other, as Bassett will not consent to his ward marrying an unbeneficed curate but also hesitates to give the curate a living. The future happiness of the curate and fiancée are entangled with power of the lay patron.

The rector of St Michael and All Angels Church on the Downton estate is a socially acceptable guest at the Crawley family's dining table but his status is ambiguous. He is not a servant, but is reminded of his feudal status in relation to the lords of the manor. An act of mild rebellion meets with rebuke from the dowager: 'Your living is in Lord Grantham's gift. Your house is on Lord Grantham's land, and the very flowers in your church are from Lord Grantham's garden'. The snobbishness inherent to the drama is also nostalgic for a period which intentional and reliable class barriers and led historian Simon Schama to describe watching *Downton Abbey* as an act of 'cultural necrophilia' (Leggott and Taddeo 2014, xxix). The clergy characters are markers of social status. The Crawley family also recognises the difference in status between a humble parish incumbent and a prince of the Church and invites the archbishop of York to officiate when Lady Mary Crawley is married. The archbishop is Dr Cosmo Lang, then the archbishop of York and in due course the archbishop of Canterbury. The wedding scenes have a televisual ancestry in *The Pallisers*, the BBC's 1974 adaptation of Anthony Trollope's novels about an aristo-cratic family, where only a bewigged archbishop is good enough to offici-ate at a ducal wedding. The appearance of Archbishop Lang at a high-society wedding also reflects the actual interactions between him and the upper classes before the Second World War. Among other aristocratic weddings, Lang officiated when the Earl of Feversham married the Honourable Anne Wood in York Minister in 1936 (*Yorkshire Post* May 11, 1936, 5).

Pre-dating both *Jeeves and Wooster* and *Downton Abbey* in production but post-dating them in setting, *To the Manor Born* (1979–1981) pro-vided a later-twentieth century instance of the close but uncomfortable relationship between the lord of the manor and the parish incumbent. The comedy and plotting of the series revolves around the economic misfor-tunes of the lady of the manor, Audrey fforbes-Hamilton. Left impover-ished when her husband dies, she has to sell her ancestral stately home to a man who is both foreign-born and nouveau riche. That double affront to her social class and social standing in the local community aligns the programme with a long-standing fixation in both British comedy and drama on social class (Wickham 2017, 201). It also involves the Church of

England in the confrontation between the gentry and the interloper. An actual lord or lady of the manor did not, by 1979, have any vestigial legal rights over the parish incumbent. However Mrs fforbes-Hamilton maintains an unofficial but iron grip over the parish and its traditions, insisting the King James Bible and Cranmer's prayer book remain in use the local church, as the Church of England elsewhere adopted modern language texts. She points to the 400 year association between the parish and her family, and to the memorials in the church, as 'the church is absolutely stuffed with fforbes-Hamiltons'. She also derides any traces of modernity in church identity or practice, telling the new owner of the manor 'we don't have any truck with this new form of service any more than we would expect the Rector to call himself a team vicar and be known to his parishioners as Pete'.

The lord of the manor's relationship with the clergy received an unusual and extreme twist in the 1972 espionage series *Spyder's Web*. In Part I of this book, the Church of England's tentative responses to perceived blasphemy was contrasted with the forthright certainties of Mary Whitehouse. The Church's unwillingness to react and its preference to 'let matters drop' contrasted with Whitehouse's determination to mobilise ancient laws and modern media campaigns to protect society from filth. *The Executioners*, the second episode of *Spyder's Web*, appears as a distillation and reinterpretation of contemporary morality campaigns. Above we saw the all-male Church Assembly as a more equivocal body compared to Whitehouse and her female supporters in the Mothers Union. *The Executioners* adjusts that impression, and dramatises a body of all-male, aristocratic and establishment figures such as judges and captains of industry, led by rogue aristocratic Lord Rothmore, working outside the law to suppress filth and vice. The espionage organisation at the centre of the series, which hides its identity behind a public veneer of being film makers, has noted that members of the permissive society have been mysteriously disappearing, with notices appearing in *The Times* proclaiming that their deaths are 'pro bono publico', for the public good. So-called high priests of the permissive society, including a student radical who defecated during Evensong at King's Cambridge and an educational radical, have vanished. The organisation, posing as a film production company, seeks to infiltrate by proclaiming they will make a lewd feature *Libido '72*, which will feature 'medieval devil worship, pagan rites, witchcraft, flagellation, incest, transvestitism, and cannibalism', all going on at the same time.

Here the Church enters the action. One of the establishment figures suppressing vice is an Anglican archbishop, addressed as 'your grace' and wearing gaiters, apron and frock coat. His participation as part of a body that takes decisive action to locate, trap and deal with the permissive society stands in contrast to the dithering inactivity of actual Anglican bishops. Members of the permissive society undergo a form of trial, with the archbishop prosecuting. The episode ends on a curiously amoral note, with the covert body of aristocrats left free to continue their campaign against the permissive society.

The episode though has a curious further intersection with the permissive society. The type of low-budget, sensationalist film making distributed in seedy cinemas that *Spyder's Web* evokes embroiled Bishop Mervyn Stockwood in controversy in 1970. A picture house in Charing Cross Road had exhibited *Legend of the Witches*, a type of soft-core film reminiscent of how *Libido '72* was described, with putatively educational aims being an excuse for prurience. However Stockwood had been duped by film makers, and had allowed himself to be filmed administering Holy Communion, only for the footage to end up in *Legend of the Witches* juxtaposed with sequences of a black mass involving a naked young woman. The film's poster promised viewers 'more exposed flesh and genitalia per square foot than virtually anything in the sex film genre' and a reviewer found that as a 'kinky nudie show' it had 'baleful of bare bottoms and breasts' and 'full frontal male nudes' (*Kensington Post* November 13, 38). An exasperated and appalled Archbishop Ramsey wrote to Stockwood, wondering how Stockwood had managed to bring 'some Christian ceremonies into a very horrible context of sexual orgy'. He ended by asking 'can you not get more adequate advice before involving yourself in a matter of this kind?' Ramsey had received a full and detailed account of the film's content, including 'naked witches dance around a fire', a 'cockerel is sacrificed and its entrails examined for omens' and 'the Bishop of Southwark baptises and confirms an adult woman. A Series 2 Communion follows' (LPL Ramsey 182, ff 95–99). The incident was quickly contained, not least as *Legend of the Witches* received a limited distribution, but also because it presents in retrospect an intriguing combination of the permissive society, grotty cinema houses, small-scale softcore porn film makers and the Church of England brought into awkward union with each other. The incident also resonates with the plot of *Spyder's Web* two years later but from a contrary perspective. In reality, Stockwood was duped and embroiled with the permissive. In fiction, an archbishop and a lord upheld social standards, exercising aristocratic privilege and wealth to suppress vice for the good of their retainers.

Later iterations of the type included the *Midsomer Murders* episode *Made to Measure Murders* (2010), where an unusually well-attended local church was due to the overweening influence of the local squire, who dominates and controls the parish priest and who is revealed in the end to be a criminal and a hypocrite. *Midsomer Murders* takes place in a fantasy version of the English countryside and the relationship between the vicar, the squire and a church going local community avoids seeming anachronistic by virtue of the hermetic unreal community where all Midsomer county crimes take place.

To an extent the crimes of *Midsomer Murders* take place in a fantasy land. Its creator, viewers and critics recognised that level of fantasy. Producer Brian True-May called the programme the 'last bastion' of Englishness, a controversial comment because he meant it contained an exclusively white cast (*Telegraph* May 23, 2011). As reviewers noted, the programme could showcase gruesome murder, incest and blackmail but contained these within a make-believe iteration of the English countryside and its community. But the unreality of characters and settings was tempered in other ways.

Although the series, like other ITV dramas such as *Inspector Morse*, was a bankable international success because of the use of picturesque historic settings (Brunsdon 1998, 229), narratives were realistic about topics such as redevelopment and the loss of greenfield land. *Sauce for the Goose* ended with a beautiful piece of woodland torn down to become a new town. The series' first episode, *The Killing at Badger's Drift* included frankly portrayed and sexualised incest as the motive for the murders. The first episode also established the milieu that would remain in place for subsequent episodes, including gossiping village spinsters who attend church.

This milieu exists in a primarily rural, conservative environment. The appeal of these settings to television makers and to viewers, both national and international, is in their immemorial aspects. The next chapter continues to consider the Church as part of communities, but in circumstances of greater social disorder. That extends from efforts to disturb social patterns by social climbing to when the Church is placed in dramatic scenarios from war to crime where it needs to be an arbiter of morality.

Middle-Class Lives and Working-Class Shame

The lay patronage discussed in the last section belongs largely to the realm of period drama; the relationship between conservative social forces and the Church of England in programmes with modern settings found expression as an ineluctably middle-class institution. Mrs fforbes-Hamilton had an impeccable gentry background, whereas the televisual snob Hyacinth Bucket comes from lower class origins and aspires to the upper middle classes. The central character in *Keeping up Appearances* (1990–1995) generates comedy from failed attempts to cultivate a more refined exterior life. Across the five seasons, church going as a social practice rather than a religious or spiritual activity serves as a core aspect of her quest for middle-class respectability. The show's second episode introduces the new vicar, who has accepted an invitation to an afternoon tea, an event that Hyacinth Bucket anticipates will be a further opportunity to elevate her social status. The visit necessitates a rehearsal, special orders of food, careful selection of clothing, including ensuring nothing too revealing is shown such as a pair of elbows. Characteristic of the entire series, the visit ends in disaster when working-class relatives appear, including a hormonally unstable sister who promptly carries off the 'dishy vicar', leaving the vicar's wife furious. The uneaten and undrunk afternoon tea is emblematic of failed social ambition.

The link between the vicar, social class and social climbing had a longer ancestry in British comedy before *Keeping up Appearances*. Situation comedies spanning the 1960s to the 1980s fixated on social class, whether the emphatically working-class accents of *Till Death Us Do Part*, the upwardly mobile middle classes of *The Good Life*, or the authentically upper class in *To the Manor Born* (Wickham 2017, 202). The birth of situation comedy on British television came in a period preoccupied with class distinctions (Dickason 2016, 25). Although scholarship on post-war television interprets the way this preoccupation registers in comedy and drives characterisation and situations, it overlooks the key way situation comedy engaged with class through the Church and its parish clergy. The appearance of a vicar making his rounds or coming to tea, created humour as working-class characters hurriedly rounded their vowels and attempted to hide any awkward signs of working-class characteristics. *Hancock's Half Hour*'s 1957 episode *There's an Airfield at the Bottom of my Garden* took place in the show's usual fictional location of East Cheam and Hancock played a distillation of himself as a down at heel comedian. Hancock's attempts to seem cultivated and to be further up the social ladder depended on the vicar, whom Hancock hoped could get him an invite to meet the lord of the manor.

Meet the Wife (1963–1966), a comedy vehicle for Thora Hird and Freddie Frinton extracted comedy from the lower class impulse to be more middle class whenever a clergyman appeared. In the episode *The Merry Widow*, the vicar calling around necessitates the instant end to a domestic dispute, changes to accent and frantic efforts to look more respectable. 'What will vicar think?' frets the housewife at the thought of the parson seeing anything resembling working-class life. *Steptoe and Son* (1962–1965, 1970–1974) presented a class-based dynamic between the plainly working-class Old Man Albert Steptoe, a rag and bone man, and his son Harold, also working class but aspiring to intellectual and social improvement. When the local vicar appears, the interactions again centre on the clergy provoking socially aspirational behaviour. *Men of Letters* (1972) is based on a sudden rivalry between father and son when the vicar asks for an article about the history of rag and bone men for the parish newsletter. While Harold writes the article, his father contributes a crossword. Unfortunately, all the words are obscene, leading to a vice raid on the vicarage, the impounding of the parish newsletter and the vicar's arrest for corrupting public morals.

In *Porn Yesterday* (1974), Harold discovers that the decades-old images in a 'What the Butler Saw' Mutoscope show his father engaging in lewd acts. The discovery that the old man had been a 'silent porn star' seemingly imperils Harold's 'whole social standing', not least as the vicar uses the old machine as a novelty for the church fete. The vicar character is a means to highlight class distinctions and social aspiration. Harold is on his best behaviour once the vicar appears. In *Men of Letters* he sees the opportunity to write for the parish newsletter as a means to social advancement.

The comedy function of a vicar as a stimulus for social climbing and a means to show off social advancement recurred across programmes and genres. The appearance of a vicar in *The Labour Exchange*, a 1973 episode of *Some Mothers do 'Ave 'Em*, instantly makes some removal men stop swearing and speak nicely. *Your Money or Your Life* (1976), an episode of *George and Mildred* sees Mildred fussing that George should display no vulgar working-class habits in front of the vicar. *Messenger of the Gods* (1978), the opening episode of the fourth season of *The Sweeney*, used a vicar and his church for the same purpose, in which a social climbing woman believed that a church wedding and the attendant opportunities to be seen with the vicar, whom she addresses with increasingly ludicrous honorifics, was a pathway to social advancement. The association between the vicar and respectability can receive simultaneous inversion and rein-forcement by the appearance of a bogus vicar. *The Con*, a 1991 episode of *Jeeves and Wooster*, featured a jewel thief impersonating a vicar at a respect-able seaside hotel. The clerical collar and an upper-class accent are both fake. Just as fake was the antique expert in *Parson's Pleasure*, a 1980 epi-sode of *Tales of the Unexpected*, where a clerical collar and a scholarly demeanour are a cover for a greedy thief.

But the contribution of a clerical archetype in class-fixated television is not straight forward. In some programmes, the connection between vicars and good manners diminishes the archetype into a stereotype of a prissy, conservative man in a collar and stock. The appearance of a vicar makes other characters class conscious by hiding signs of working-class life and accents. These reactions are spontaneous and the vicar has not explicitly demanded changes in accent, mannerism or outlook. These appearances intersect with Callum Brown's impression of the way religious practice and religious identity are discursive as much as they are institutional. An example such as 'Sunday Best' is a religious practice that the Church and clergy have not insisted on but were essential aspects of how lay people performed their religion (Brown 2000, 115). The expectation that meet-ing a vicar meant being posh is not sought by the clergy, but enacted by the laity. A further layer of complexity is how occasionally the comedy makes the vicar complicit in lowering standards. Galton and Simson, script writers of *Steptoe and Son*, proved adept at using stereotypes, among them the 'vague vicar', but taking these in unexpected and original directions (Stevens 2011) At the end of *Porn Yesterday*, Old Man Steptoe causes a sensation when he appears at the church fete and is recognised as the silent porn star from the titillating images.

The flip cards inside the Mutoscope are spilled, causing people to scramble to get Old Man Steptoe's autograph on them. The episode ends with the vicar, far from being shocked, enthusiastically upping the price for the pornographic cards from one to two shillings once autographed. Until this point, Galton and Simpson had not offered anything different from the vicar as the unwitting enforcer of middle-class behaviour, before the final line of the episode subverts the character and the expectation.

The vicar's enthusiastic auctioning of the dirty pictures in *Steptoe and Son* indicates the complex intersection of television clergy and middle-class morality. While appearing as bastions of morality that make other characters drop working-class accents and draw a veil over any domestic discord, clergy are participants in the subversion of standards. Notably in *Georgy Porgy* (1980), an instalment of *Tales of the Unexpected*, the vicar is central to the subversion and collapse of middle-class morality. The repressed Reverend George Duckworth preaches stern sermons on morality and against the age of permissiveness, and remarks unctuously on St Paul's moral strictures being out of fashion. But he is also beset by lewd daydreams, including one where from his pulpit he imagines all the women in his congregation sitting naked (except for their hats) in the pews. He tries to sing the pious hymn 'Lord Jesus think on me', which includes the lines

> And purge away my sin;
> From earthborn passions set me free
> And make me pure within.

But he loses his focus and begins playing a jaunty secular song.

The Church's distinctive capacity to be central to both the pursuit of middle-class responsibility and its destruction recurs in *The Worst Week of My Life* (2004–2006). Across several significant life events, including a wedding and the birth of their first child, an ill-matched couple (she is the daughter of a High Court judge married to a social climbing wife and he is the son of a working-class labourer) are preparing to have their child baptised. For the judge's wife, the Church of England is core to her social elevation and tea with the vicar an opportunity to lobby to have the bishop conduct the christening in Winchester Cathedral. The pursuit of social glory backfires through a sequence of farcical events, when an ill-repaired jug breaks and spills scalding hot mulberry wine in the vicar's crotch, and the judge's wife is compelled to rub butter on his genitals to soothe deep burns.

This chapter examined television drama that makes the Church part of its local communities, but further where the institution and its clergy are called on to be arbiters of morality, from appropriate domestic conduct but where clergy can also be subversively positioned, where their very presence provokes social aspirations but good taste can be breached. The following chapter retains a focus on television's dramatisations of the Church in communities, in this instance communities broken by conflict and war and where the Church's role is sometimes but not always to heal.

REFERENCES

NEWSPAPERS, PERIODICALS AND TRADE PAPERS

Independent
Telegraph
Yorkshire Post

ARCHIVES

LAMBETH PALACE LIBRARY (LPL)

LPL Ramsey 182, ff 95–99

PRINTED SECONDARY SOURCES

Bacqué, M., G. Bridge, M. Benson, T. Butler, E. Charmes, Y. Fijalkow, E. Jackson, Lydie Launay, and Stéphanie Vermeersch. 2015. *The Middle Classes and the City: A Study of Paris and London*. Springer.

Baker, D.L. 1991. Turbulent Priests: Christian Opposition to the Conservative Government since 1979. *The Political Quarterly* 62 (1): 90–105.

Bale, Tim. 2012. *The Conservatives Since 1945: The Drivers of Party Change*. Oxford University Press.

Brown, Callum. 2000. *The Death of Christian Britain: Understanding Secularisation, 1800–2000*. Cambridge: Cambridge University Press.

Brunsdon, Charlotte. 1998. Stricture of Anxiety: Recent British Television Crime Fiction. *Screen* 39 (3): 223–243.

Burns, Arthur. 2013. Beyond the "Red Vicar": Community and Christian Socialism in Thaxted, Essex, 1910–84. *History Workshop Journal* 75: 101–124.

Dickason, Renée. 2016. Social Class and Class Distinctions in "Britcoms" (1950s–2000s). In *Social Class on British and American Screens: Essays on Cinema and Television*, ed. Nicole Cloarec, David Haigron, and Delphine Letort. McFarland.

Leggott, James, and Judie Taddeo. 2014. *Upstairs and Downstairs: British Costume Drama Television from The Forsyte Saga to Downtown Abbey*. Rowman & Littlefield.

Moore, Campbell. 2015. *Margaret Thatcher: The Authorized Biography, Volume Two: Everything She Wants*. Penguin.

Stevens, Christopher. 2011. *The Masters of Sitcom: From Hancock to Steptoe*. Michael O'Mara Books.

Strong, Roy. 1997. *The Roy Strong Diaries 1967–1987*. Weidenfeld & Nicolson.

Wickham, Phil. 2017. Twenty-First Century British Sitcom and "The Hidden Injuries of Class". In *Social Class and Television Drama in Contemporary Britain*, ed. David Forrest and Beth Johnson. Springer.

Williamson, Cliff. 2012. The Church of England and the Falklands War. In *God and War: The Church of England and Armed Conflict in the Twentieth Century*, ed. Stephen G. Parker and Tom Lawson, 165–185. Ashgate.

Wolffe, John. 2013. Anglicanism. In *The Encyclopedia of Politics and Religion*, ed. Robert Wuthnow, 35–39. Routledge.

CHAPTER 10

The Church and Its Moral Communities: Conflict and Crime

A priest can expect to be surrounded by death, especially from being at the bedside of the dying and officiating at funerals. Social relations between the Church and its communities can be disrupted or strained in drama based around encounters with death and dying and this chapter studies drama that has situated the Church and its clergy in communities troubled by wartime disruptions or sudden death. In the previous chapter we saw clergy expected to the signifiers and arbiters of good taste. Here *Foyle's War* is the fulcrum on which this chapter turns, as a transition from the deaths caused by war to the investigation of murder as television shows communities fractured by death.

THE CHURCH IN WAR

The Church of England was an active contributor to the war effort in both the First and Second World Wars. Military chaplains were deployed in these conflicts and some died (Parker 2013, 2). After the Wars, the Church organised services of remembrance. During the Second World War, when bombing destroyed so many churches, St Paul's Cathedral survived. During the War, the famous newspaper picture 'St Paul's Survives' taken by Herbert Mason and published in the *Daily Mail* in December 1940 became instantly famous but also was swiftly read in religious terms. Linda Colley calls it an image of a 'Protestant citadel' showing not just resilience in the Blitz but the resilience of London's Anglican cathedral and the

© The Author(s) 2020
M. Harmes et al., *The Church on British Television*,
https://doi.org/10.1007/978-3-030-38113-4_10

'parish church of the Empire' (Paxman 2007; Richards 1997, 110). The firestorms of that night's bombing become in the photo a mysterious source of illumination of the cathedral dome and the image itself a mystical combination of the Church and the British communities fighting the War.

This triumphant image is in line with some but not all Anglican responses to the War, in which the Church appears as an 'arm of government public relations' cheering on the war (Webster 2014, 129). When Britain declared war in 1939, George VI broadcast on the BBC but as the historian Andrew Chandler points out, the Church of England became a critical communication channel; war was declared on a Sunday, December 3, 1939, and the first many heard about it was from the pulpits of their parish churches. The 1998 drama *Goodnight Mister Tom* dramatised that circumstance, when villagers learn there is to be a war when attending church.

The same evening that the king broadcast, so did Cosmo Lang the archbishop of Canterbury. While Lang's address was partly ambivalent, such as not laying claim to the new war being a holy one, he urged the British people to pray for victory. The archbishop of York pursued a different line and urged people to pray 'thy will be done' (Chandler 2016, 74). What senior clergy thought about war and said about war resonated because of the Church's establishment status. Between the world wars, English bishops largely shared the educational and social backgrounds of secular politicians as well as their outlooks. Some bishops enjoyed especially close relationships with ministries, including Cyril Garbett's close ties to the Foreign Office (Kirby 2012, 125). Garbett and Fisher, the two primates after the Second World War, therefore spoke guardedly, with accountability not just to the Church but also to the state for what they said about conflict during the world wars and Cold War and about alliances with the communist Soviet Union. Fisher in particular spoke with acute consciousness of the links between Church and state and the obligation of bishops not to make the Government's 'task harder by coming out with provocative denunciations of Russia' (cited in Kirby 2012, 126). Some bishops had 'ready access to the very corridors of power', according to Dianne Kirby, and made the Church an active participant in the dissemination of information and messages about conflict during war and social development after it (Kirby 2012, 122). This involvement extended beyond the informality of shared social outlooks to the formalised structures of the Religions Division section of the Ministry of Information (Kirby 2000).

As Corinna Peniston-Bird points out, British film and television had continuous resort to the world wars, and 'filmic constructions' of the Second World War are enduringly popular (2007, 184). These represent conflict as well as national reactions and life on the home front, but subject them to re-interpretation and re-worked meaning. The Second World War is rarely absent from the big screen and period wartime drama also proliferates on television. These include evocations of how the clergy reacted to hostilities and to the mobilisation of their communities. While providing the substance of drama, the War also inspires comedy. The characters, settings and plots of *Dad's Army* celebrate small-scale resistance to the Nazis during the Second World War. The scale is deliberately small but Walmington is located in a coastal area vulnerable to invasion. The quotidian lives of the men in a small seaside town and their often comically disastrous efforts to achieve a degree of military effectiveness in case of invasion are the basis of all episodes. However, apart from *All Gas and Gaiters*, *Dad's Army* is also the most sustained and successful ecclesiastical comedy made on British television, as a central character is the vicar of Walmington-on-Sea.

Including a priest as part of the programme does not mean that *Dad's Army* explored the morality of war or fighting. The bombing of English towns and cities is a commonplace of the series and the drone of an air raid siren is in the theme song. The pay back is also apparent, as British planes fly off to bomb German cities and German civilians with the characters' evident approval. Occasionally there are suggestive references to a wider and more challenging theatre of war than Walmington, such as the evacuation from Dunkirk, but the fighting and the bombing are sources of humour, not reflection on the morality of war.

That is not necessarily because, as a comedy, *Dad's Army* was not have been the place for darker moments. *Dad's Army*'s comedy was often balanced by significant moments of seriousness. The possibility that the members of the Platoon will die should the Germans invade is played straight, as the town is on the coast and would be a target for attack. There is also a degree of bleakness in Arthur Lowe's characterisation of Captain Mainwaring. His marriage is profoundly unhappy, a point poignantly underscored in the episode *Mum's Army*, when he meets, falls in love with and then loses a sophisticated middle-aged woman in scenes deliberately echoing *Brief Encounter*. The character's class-consciousness, professional envy, and resentment of characters with more social cachet also come to the surface with a degree of venom that is not comical.

The vicar and the Church however are emphatically and unvaryingly part of the comedy in this small community, detached from any of the darker themes. For the vicar of Walmington-on-Sea, the War is a source of exasperation more than a moral conflict. He has lost use of his church hall because of Home Guard and ARP exercises. Military field training takes place in the vicarage garden, and he cannot use the church bells as that would signal an invasion. Brett Mills points out that sitcoms are not simple in their structures, conventions or what audiences need to understand to enjoy them. But as he further indicates, they can endorse rather than challenge the society they portray, which was the approach *Dad's Army* took towards the War, to bombing and to the morality of fighting (Mills 2009, 5).

The vicar of Walmington-on-Sea stands distinctively apart from rather than analogous to the actual Anglican clergy during the Second World War. The obliteration bombing of German cities was inescapably part of the British conduct of war. Sustained consideration of the moral implications of these actions came from Bishop George Bell of Chichester. As a bishop he had a seat and a voice in the House of Lords. His arguments there and in other addresses were two-fold. One was that the bombing of civilians appeared contrary to the notion of a just war in ways that were intolerable to someone professing a Christian conscience. As an ecumenicist with many international contacts, including Dietrich Bonhoeffer, Bell's second point was the possibility of German people achieving an honourable peace should the Nazis be removed from power. That possibility was in opposition to the pursuit of unconditional peace by Churchill and Roosevelt (Edwards 1971, 338). The scale of disagreement against Bell was considerable; his comments during the War turned Churchill against appointing him to Canterbury when William Temple died in 1944.

That was an indirect action but Bell received forthright opposition to his face. His own cathedral dean in Chichester vehemently disagreed with him (Edwards 1971, 338). The bishop of Monmouth, Alfred Monathan praised the bomber pilots as 'gallant knights' and in *The Times* he urged: 'Let the bombing go on, and be increased, until the Germans have learned the lesson that wars of aggression are devilish and in the end do not pay' (Chandler 2016, 178). In the House of Lords, which has long adhered to the tradition that its debates are restrained in comparison to the 'other place', meaning the House of Commons, all pretence of cordiality vanished in a splenetic debate in which Labour and Conservative peers turned on Bell. The flashpoint was also two-fold. One was the bombing of Monte Cassino monastery in Italy and the ensuing destruction of this ancient Benedictine site, which moved Lord Lang, the retired archbishop of Canterbury to put a motion asking about measures to preserve sites of historical importance. The other was Bell's more general call to change bombing policy to spare the lives of German civilians (*Birmingham Gazette* February 17, 1944, 4). The gloves came off. The Lord Chancellor called Bell's comments a 'pestilential heresy'. Lord Samuels taunted Lang that more historic buildings would likely be destroyed in the fighting with 'the likelihood of our having to fight street by street in Rome and in the Forum, Collosseum [sic] and other preserved ruins'. The Labour peer Lord Latham was demotic, mocking the prelates for not caring about the 'little homes of little people' and several peers argued that the propaganda machinery run by Goebbels had received assistance from the two bishops (*Birmingham Gazette* February 17, 1944, 4). Observers at the time felt the House of Lords was stridently departing from its usual civilised tone.

This debate belongs in a history of the Church on television for these reasons. The Second World War has rarely been absent from British television screens; *Dad's Army* itself is still frequently repeated. Retaliatory bombings and the struggles to conscience provoked by the possibility that the war may not be a just war are themes carried onto the small screen in war-set drama where the clergy act as a point of discussion about the rightness of the war. Bell's mostly solitary efforts to moderate the impact of British bombing prompted televisual afterlives. Not comedy but science fiction suggested clerical anguish and doubt about the rightness of the war effort. The 1989 *Doctor Who* serial *The Curse of Fenric* is set during the Second World War, and brings the Doctor to a military base in Northumbria, which is near a church. The local vicar, Mr Wainwright, soon contends with a number of issues, as the dead rise up from the graveyard and from under the sea and vampiric creatures attack him and his church. Yet amidst the science fiction chaos, the serial also highlights the spiritual confusion of a Church of England clergyman attempting to preach and minister during a war. As the story opens, an angry parishioner assails the vicar after the Sunday morning service, during which Wainwright has clearly preached an unpatriotic sermon. 'There's no doubt about it, Mr Wainwright, of course we'll win the war. Right is on our side', says the elderly woman, and the vicar's ambivalence shows in his response that 'I don't think that right is on anyone's side in war'. The argument escalates in profound ways. While the presence of alien science and supernatural events could be sufficient to shake Christian faith, man-made atrocities first weakened and then finally destroyed the vicar's faith (Jones 2013, 49). When reading the Bible in church, he falters and eventually chokes on his ability to read out the word 'love', and later vampiric creatures taunt him: 'you stopped believing when the bombs started falling....British bombs killing German children'.

The vicar's doubts about the bombing of German civilians brings onto screen echoes of the torrid debates in the House of Lords over 40 years earlier involving Bishop Bell. The serial was daring in its Thatcherite context for making these points and in even raising, through dialogue and characters, doubts about the morality of the British bombing campaigns. The Thatcher government's history curriculum strongly reinforced a contrary and far more patriotic impression. Within the serial, all the other characters have faith, from the Doctor's faith in the friendships he has with his companions and the faith Russian soldiers have in the Communist revolution. The vicar stands apart, denuded of faith and shattered morally by the actions of Bomber Command.

Bishop Bell's controversial wartime actions received a further televisual afterlife in *Foyle's War*. The episode *Plan of Attack* (2008), set during the Second World War included an Anglican bishop campaigning for peace. As in other scripts, the episode demonstrated close attention to historical detail. One clerical character voices concerns that distil Bishop Bell's actual concerns about an honourable surrender. 'It's this question of total and unconditional surrender. Everyone knows the Germans have lost the war, it's just a question of how many more innocent people have to die before they accept it'. Anglican clergy criticise British bombing raids on Hamburg and struggle to reconcile the Bible's demand 'thou shalt not kill' with the act of war. The character of Bishop Francis Wood, the bishop of Cirencester, has a frame of reference based around Bishop Bell. Wood is touring the country preaching peace and reconciliation, although others question if he has chosen his time well. The characterisation draws on Bell's ecumenical efforts, as the fictional bishop is busy organising a pan-European famine relief scheme.

The episode also positions the peace campaigning bishop as at odds with much of the establishment and the wider community. The local police superintendent mounts a police guard, having heard that protests in London against the bishop caused a riot. The same senior policeman scorns the bishop's claims that war and bombing represents the degradation of the spirit, viewing it instead as sedition. As James Chapman points out, a murder mystery detective series set during wartime is a thematically rich way to bring moral questions into drama (2007, 32). Anthony Horowitz's inspiration for creating Superintendent Foyle and his wartime milieu came from the contradictions of bothering to solve a small number of murders during a war when millions were dying anyway. An earlier episode, *Eagle Day*, made this point through the point of view of another clergyman, father of the lead character Samantha Stewart. Stewart, daughter of a vicar, has mobilised for war and joined the Mechanised Transport Corps. Her father frets that young women in uniform lead dissolute lives and Samantha would be better off at home, believing 'any sort of morality has been shot to pieces by this dreadful war'. The vicar's narrowmindedness receives a rebuke from Foyle, who ponders that 'People are being killed in bombing raids every day of the week and we spent all our time trying to solve small domestic murders… But on the other hand should we be ignoring innocent victims simply because we're in the middle of a war?' Foyle reasserts the continuing importance of these actions, even in the chaos of war. As Chapman points out, detective stories can be inscribed within a moral and even religious framework as good is restored over evil and order over chaos (2007, 32).

'High Mass Murder': The Church, The Police and The Law

By bringing together period-set criminal detection and the Second World War, *Foyle's War* synthesised two major strands of British television drama about the Church and its communities. That law making and law breaking has a religious dimension is reinforced by the portals of the Old Bailey, arguably the most famous courthouse in Britain, which has words from the 72nd Psalm carved in stone: 'defend the children of the poor and punish the wrongdoer'. The association of the religious and the legal carries over into crime fiction. The Church of England is central to television programmes about the law, the police, solving murders and punishing wrongdoers. Many of the 'golden age' crime writers in the 1930s were Anglican and consequently clergy abound in environments where there are high death counts. Agatha Christie and Dorothy L. Sayers, two queens of the golden age of detective fiction, were practising Anglicans and often turned to the Church as their setting. Television makers later responded to the nostalgic appeal of their writing and the opportunity for productions showcasing the picturesque mingled with the murderous. In 1974 the BBC adapted Sayers' *The Nine Tailors*, using the spectacular medieval church in Walpole St Peter as the principal filming location. Following the novel, the miniseries made the church part of the narrative as the church's bells are the unlikely murderers and the medieval angels high in the ceilings are concealing a fortune in stolen jewels. While singing the hymn 'Holy, Holy, Holy' during Matins, Lord Peter Wimsey has a moment of epiphany (prompted by the line 'cherubim and seraphim bow down before thee') about the whereabouts of stolen jewellery. Other adaptations of vintage detective fiction made the Church and its places of worship part of the fabric of drama. Also in 1974, location filming for *Father Brown* in St Peter and St Paul's Church in Easton Maudit included lingering shots over the deaths heads on a Jacobean tomb, creating a suitably gruesome atmosphere.

After the golden age, popular detective series such as *Midsomer Murders*, *Inspector Morse* and *Grantchester* were series steeped in nostalgia and filmed in photogenic parts of England around East Anglia and Oxfordshire and showcasing vicars, rectors and college chaplains in narratives. Detective drama is one of the major ways television brings the Church onto the screen. The circumstance of writers of detective fiction being committed Anglicans also ensured a place for the Church on television as these popular novels were adapted. P.D. James' novels about Commander Dalgliesh reflect the writer's personal interest in the Church and ecclesiastical minutiae. The architectural peculiarities of an Anglo-Catholic church in *A Taste for Death*, the irregularity of an Anglican monastic order in *The Black Tower*, the internal politics of a theological college in *Death in Holy Orders* among others are richly described in prose. Although a television adaptation cannot bring all that onto the screen, Anglia Television's adaptation brought the churches and clergy of her books onto screen as distillations of her personal interest.

Mayhem Parva

English crime drama brings onto screen a Church in the midst of its community. The signifier Mayhem Parva, coined in *Snobbery with Violence* by Colin Watson, is a small village like St Mary Mead where a large number of murders take place. St Mary Mead appears in Agatha Christie's detective novels and therefore in television adaptations of her work. Christie created two especially popular detectives, M. Hercule Poirot, and Miss Jane Marple. Poirot, being a Belgian wartime refugee, is a Catholic. Miss Marple, however, is a member of the Church of England. The character had appeared occasionally on film, but in 1984 the BBC commenced a series of lavish and faithful adaptations of all the Marple novels, filmed in the Home Counties (Aldridge 2016, 220). These adaptations, which included the authoritative input of Agatha Christie's family (Aldridge 219), took the source material more seriously than the campier ITV adaptations that commenced in 2004, which deviated significantly from the books. As such, the 1980s adaptations faithfully bring onto screen a world dominated by the Church of England. Wherever Miss Marple goes, she is in the company of Anglican clergy, including the vicars in *The Moving Finger* (1985) and *A Murder is Announced* (1985) and the archdeacon in *Nemesis* (1987). Even when Miss Marple steps outside her familiar surroundings of small English villages, she is still normally consorting with clergy, such as the canon she meets in *At Bertram's Hotel* (1987).

The Church received its most sustained appearance in the 1986 adaptation of *Murder at the Vicarage*. The setting is not incidental; instead the Church, its clergy and its officers are all central to the narrative. The BBC's adaptation brought onto screen the ecclesiastical detail in the original novel, including the tensions caused by the curate's ritualism and the presence of medieval wall paintings in the parish church. Aspects of village religious life permeate the story. The victim, Colonel Prothero, was a churchwarden who was investigating the financial irregularity of the parish accounts. He was involved in a dispute with the curate, whose high-church ceremonialism incurred the Colonel's ire. Central to the narrative is the Reverend Leonard Clement, whose vicarage is the site of the murder.

Yet it is not the Reverend Clement who solves the murder of the Colonel, nor is it the police, the other source of male authority in the novel. The elderly Miss Marple, one of Clement's parishioners, ultimately deduces the killer's identity and brings her to justice. The Reverend Clement is a passive witness to the killing and to the restorative justice achieved by Miss Marple. His curate appears even weaker, as his overwrought sanity snaps when suspicion falls on him, and he attempts suicide.

In *A Murder Is Announced* and *The Moving Finger* Miss Marple solves crimes in the company, but not with the assistance, of vicars of the Church of England. Two further novels, *Nemesis* and *At Bertram's Hotel* consolidate this impression. In the former, a clerical character Archdeacon Brabazon imparts vital clues to Miss Marple, but he is an instrument of Miss Marple's justice, not the agent of it. As the narrative makes clear, the Archdeacon has responded to the summons to come to England and speak to Marple given to him by a reclusive millionaire, and at all points the

Archdeacon acts in reaction to instructions given to him rather than taking action himself. In *At Bertram's Hotel* the character of Canon Pennyfather is weaker still. He is irredeemably befuddled (as is recounted, even sitting in his stall in the cathedral, he once forgot the text of his sermon) and his confusion means he is the victim of crime, being attacked, kidnapped and his place being taken by a doppelganger. It falls to Miss Marple to act dynamically to bring order to chaos.

However the clergy do provide a moral centre. Aldridge's study of the entire set of BBC adaptations points out that they are not cosily nostalgic. The graphics in the title sequence hint at darkness and viciousness that may be present in the green and pleasant countryside. The plot dynamics point to community tensions, vicious gossip and the impact of post-war social change such as migration that are far from being cosily nostalgic. The vicar in *Murder at the Vicarage* also beings onto screen extended moral and theological speculation on the impact of murder on a small community and the rupture of neighbourliness. After Colonel Prothero's murder, the community, including Miss Marple, comes together for Matins at the parish church in St Mary Mead. Preaching on the penitential overtones Psalm 50, the vicar questions the meaning of being a neighbour when 'an act of horrible violence and cruelty' has taken place at the heart of the village. Regardless of the actual motive and identity of murderer, the vicar implores the congregation to see their collective community as involved in the murder through gossip, intrigue and anger. The sermon moves to the eschatological, to the time when all the parishioners will be judged under the gaze of the 'eternal judge' and to the reminder that an act of murder is a religious affront, the 'breaking of the mightiest of all commandments' and committing the deadly sin of anger. Close ups show the different reactions of the entire community, with village gossips squirming, bored schoolboys playing with toys, Miss Marple watching everyone shrewdly and the murderer becoming receptive to the message of judgement and redemption. It may be Miss Marple who solves the murder, but the BBC adaptation gives time and space to an earnest and searching sermon on sin, death and contrition. It is an aspect of the overall seriousness of the productions which so pleased Christie's family. It also is part of a trajectory that leads to *Grantchester*. This detective series is a period work that eschews nostalgia, foregrounding the agony of closeted homosexuals, the presence of racism and the hypocrisy of respectable men who beat their wives or commit fraud. It shares that subversive approach to the post-war era encountered in the BBC's Marple adaptations, and the programme gives space to the religious commentary on crime. The sleuthing of the vicar Sidney Chambers is only part of the fabric of the drama. The other is the showing Chambers preaching to his community in the aftermath of a crime to bring moral coherence back into light.

The Kinky Vicars' Court

The possibility that Anglican clergy will misbehave with members of their communities and bring official sanction down on is another avenue for the Church to have been brought onto the screen. The dramatic potential of clergy involved in sex scandals is also evident in soap opera from the grittier *Coronation Street* to the outlandish *Revelations*. Clerical misdemeanours that require ecclesiastical sanctions bring the Consistory Court's awesome and even supernatural powers onto the small screen. A bishop's Consistory Court is an ancient foundation. A diocesan chancellor presides over it and the court sits to deliberate on multiple issues, many mundane parts of ecclesiastical administration such as granting faculties (Briden 1993).

Occasionally the consistories have tried more dramatic and sensational cases. These provide a context for the appearances of chancellors and wayward clergy in television drama. The background of television drama shows some embarrassing cases in Church legal history. In 1932 the rector of Stiffkey in Norfolk appeared in the court of the bishop of Norwich charged with immoral conduct in a widely reported case that had something of everything. The rector was eccentric, young women accused him of making secret assignations in London for making love, and somehow a mysterious Indian servant was involved in the scandal (*Sheffield Daily Telegraph* April 1, 1932, 6). In 1940, the chancellor of St Alban's and his assessors found the rector of Blunham guilty of drinking, resorting and accosting women (*Evening Express* December 4, 1940, 1). In 1956 the bishop of Chester prosecuted the vicar of Woodford for faking a drowning, abandoning his benefice, absconding to Switzerland, and having 'habitually committed adultery' (*Birmingham Daily Gazette* November 23, 1956, 3). When the bishop of Chester sat in judgement on the vicar of Woodford, proceedings began with a grand procession of the bewigged chancellor, the bishop, the bishop's chaplain and the archdeacon of Macclesfield in academicals.

In 1961, the vicar of Balham Hill fought charges of adultery by arguing a 40-year-old woman had been pursuing him (*Belfast Telegraph* March 20,

1961, 4). The bishop's consistory court tried him according to the Clergy Discipline Act of 1892 (Knight 416), old but still powerful legislation, and the trial itself filled column inches with details of the exchanges in court and the scandalous evidence (*Liverpool Echo and Evening Express* March 15, 1961, 14). The details that kept emerging over weeks of trial, of adultery, allegations of assaulting the curate's wife, acrimony in the parish council meetings and conspiracies about who read the lessons, made sure it remained in the press for weeks. The case, occurring as it did the consistory of the bishop of Southwark, was also another media opportunity for Mervyn Stockwood, who as ordinary of the diocese was the man in whose name the prosecution took place and the judgment given. The court's sentencing preceded awesome ritual; when the court found the vicar of Balham Hill guilty, Stockwood presided over the unfrocking and deposition from Holy Orders in Southwark Cathedral, with the time and place advertised in advance in the press (*Liverpool Echo* April 28, 1961, 19).

A trial in a consistory court functioned in its format and external appearances much like other trials, with a presiding officer and wigged and gowned counsel representing the parties. Occasionally the scandalous details could be kept private if the accused clergyman admitted the crime and the bishop dealt with the case privately (*Yorkshire Post and Leeds Intelligencer* December 4, 1954, 4). However if the accused fought the accusation, the case went to full and public trial.

Following the Balham Hill case, where the trial had lasted so long, produced such scandalous evidence, and prompted so much in-depth media coverage, the Church of England became acutely conscious that the interest of the media in their ancient courts was harmful. It is with this possibility that the Church of England consistory courts enter the domain of television drama. The television dramas placing the vicars in their Church's own courts are opportunities for extended televisual meditations on justice. By the late twentieth century the Church's Ecclesiastical Jurisdiction measure seemed old fashioned and unusable, an impression especially reinforced by the expensive and damaging Lincoln Consistory trial of Dr Brandon Jackson for adultery. The Consistory Court found Jackson, the dean of Lincoln, not guilty of adultery with a verger (*Independent* July 20, 1995), after a dramatic trial which raised lurid allegations, such as the dean jogging to have sex with the verger after Evensong (*The Times* July 12, 2000).

Although the Consistory Courts were also sources of embarrassment for the Church, as public spaces for airing very dirty linen, they are also positioned in television drama as socially elevating for the lawyers involved. John Mortimer's fictional barrister Horace Rumpole in the television series *Rumpole of the Bailey* was a child of the vicarage who largely rejected his father's religion, while still being able to quote from scripture as much as he could from English poetry. Rumpole belonged to an old and well-established set of barristers' chambers, the same professional milieu used in *Kavanagh QC*. For Samuel Ballard QC, Rumpole's head of chambers, the invitation to become a diocesan chancellor is an appointment that will add lustre and distinction to the chambers. Indeed, Ballard speaks of the 'singular honour' in such pompously elevated terms Rumpole initially believes he is referring to the lord chancellorship (*Rumpole and the Age of Miracles* 1988). John Mortimer's script toys with the different types of scandal that surrounded the Church by the 1980s, exemplified by the reports in *News of the World*. In an earlier episode *Rumpole and the Man of God* (1979), a cathedral canon appears in chambers to brief Rumpole for the defence and another barrister assumes 'it's the choirboys again'.

In *Kavanagh QC: Innocency of Life* (1998) the Consistory Court appears poised equally between bringing social cachet to lawyers and embarrassment to the Church. The bishop of Norfolk, described by the head of chambers as an 'exceedingly distinguished visitor', whose business will be 'very good for chambers', comes to the barristers' chambers to initiate a trial of a vicar. The bishop himself fails to put people at ease; when asked how he prefers to be addressed, he suggests 'My lord bishop' will do. But conversation between the bishop and the Queen's Counsel also turns to the possibility of the church courts to raise up scandal. The bishop boasts that he enjoys unfrocking clergy and that his diocese has a long tradition of scandal, including a notorious case from the 1930s.

The episode also captures the Consistory Courts at a moment of reform, one resisted by clerical characters on screen who blame reform on a managerial age. It is as inadequate tribunals though that they primarily appear. A crime has been committed by a clergyman in *Innocency of Life* but it is not the Consistory Court that uncovers it or brings him to justice, but the enterprising investigations of the title character James Kavanagh, a barrister at the criminal bar. The same limitation prevails in Ballard's Consistory Court. The ecclesiastical crime the tribunal has been assembled to try is exposed as malicious, but Rumpole's shrewd investigations were extrinsic to the tribunal's deliberations.

This chapter started by considering television which made the Church the arbiter of morality and decency, frequently exemplified by standards of middle-class conduct. Where it ends, with the consistory courts, is with the Church as arbiter of itself, in cases where embarrassing scandals could air in public. Between these two points are television programmes showing the Church and its clergy intersecting with its local communities, often communities under strain from conflict, war or crime. The consistory courts, actual or fictional, could expose the inner lives and inner scandals of clergy. The next chapter moves to those inner worlds, where television has found drama inside the vicarage.

REFERENCES

NEWSPAPERS, PERIODICALS AND TRADE PAPERS

Belfast Telegraph
Birmingham Daily Gazette
Birmingham Gazette
Evening Express
Independent
Liverpool Echo
Liverpool Echo and Evening Express
Sheffield Daily Telegraph
The Times
Yorkshire Post and Leeds Intelligencer

PRINTED SECONDARY SOURCES

Aldridge, Mark. 2016. *Agatha Christie on Screen*. London: Palgrave Macmillan.
Briden, Timothy. 1993. Recent Consistory Court Cases. *Ecclesiastical Law Journal* 3: 117–122.
Chandler, Andrew. 2016. *George Bell, Bishop of Chichester: Church, State, and Resistance in the Age of Dictatorship*. Wm. B. Eerdmans Publishing.
Chapman, James. 2007. Policing the People's War: *Foyle's War* and British Television Drama. In *Repicturing the Second World War: Representations in Film and Television*, ed. Michael Paris, 26–38. Palgrave Macmillan.
Edwards, David L. 1971. *Leaders of the Church of England 1828–1944*. London: Oxford University Press.
Jones, Tim. 2013. Breaking the Faiths in *The Curse of Fenric* and *The God Complex*. In *Time and Relative Dimensions in Faith: Religion and Doctor Who*, ed. Andrew Crome, 45–59. London: Darton, Longman & Todd.

Kirby, Dianne. 2000. The Church of England and "Religious Division" During the Second World War: Church-State Relations and the Anglo-Soviet Alliance. *Electronic Journal of International History* 1: 1.

———. 2012. The Church of England and the Cold War. In *God and War: The Church of England and Armed Conflict in the Twentieth Century*, ed. Stephen G. Parker and Tom Lawson, 121–145. Ashgate.

Mills, Brett. 2009. *The Sitcom*. Edinburgh University Press.

Parker, Linda Mary. 2013. Shell-Shocked Prophets: The Influence of Former Anglican Army Chaplains on the Church of England and British Society in the Inter-War Years. PhD diss., University of Birmingham.

Paxman, Jeremy. 2007. *The English*. Penguin.

Peniston-Bird, Corinna M. 2007. I Wondered Who'd Be the First to Spot That. *Media History* 12 (2–3): 183–202.

Richards, Jeffrey. 1997. *Films and British National Identity: From Dickens to Dad's Army*. Manchester University Press.

Webster, Peter. 2014. God and War: The Church of England and Armed Conflict in the Twentieth Century (Review). *Journal of Beliefs and Values* 35 (1): 129–130.

CHAPTER 11

The Church and Its Communities: The Church Domestic

This chapter continues to examine the Church as it appears in drama in the midst of its different communities. The focus is on the domestic tensions inside the episcopal palace and the vicarage and the way domestic tensions reach outward to community tensions regarding human sexuality.

MEET THE VICAR

The fact that Anglican clergy can marry and therefore have private and family lives is important to what television can show. The possibility that there could be misery, mental illness or domestic abuse taking place inside the vicarage or bishop's palace appeals to makers of drama, comedy and soap. Documentary makers have been invited into the domestic lives of the clergy since Archbishop Fisher and his wife consented to be shown at home. Thereafter television crews have taken opportunities to show clergy and their family up-close. The Reverend Peter Pearce Gould, the rector of Backwell near Bristol, became the subject of a BBC documentary in 1974, of interest owing to his transition from army officer to priest. Higher up the hierarchy, BBC cameras entered the domestic spaces of the Church's leaders. In January 1980, BBC One showed *Bishop's Move*, capturing Robert Runcie and his family preparing to move from St Alban's to Lambeth. In 1986, viewers again saw Runcie at home in *Home on Sunday*, when Cliff Michelmore visited him at the Old Palace in Canterbury and talked with him about his war service. These actual clergy sit on screen alongside fictional analogues presented in drama in intimate close up.

THE CHURCH DOMESTIC

Drama producers have yet to produce an adaptation of any Barbara Pym novel. Pym (1913–1980) was a successful novelist of the 1950s although her works fell from favour with publishers in the 1960s. Her triumphant return to publishing in the next decade was marked by accolades from David Cecil and Philip Larkin and a Booker nomination in 1977. Her absence from television however, is striking, given television's fruitful use of Mary Gaskell, Jane Austen and other women writers who delineate and celebrate small-scale rural English life. Pym, a committed member of the Church of England, is also the most Anglican novelist of the twentieth century and her books are almost invariably set around country or city churches. Clergy appear in most of her books as do the women who attend church and perform the good works associated with them from acts of charity to the flower arranging (Bede 1993). Pym wrote with the greatest of insight into Anglicanism's ethos and its peculiar mixture of the prayerful, cheerful and worldly, such as her dry observation in *Some Tame Gazelle* (her debut novel of 1950) that a village congregation settled comfortably in their pews for a sermon, 'having just sung with great vigour that the world was very evil' (Pym 1978, 108).

The one exception to television's non-use of her fiction is *Miss Pym's Day Out*, a 1992 instalment of *Bookmark*, a programme about books and writers. Patricia Routledge played Pym, and the remainder of the cast was a deft mingling of actors and amateurs, the amateurs being people who had known the real Pym, including her sister and colleagues from the International African Institute. The script by Robert Runcie's son James Runcie also weaves together the actual people with characters from Pym's novels. The approach had an antecedent in Pym's own novels, in which characters from one book could make a cameo appearance in another, and in one of her novels, Pym appeared herself interacting with her fictional creations. *Bookmark* remains to date the only time the small screen has brought to life Pym's characters, and the show's hybridity of documentary and drama evokes the rural English church-going communities that Pym knew. The action opens with Pym attending her village church in Finstock alongside other villagers and hearing a sermon preached by a vicar from one of her books. Later, in London, she visits the African Institute and attends a lecture by another of her creations, Bishop Grote of Mbwawa. She prays in a city church from the *Book of Common Prayer*'s Order for the Visitation of the Sick, imploring 'O most mercifull God, who according to the multitude of thy mercies, dost so put away the sins of those who truly repent, that thou remembrest them no more; open thine eye of mercy upon this thy servant, who most earnestly desireth pardon and forgivenes.' At the end of the story, Pym returns to her country cottage in Finstock, having failed to win the Booker. Runcie's script locates Pym, her fiction and her sympathies firmly within the small-scale community in the Oxfordshire village. Pym's insistence on the Church as intrinsic to the fabric of a community is a precursor of the television dramas that have shown but also questioned the role of the Church's domestic spaces, especially the women who do the Church's good works and the tensions that may beset the lives of the clergy.

Until the early 1990s, the Church's clergy were all male. Female involvement in Church life until that point had taken a number of forms, both official and voluntary, including the parochial or diocesan mainstay represented by the vicar's wife or bishop's wife. Television introduced some of these women to a wider audience. Geoffrey Fisher's wife occasionally broadcast, and the families of bishops could appear alongside husbands and fathers. A newsworthy exception to many quieter clerical marriages was the press treatment meted out to Rosalind Runcie, wife of Robert Runcie. Before Robert Runcie became archbishop of Canterbury in 1981, his wife already had a small degree of notoriety after winning an obscene crossword competition for *Private Eye*. After her husband became archbishop, his wife became of media interest in her own right but in mostly critical ways. The publication of photos of Rosalind Runcie 'including one of her in evening dress draped, vamp-like, across a piano, and another in a swimsuit', as noted in her *Telegraph* obituary, provoked mockery; a press campaign to portray the Runcie' marriage as in crisis with divorce pending carried across the 1980s (*Telegraph* January 13, 2012). The Runcies never did divorce; however, the significance of their turbulent relationship not with each other but with some newspapers lies in the televisual possibilities that opened up through the association of the life inside a bishop's palace or domestic drama in the vicarage.

In the early 1990s circumstances converged that made the domestic interiors of the Anglican Church a source of dramatic opportunity for programme makers. One was the press-driven Runcie dramas. The other was the ordination of women, which disrupted settled patterns of Anglican domestic arrangements, as the woman was no longer automatically the vicar's wife but could be the vicar. Early 1990s drama that ranged in approach and intention from the serious to the deliberately scandalous responded to this potential.

Alan Bennett found rich potential in excoriating misery in the vicarage in *Bed Among the Lentils*, in 1988's *Talking Heads*. Matched with Maggie Smith's acting intensity, the script of the monologue unveiled the loneliness, bitterness, alcoholism and indignities of a vicar's wife, as well as her partial salvation through alcohol and sex with an Indian man (Hunt 1993, 29; O'Mealy 2013, 99). The domestic tensions within a clergy family became the basis of the drama series *The Rector's Wife*, a 1994 series based on the 1991 novel by Joanna Trollope. The series faithfully adapted the plot, dialogue and characters from the book and brought to the screen the spiritual disintegration of an overworked clergyman Peter Bouverie, which occurs as he fails to obtain a promotion and his wife Anna gains new meaning and a fulfilling purpose to her life by taking a low-status job in a supermarket and embarking on an affair with an archdeacon's brother. Trollope's story was attuned to recent and ongoing changes in the Church. In the series, the Church Commissioners have sold the large and elegant old rectory and the rector's family lives in a poorly built modern house, a fictional analogue to the actual sale of large numbers of village and urban parsonages and their replacement with more modest dwellings (Jennings 2018, 13). The profile of the clergy is changing, as the new deacon is a woman, and the rector is no longer responsible for just one parish but has to work in a five-point parish of joint benefices (Sorensen 2014, 228).

At the end, the Reverend Bouverie dies in a car accident, possibly suicide, after learning his wife had an affair with his archdeacon's brother. The miniseries included adultery and suicide and foregrounded an association between scandal and the private lives of clergy family that recurred a decade later in *The Book of Daniel*, a 2005 American drama (of which more below). In *The Rector's Wife*, the clerical family's poor standard of living and straitened finances are central to the plot. At the beginning, the rector fails to gain an archdeaconry that would have meant more money for the family and more status for himself. The series insists on the hypocrisy of the Church and the community in their reactions to Anna taking on a publicly visible job at a supermarket compared to her previously discreet work translating texts, which was tolerated so long as it was covert (Sorensen, 228). The miniseries indicts the Church of England, in particular its bishops, for not giving pastoral support to clergy families. The series ends with Anna, now the rector's widow, seeking help from the bishop for a support network for clergy wives but learning there is no funding for it.

The following year the BBC turned another Trollope novel *The Choir* into a miniseries. The setting and narrative moved from a village rectory to a cathedral close and to the personal and financial struggles of the bishop, dean, and choirmaster of Aldminster Cathedral. The shift to life among higher ecclesiastical echelons focused on higher institutional stakes than one parish priest. The dean and chapter discover that their cathedral requires drastic and expensive repair to its stonework. The plot thereafter is driven by conflict between the cathedral dean on one side, and the choirmaster and the headmaster of the choir school on the other about a plan to save money by shutting down the cathedral choir. Sitting underneath the factional conflict in the cathedral close, the stakes are the emotional well-being of women in the cathedral close. Trollope again channelled recent controversies in the Church of England. The vision of a cathedral close at civil war had appeared in the press as the dean and chapter of Lincoln Cathedral had brawled publicly, as personality clashes between the dean and chapter treasurer and the treasurer's wife and allegations of financial impropriety were leaked first in the *Church Times* then in the national press, including *Private Eye* (*Independent* October 15, 1994). Like *The Rector's Wife*, *The Choir* criticises a male hierarchy for being largely oblivious to other people's emotional wellbeing. By the end of the series, the dean's imperious wife has suffered a nervous breakdown, but the emotional trauma is contained within the walls of the deanery.

Even the fantasy land of Midsomer County suggested the troubled inner lives and private lives of clergy. The portrayal of the Church of England as part of rural communities is a way that elements of fantasy in *Midsomer Murders* are moderated by flashes of reality. The rural church buildings are picturesque, but the series also engages with the reality of declining rural congregations and the disconnect between the institution and its surrounding communities as much as drama set in the inner city does. In *Second Sight* a popular and successful inner-city vicar has been brought to Midsomer Mere to revive the congregation in the empty church. His mission however fails and his career in the parish ends in disgrace.

The series did not shy from the frank presentation of different sexualities and foregrounded the awkward position of clergy who were gay in their private lives. Two gay clergy in *The Straw Woman* (2004), the vicar and curate, are the victims of crime but they are victimised in other ways. The series is alert to other ways the clergy's position in society is weakened. The narrative includes reference to the sale of the historic vicarage and the downscaling of the clergy's lifestyle. Where the clergy are the victims of murder, a local pagan and libertine is by contrast a forthright and charismatic figure. The clergy in this story are at the heart of a complex interplay of factors: their sexuality, their victimhood and their weakness compared to non-Christian religion interact in negative ways. In other episodes the clergy are more dynamic but as the agents of crime. *Death's Shadow* (1999) ended with the revelation that the vicar of Badger's Drift had committed a series of brutal murders. Casting Richard Briers as the vicar is indicative of an industry-awareness of certain archetypes, as Briers was by that point known for playing amiable clerical types including *All in Good Faith*, but the excoriating domestic misery that turns the vicar into a murderer uses but then subverts that televisual familiarity.

Spiritual darkness and black comedy also surrounded a clerical household in *The Vicar*, a 2001 episode of the comedy series *People Like Us*. Chris Langham's mockumentary series highlighted a different profession each week to similar effect. A disjointed commentary and set of interviews purportedly investigated the person and their role, but inept questions and gauche comments from the interviewer (played by Langham) disrupted and disturbed the interviewee's peace of mind and sense of self-worth. 'No-one know how many churches there are in England, or exactly where they are' is the unhelpfully incoherent opening to *The Vicar*. By the end of the episode, the vicar has accidentally realised his own atheism, the vicar's wife has concluded 'isn't life disappointing' as she reflects on the misery of being married to a 'good man', and the generally dismal ambience of the church and its tiny congregation prevails throughout. The episode also insists on reducing the sacred to the banal. A house blessing includes liturgical language invoking God's blessing on 'this lounge-stroke-dining room' and 'this bathroom with separate shower'. A wedding rehearsal from which the prospective bride leaves in tears becomes a garbled mess and the pre-wedding counselling session signally fails to achieve spiritual meaning. The vicar attempts to explain the bond of married life by using the RSPCA slogan 'a dog's not for just for Christmas but for life'; the groom assumes marriage is like a dog. The black humour cuts uncomfortably close to domestic misery and spiritual emptiness and as the episode ends, the vicar realises his vocation was a mistake.

The Church and Soap: Inner Cities and Inner Lives

The dramatic potential of life within a clerical household reached more extreme form in *Revelations*. The 1994 soap opera remains distinctive in British television as, so far, the only soap opera with an explicitly ecclesiastical focus and takes place within a bishop's palace and involves the bishop, his wife and their children. The advance publicity and the late night scheduling led reviewer Harry Venning to hope for something 'a bit raunchy' (*Stage and Television Today* October 13, 1994, 24). The tone of *Revelations* grew darker while the plots became more outlandish; episode one established that the bishop's son had 'dark secrets' he was keeping from his new wife, including his drug addiction.

Revelations remains the only effort so far to build a soap opera around the private life of a churchman; the local and close-knit communities in mainstream soap operas however have served as means to include a local clergyman interacting with parishioners. Soap operas have further served to present a rich variety of clerical types, including minorities, and the positive presentation of gay and women clergy. Because of their emphasis on small-scale communities and a particular vision of everyday life, soap operas are also the one recurring means to televise the Church as part of a community's lifecycle of birth, marriage and death, including the clergy's own private domestic dramas. Episode one of *Coronation Street* (broadcast in December 1960) immediately located the small community not just in a specific northern geography but in a set of social parameters defined by religion. The character Ena Sharples bursts into the corner shop and begins to interrogate the new shopkeeper, demanding to know 'where's your place of worship?'. The shopkeeper's vague response that she doesn't really worship anywhere leads Sharples to assume 'Oh I know, C of E'. Further, being 'C of E' is instantly and negatively associated with social climbing and aspiration: 'Oh it's like my sister's husband', who on her husband receiving a promotion at work said '"we're civic dignitaries now. We must head for church"'. Within a week they were received, christened and confirmed and within a fortnight she was sitting up all night sewing surplices'. The type of sudden and facile attachment to the Church of England that Ena derided as a form of social climbing contrasts with the earthier nonconformity that initially defined religion in *Coronation Street*. Sharples was caretaker of the Glad Tidings Mission on Coronation Street. The Hall's nonconformity evoked 'quintessential working class Englishness' (Sassoon 2006, 1197) that the Church of England did not, with the established Church being the means of social advancement out of the northern working-class milieu that the series' creator Tony Warren carefully crafted (Kynaston 2014, 116). Sharples's strict puritanism, including her belief that Elsie Tanner was likely damned, was *Coronation Street*'s sharpest portrayal of the nonconformist attitudes in the community. On screen, the Glad Tidings Mission Hall closed down and Ena Sharples worshipped at the Victoria Street Mission, which in time closed as well. *Coronation Street* became more religiously mainstream and Anglican and less nonconformist, as it moved away from Warren's scrupulous evocation of what made life in small northern communities. Behind the scenes, production decisions about the standing sets led to changes to the original sets that led to the storyline in 1968 of the Mission Hall being demolished. St Mary's Church of England is now the venue for baptisms, weddings and funerals.

Soap opera also has served to bring onto the screen Church and faith-based controversies. The vicar of Weatherfield in *Coronation Street* is gay and his storylines have involved tensions between his sexuality and his priestly calling. A female vicar in *Emmerdale* blessed a same-sex union and was removed from her parish. The threat of church redundancy, the introduction of female clergy and changing moral teachings have been mobilised in soap opera narratives, including the planned closure of St Mary's Church in *Emmerdale*. What soap operas choose to showcase regarding the Church has a distinctive level of importance. Stephen Coleman's study of political characters in British soaps make a number of points equally relevant to the vicars and the Church, in that television presents a mediated reality but is also the public's primary source of information about social realities. These realities can include (given Coleman's focus) their political representatives, political institutions and other professions including the police and the medical profession (Coleman 2008, 199).

Equally significant is that soap operas, poised between the demotic and the sensational and purportedly offering a slice of life that moves at slow increments, allows for all possible dramas to surround a character. That includes clerical characters, and two examples will suffice. The Reverend Ashley Thomas of St Mary's Church in Emmerdale dies of complications from vascular dementia. Before that, his major storylines included extra marital affairs, illegitimate children, elder abuse, church redundancy, homelessness and male rape. In *Coronation Street*, the incumbency of the Reverend Billy Mayhew of St Mary's Church in Weatherfield has been disrupted by broken love affairs, being kidnapped, falling off a cliff, heroin addiction and house breaking.

The drama echoes to an extent the more moderately scaled issues experienced by clergy in other series. The young vicars in both *Grantchester* and *Broadchurch* are conflicted by past involvement in traumatic incidents and troubled by alcoholism. The incidents involving the clergy need to be understood in context, in that all other major characters have storylines with equally intense and lurid developments. They are however significant markers of changes in television not only in soap but more generally. In earlier decades clerical characters were more peripheral in soap, even if present at key moments but did not participate as characters to the extent they do now. The staff of *Crossroads* attended church at Christmas and clergy conducted funerals, weddings and baptisms. Clerical appearances could also serve as benchmarks of traditional morality compared to the dramatic private lives of the soap leads. In *Coronation Street* in 1981, the then vicar of St Mary's had refused to marry the divorced Ken Barlow in church. Moments such of those used bit-part actors to play the clergy, in comparison to the sustained space now open to clerical characters in soaps, with the consequence however that these scenes of their lives are as outrageous as other characters.

The Episcopal Church Welcomes You?: An American Excursus

Ecclesial and theological controversies such as the ordination of women and the treatment of gay clergy made the Church useful to British programme makers including soap producers. In the United States, the numerically small but high-profile Episcopal Church became a useful dramatic site for television makers wanting to bring conflicts around human sexuality and family tensions onto the small screen. The Episcopal Church is small but mainline, and in fictional guise sometimes appears in mainstream and prestigious dramas, including the 'quality' drama associated with HBO (McCabe 2007, xviii). Beyond the quality dramas, the Episcopal Church had made occasional appearances across other genres. The family in the animated *American Dad* (2005-present) worship in an Episcopal Church, a location for strange events including the Rapture and in the 2011 episode *Season's Beatings* an animated version of Bishop Jefferts Schori appeared. A macabre serial killer in *NCIS* (in the 2004 episode *The Good Wives Club*) was an Episcopal navy chaplain. These fleeting appearances do not lead to any meaningful impressions. Where the Episcopal

Church attracted more sustained interest was with human sexuality. Crises in the Episcopal Church over sexuality ran parallel to similar tensions in the Church of England. In 2003 in England, the proposed consecration of the gay clergyman Jeffrey John as a suffragan bishop was a flashpoint of controversy, damaging the standing and authority of the new archbishop of Canterbury Rowan Williams and further exposing the tensions within the Anglican Communion that had defined the 1998 Lambeth Conference (Sachs 2009, 240). Also in 2003, the Episcopal clergyman Gene Robinson became a bishop coadjutor (or assistant) and in 2004 became the first openly gay serving diocesan bishop in the Anglican Communion upon his election as the Bishop of New Hampshire. The drastic changes to the internal structures of Anglican dioceses and provinces and to the wider Communion are significant aspects of modern scholarship on organised Christian religion and human sexuality. We do not propose to revisit them here, except to note that they served to keep the Anglican and Episcopal Churches in the media as part of a protracted narrative of chaos and division. Specific actions included the defection of Episcopalians to form a new denomination, the Anglican Church of North America. This schism interacted with and was fed by the rise of the so-called Anglican Re-alignment around a power base in the Global South. The departure of conservative congregations from their own ecclesial structures to the authority of African and South American bishops, and the boycotting of many conservative bishops of the 2008 Lambeth Conference maintained the Anglican Church's newsworthy status but meant the press narrative revolved around crisis and decline (Sachs 2009, 245). How did that refract in drama?

For a small denomination, the Episcopal Church's public profile in the United States is disproportionate. Gene Robinson's diocese numbered only about 11,000 people, yet Robinson became the seventh most influential LGBT person in America in 2009, as judged by *Out* magazine. By then he had already played a part in the kick-off for Barack Obama's first inauguration. Even that participation involved him in television controversy when organisers omitted Robinson's inclusively worded prayer from the broadcast, an action prompting the Obama team to issue an official explanation (*San Francisco Chronicle* January 19, 2009). While the proportion of American drama to feature Episcopal clergy is not large, it is telling in terms of reception, status and approach. Earlier in the twentieth century, Episcopal clergy made appearances in film and television in line with the public profile of their small but wealthy and prominent denomination. *Green Light*, a 1937 melodrama based on a successful novel, included an Episcopal cathedral dean played by Sir Cedric Hardwicke. The character was the purveyor of wise advice to both the lead character, in this case a troubled doctor played by Errol Flynn, and to the wider community as a radio preacher. *The Bishop's Wife* (1947) cast David Niven as a smooth and urbane bishop, whose ministry and marriage receive divine intervention from an angel played by Gary Grant, but whose social status and public effectiveness would never be in doubt. Both *Green Light* and *The Bishop's Wife* end with the Episcopal clergyman preaching wisely and profoundly to an enlightened congregation. The calm, stable and prosperous world these films evoked carefully matched the actual Episcopal Church as it existed for much of the twentieth century. 'Astors, du Ponts, Morgans, Vanderbilts, Mellons, Roosevelts—Episcopalians all' is how the *New York Times* recalled the denomination's glory days, when 'a third of the most powerful banking concerns were headed by Episcopalians, as were one-fifth of the nation's major corporations', and Vice-President George H.W. Bush (September 1, 1985). Those same glory days were when episcopal bishops were preeminent social and spiritual figures in places like Maryland and whose congregations included many political leaders (Hein 2001, 108–109).

The trappings of these earlier Episcopal appearances such as the WASP congregations, the swanky private lives of the clergy and the general atmosphere of wealth and privilege that surround Episcopalians prevail in later fictional portrayals of the Episcopal Church. But they now offset an important distinction. In place of moral certainty and clerical authority, the wealthy trappings are the context for a Church in crisis, ripped apart by disputes over human sexuality and seeing influence and numbers decline. In this regard, television drama including *Six Feet Under* and *The Book of Daniel* distil the Episcopal Church as it travelled through the early twenty-first century, often with its real estate portfolios intact but its doctrinal integrity in doubt and some dioceses irrevocably in schism.

A wealthy, WASPish Episcopal family provided the central focus of *The Book of Daniel* that appeared on network television briefly in 2006, but the intended eight episodes did not extend beyond four. The series placed profound dysfunction within the rectory of St Barnabas' Episcopal Church. The rector is the son of a bishop and traces his descent from Daniel Webster the nineteenth-century senator. He also married into old money. His large rectory, African American domestic staff and descent from a great man in American history, are in tension with his current realities of a drug dealing daughter, an alcoholic wife, drug addiction, fraud, entanglement with the mafia, money laundering, gay bashings and extra marital sex between two elderly bishops. Wolff points to the resemblance between the series and the more successful *Desperate Housewives* in its 'over the top' account of family life, yet *Desperate Housewives* became an international hit while *The Book of Daniel* sank without trace (Terrace 2014, 124). Wolff also notes the significance of the programme in showcasing a number of 'firsts' for American television, although there were perhaps too many of these. It was the first to make the Episcopal Church the central and explicit focus of a drama series. The actual Episcopal Church's news service was one of the few outlets to take any interest in the series and even spoke hopefully of *The Book of Daniel* offering 'the Episcopal Church a rare product placement opportunity' on NBC (Episcopal Church August 16, 2005). A further oddity in the programme's reception was the generally positive response from the Episcopal Church to the series' juxtaposition of the Church with various personal, legal and social crises. If anyone had a right to be outraged it would have seemingly been Episcopalians; instead *The Book of Daniel* outraged non-Episcopal religious groups including family values associations (Cowdell 2010, 182). Its appeal to some quarters of the Episcopal Church, which after all had the most to lose from a mainstream drama series about sex, drugs, divorce and dysfunction inside a rectory, came from its distillation of the Church at that particular moment in its history. For all the rector's personal problems, his espousal of socially liberal causes aligned with the priorities of its Presiding Bishop and some prominent congregations. In 2006, Katherine Jefferts Schori became Presiding Bishop. Although her election was not the cause of tensions in the Episcopal Church on a range of social issues such as blessing same sex marriages, her more direct espousal was a catalyst for large scale schisms from the Church and long-running legal disputes about real estate (Caldwell 2017, 240).

The Book of Daniel was timely in portraying the Episcopal Church with a woman bishop who spoke worryingly about a her Church being 'in crisis', but also inverted its leadership by showing female leadership as stridently controlling and conservative compared to the rector. The female bishop's conservative disquiet at this crisis provided a big picture impression of institutional problems contrasted with the micro level domestic concerns taking place in the rectory. This characterisation of female leadership was at odds with the Church's actual Presiding Bishop but also was an aspect of the drama that made the series less progressive than

Episcopalians might have hoped for before broadcasting started. According to one clergywoman, the Reverend Susan Russell, her expectation of the series was that it would be 'cool...that a progressive Episcopal priest has a shot at being a prime-time drama protagonist'. In addition, the series seemed an opportunity to realise 'How surprising might it be to many who tune in to find out there actually IS a church where women can be bishops—clergy can be human—and there's enough Good News around to extend to everybody?' (Episcopal Church August 16, 2005).

For other Christian groups, the series was proof of NBC's 'anti-Christian bigotry' (Wolff 2010, 191). Far from providing an opportunity for product placement, the network struggled to sell advertising space during the commercial breaks and the series faltered then died after only four episodes. Different explanations have been suggested for the rapid demise of what had been a lavishly produced and expensive series, including the outrage caused by the juxtaposition of Christianity with drugs, crime and alcoholism although, as noted, this outrage did not come from within the Episcopal Church. The way the rector spoke easily and informally to Jesus, played as a laid back white man, caused offence that transcended denominational boundaries.

The programme's failure to rate may also indicate that people in general are not especially interested in the Episcopal Church. The momentary elation felt within the real life Church that a major network was making a whole programme about them was very short lived. *The Book of Daniel* failed to rate and to viewers it failed to say or do much that was significant. *The Book of Daniel* made the Episcopal Church the focus of the setting and the drama; *Six Feet Under* was not a programme about the Church; the institution was one smaller aspect of a much larger narrative palette. The failure of the first and success of the second therefore seem to conform to Wolff's argument that few Church-based dramas succeed, either as gaining and consolidating a space in schedules and appeal to audiences, or in presenting a reasonably authentic vision of Church life such as worshipping, praying or showing denominationally meaningful liturgy (Wolff 211). If a programme about the Church does succeed, it is only through denuding the television version of the Church of distinctive character.

However, Wolff's ideas can be augmented and modified, as the focus on the Episcopal Church is a more tightly specific reason for failure. Although not writing specifically about *The Book of Daniel*, a piece by the religious studies professor (and son of an Episcopal priest) Walter Russell Mead, points to a number of reasons that the Episcopal Church and its domestic dramas would fail to interest the consumers of popular culture and media. Characterising its clergy as of 'upper middle-class background' and 'educated professionals', such as defines the characters in *The Book of Daniel*, he also suggests it has been many decades since an Episcopal leader said something that would be of interest to viewers and listeners. He suggests (2010) the sarcastic headline that would never appear: 'Liberal Official of Small, Declining Liberal Denomination Endorses Liberal Idea' as summing up an institution whose liberal clergy's preaching to the government and state is critically weakened by their Church's numerical collapse and internal disorders, and who fail to attract or hold the attention of their own flocks or the wider world.

The Book of Daniel stands alone as a drama series highlighting the Episcopal Church, although the denomination had earlier been an essential part of the narrative fabric of *Six Feet Under*. This programme debuted in 2001, and the first season included an Episcopal priest and his congregation and the internal squabbles within the parish about human sexuality. Lead character David Fisher was a practising Episcopalian, deacon of St Bartholomew's Church, but also homosexual. Throughout the first season, tension grows both within David and between him and the Church authorities who are concerned that a new assistant priest might be gay and seek to block his appointment while quoting the resolution from the 1998 Lambeth Conference that declared homosexual relations to be 'incompatible' with scripture. *The Book of Daniel* located tensions about human sexuality and same sex identities within the rectory, but did posit that a liberal Episcopal minister would be able to work through these issues.

In *Six Feet Under* the message about the Episcopal Church is bleaker, suggesting that personal happiness for a gay man lies outside the Church and requires rejection of the denomination as bourgeois and straight laced. Television scholar Sally R. Munt considers the storyline of David Fisher's coming out to friends, family and his church congregation across the show's first season as a narrative based on equivocation. David Fisher's dramatic public outing of himself is placed within the Church, not only spatially, when he is standing at a church lectern, but ontologically, as he accepts his own gay identity at the same moment in time that he repudiates his Episcopal heritage (Munt 2006). Writing and editing combine to show that David Fisher's acceptance of his sexuality is coterminous with his rejection of the Church. He breaks off from reading Psalm 31 ('In thee O lord do I put my trust let me never be ashamed') to out himself. A brief fantasy that the congregation is applauding is shattered and an abrupt edit takes us from David's fantasy of applause to the actuality fi the congregation sitting in silent judgement.

The narrative situates the Episcopal Church within a longer institutional trajectory along with military and state organisations where the 'open secret' of a person's homosexuality is known to those in authority, but the same authorities demand the homosexual identity be publicly denied (Munt 2006). Ultimately, *Six Feet Under* made the Episcopal Church an important but morally compromised and eventually rejected part of a character's coming out story. It remains with *The Book of Daniel* the only prime time network series to deal seriously and at length with the Episcopal Church and in both cases programme makers were attuned to the Church's then current struggles with same sex relationships and a denomination unable to do much more than discuss sex in fraught and fracturing terms. In both cases the Church's 'product placement' conduced to an anguished and uncertain institution.

INNER LIVES AND COMMUNITY CONFLICTS

A Church that is anguished and uncertain is shown in drama about the Episcopal Church, but its impression is associated with two further programmes that take viewers inside a priest's private life. *The Vicar of Dibley* and *Rev* can be mentioned in the same breath as the BBC's two most successful comedies about vicars. There are substantial differences as well as some points of connection. Both *Dibley* and *Rev* feature a clergyperson struggling with their pastoral roles and their parishioners.

Beyond the obvious differences of a female and male central character and the contrast between the countryside and inner city, *Dibley* dealt more with the shock of the new as the rural congregation adjusted to a female vicar, and Richard Curtis's scripts were timely responses to the ordination of the first women priests, which had come after a five and half hour debate and an initial vote at the 1987 General Synod (Sorensen 2014, 194).

The ordination of women as a source of controversy and possible renewal registered across genres. If the *Vicar of Dibley* does have a counterpart in that regard, it is the Reverend Bernice Woodall in *The League of Gentlemen*. Her rural ministry is exercised in Royston Vasey, and like other inhabitants she is a grotesque who is prone to abusing her parishioners and deriding the disabled and minorities. Still in the realm of the sinister and grotesque, the detective series *Inspector Morse* used the issue as the basis of drama and mystery in *Fat Chance* (1991). A female candidate for ordination is murdered and an Oxford college is thrown into uproar over a vote for a new chaplain when one of the candidates is a woman. The episode also toys with cruel ironies about the divisions. By the end a male priest viciously opposed to the ordination of women has gone mad and been confined to an Anglo-Catholic care home, where Inspector Morse remarks on the irony of a misogynist priest being cared for by controlling nuns.

The comedy of the Church's divisions registered in *Dibley*. The series directly confronted the tone and content of much real-life opposition to women priests. An oft-quoted line from the first episode has the new vicar declare 'You were expecting a bloke. Beard, bible, bad breath. And instead you got a babe with a bob cut and a magnificent bosom'. Her emphasis on body and appearance appropriated the way female clergy had been objectified and sexualised by their opponents and in the media, such as the *Sun* headline: 'The Church says yes to vicars in knickers'.

However an aura of comic unreality hung over *The Vicar of Dibley*, with humour coming from broad rural stereotypes and accents. The series itself tended to revel in being old fashioned, down to the more theatrical style of acting and the studio-based production. The scripts rarely intersected with actual concerns shaping the Church of England and seldom made jokes at the expense of the Church (Kramer 2016). Beyond the single issue of the ordination of women, the series eschewed seriously grounding its stories in ecclesiastical realities, suggesting instead considerable nostalgia expressed via an 'unthought about backdrop' (Brown and Lynch 2012, 344). For instance, being vicar of just one single parish is far removed from the four or five point parishes and joint benefices that defined the rural ministry by the time *The Vicar of Dibley* entered production.

Much of the dramatic tension and darker comedy in *Rev* stemmed from the old and the worn-out aspects of the inner city Church of England as it struggled to engage with its community. Elsewhere on the BBC, the popular series *Call the Midwife* also placed Anglican clergy and religious in an inner city setting. Following the memoirs of the midwife Jennifer Worth, whose work recalled the respect the people in Poplar had for the Anglican sisters of St Raymund, *Call the Midwife* dramatizes the medical care and the religious devotions of the sisters (Wilder 2017, 10). The sisters at Nonnatus House coped with a world changing around them. Post war immigration, multi-racial marriages, adulteries, homosexuals, prostitution and mental illness are among the social and medical issues converging around the convent. The Anglican sisters though are a respected moral force and place of comfortable resort for the people in the East End. On screen, a recurring editing juxtaposition is the nuns at prayer with the midwives working, suggesting the mutual importance of the religious lives of the sisters and the care they provide (Wilder 2017, 11).

Rev, courtesy of Tom Hollander's scrupulous ethnographic research among inner-city vicars, including the vicar of the filming location St Leonard's Shoreditch (Ornella 2016, 101; *Guardian* August 2, 2012; *Daily Mail* July 24, 2010), is engrossed with the painful realities of urban ministry. Its multi-faith and multi-cultural milieu is distinct from the rural stereotypes in Dibley and characters in *Rev* use the correct terminology from stipends and area deans to canon law and redundancy.

A crisis point comes with the vicar's emotional disintegration, his mental state shattering completely during a Christmas Midnight Mass when a drunken congregation and a lost taxi driver reduce the service to a raucous and banal mess. But *Rev* is also tinged with a metaphysical intensity, most notably when the titular vicar, the Reverend Smallbone encounters and dances with a track-suit wearing man who may well be God, and who turns banal clichés into a spiritually meaningful exchange. The reviewer James Mumford criticised the series for presenting essentially an outsider perspective that disregarded faith or the supernatural, a strange comment because it overlooked the mystical aspects of Smallbone's ministry (*Guardian* April 28, 2014).

HTB and 'Doing Church'

The central character in *Rev* undergoes excruciating personal, professional and spiritual trials when serving his inner city parish, in a large old church with a small congregation and largely irrelevant to the surrounding community. The scenario in *Rev* repeats the main plot dynamic of *All in Good Faith* (1985–1988), when a country vicar moves to, and struggles with, an inner city parish. The comedy of *Rev* is more poignant and much grittier than the Richard Briers comedy, with one character calling the parish 'heroin alley'. Hollander's alertness to the professional realities confronting inner city vicars allowed him to build episodes around key changes in the profile of the Church. In one early episode, the tiny, aged congregation attending St Saviour's is augmented but affronted when the large youthful congregation of an evangelical Anglican Church begins sharing the building. As is the case with the series in general, the script gains a patina of reality from the use of ecclesiastical buzzwords and terminology. When the younger congregation begins reorganising the interior to shift pews and make a more flexible worship space, Smallbone frets that there is no faculty (a licence from a church court) to allow the changes.

The incursion of the evangelical congregation on top of the older, failing church community also brings onto the screen the tensions experienced in the real Church of England about the church planting by Holy Trinity Brompton, a large church known colloquially as HTB and which plants new congregations in churches deemed to be have failed. The HTB church plants attract varying responses. In some quarters they appear to be the last hope of the Church of England, but they are also viewed as parasites riding rough shod over existing faith communities and their traditions (*Church Times* November 2, 2006). In *Rev*, sympathies lie with the older, smaller traditional congregation, while also not shying away from showing Smallbone's weaknesses compared to the younger and more charismatic evangelical pastor.

The contrast between the large evangelical congregation and the shrivelled community at St Saviour's also ominously presages concerns that pervade all three seasons of *Rev*. Another reality that Hollander knew and used was the threat of redundancy hanging over many old inner city churches. Again the script knowingly uses the Church of England's own terminology while also playing with meaning. The area dean identifies the Muslim-dominated neighbourhood as one difficult to 'do church' in, using a buzzword from the actual Anglican Church. As redundancy seems to come closer, Smallbone worries that his church may become 'toast', the 'ecclesiastical term for redundancy'.

God Loves Poofs

The Vicar of Dibley, focussed as it was on the ordination of women and their gradual acceptance by a conservative rural community, only occasionally touched upon same sex controversies in the Church. Some dialogue hinted that Geraldine's diocesan bishop was homosexual and a BBC producer mistook David Horton for a repressed gay Anglo-Catholic. *Rev* embedded its narratives in painstakingly researched and painful realities. Series writer and star Tom Hollander, who played the titular Reverend Adam Smallbone, assiduously researched the lives and work of inner city vicars. The result was a series written with considerable empathy for the

demands on vicars' time and emotional well-being, but also acute awareness of the flashpoints of controversy in the modern Church.

One of these is human sexuality. The vicar of St Saviour's is straight, but
both his archdeacon and lay reader are homosexual. The implication of
being gay and in orders is forcefully suggested when the archdeacon fails
to progress to a bishopric after he reveals his sexuality to an interviewing
committee (Ornella 2016, 105), an incident among others in the series
showing the characters' failed ambitions and dark inner lives. The series'
most sustained engagement with same sex relations and the Church came
in the second episode of season three (2014) when gay congregants ask
for the vicar to conduct their wedding. The background to this narrative
comes from the Diocese of London's controversial encounter with a
church-based gay wedding in 2008, conducted by the Reverend Martin
Dudley in St Bartholomew the Great. The aftermath of that occasion
played out in ways reflected in *Rev*, specifically in an archdeacon investigating if any breach of Canon Law had taken place. The preparation was
different however. Dudley thoughtfully prepared the liturgy for the occasion in 2008, making sensitive changes to the language of the 1662 prayer
book to enable its use for this purpose (*New Statesman* June 17, 2008). In
Rev, Adam Smallbone's preparation is haphazard and he produces a hurriedly revised service on the back of an envelope a few seconds before the
service starts. Initially, Smallbone insists to the participants that all he can
offer is a few prayers in the context of a Eucharist, not a gay wedding. By
the end of the episode he has had a change of heart and found the courage
of his convictions and officiates over an actual wedding service for the
two men.

The difficult journey that Smallbone, the gay couple and St Saviour's
take towards performing the wedding service enables the episode to peel
away tensions and contradictions. Smallbone acknowledges, when initially
refusing to perform an actual wedding service, that while God will bless
their union, the Church of England cannot. Later, having attempted an
improvised and compromised set of prayers, his anguish lies in trying to
please the gay couple and follow Church law at the same time, and failing
in both.

Failure of different kinds runs through *Rev*. The third and final season
ended with Adam no longer a vicar, his church declared redundant and
boarded up, and his tiny congregation dispersed. Seemingly the triumph
lies with the area dean, who is alert to the monetary value of every square
foot of internal space in the doomed church but cannot see its spiritual

and community importance. The failure though is qualified. *Rev* based its comedy on the thoughtful and accurate use of Anglican ritual, culture and ethos. The final episode follows set days in the Church calendar from Good Friday to Easter and therefore from death to resurrection. The last episode ends with the tiny congregation reassembled on the church porch and holding aloft a Paschal candle.

That Easter service, and the symbolic representation of the Light of Christ, ends *Rev* on a tentatively hopeful note, at least suggesting that a faith community will continue in the twenty-first century even if the organised religion has died away. The programmes, both British and American, considered in this chapter locate the Church in the midst of different communities, rural and urban, committed and indifferent, and suggest the challenges faced by the institution and its clergy. On that note, the final chapter now examines the Church in the twenty-first century as an institution that is also a broadcasting entity.

REFERENCES

NEWSPAPERS, PERIODICALS AND TRADE PAPERS

Church Times
Daily Mail
Guardian
Independent
New Statesman
San Francisco Chronicle
Stage and Television Today
Telegraph

PRINTED SECONDARY SOURCES

Bede, Belinda. 1993. A 'Kinder, Gentler' Anglican Church: The Novels of Barbara Pym. *Anglican Theological Review* 75 (3): 387–398.
Brown, C., and G. Lynch. 2012. Cultural Perspectives. In *Religion and Change in Modern Britain*, ed. L. Woodhead and R. Catto, 329–351. London: Routledge.
Caldwell, Ronald James. 2017. *A History of the Episcopal Church Schism in South Carolina*. Wipf and Stock Publishers.
Coleman, Stephen. 2008. The Depiction of Politicians and Politics in British Soaps. *Television and New Media* 9 (3): 197–219.
Cowdell, Scott. 2010. *Abiding Faith: Christianity Beyond Certainty, Anxiety, and Violence*. James Clarke and Co.

Hein, David. 2001. *Noble Powell and the Episcopal Establishment in the Twentieth Century*. University of Illinois Press.

Hunt, Albert. 1993. *Talking Heads*: "Bed Among the Lentils" (Alan Bennett). In *British Television Drama in the 1980s*, ed. George W. Brandt, 19–39. Cambridge University Press.

Jennings, Anthony. 2018. *The Old Rectory: The Story of the English Parsonage*. Sacristy Press.

Kramer, L. 2016. Comic Strategies of Inclusion and "Normalisation" in *The Vicar of Dibley*. In *British TV Comedies: Cultural Concepts, Contexts and Controversies*, ed. J. Kamm and B. Neumann, 212–224. Palgrave Macmillan.

Kynaston, David. 2014. *Modernity Britain: Book Two: A Shake of the Dice, 1959–62*. Bloomsbury.

McCabe, Janet. 2007. *Quality TV: Contemporary American Television and Beyond*. I.B. Tauris.

Mead, Walter Russell. 2010. Sunday Jeremiad: Petty Prophets of the Blue Beast. *The American Interest*. https://www.the-american-interest.com/2010/02/21/sunday-jeremiad-petty-prophets-of-the-blue-beast/.

Munt, Sally. 2006. A Queer Undertaking: Anxiety and Reparation in the HBO Television Drama Series Six Feet Under. *Feminist Media Studies* 6 (3): 263–279.

O'Mealy, Joseph. 2013. *Alan Bennett: A Critical Introduction*. Routledge.

Ornella, Alexander D. 2016. Losers, Food and Sex: Clerical Masculinity in the BBC Sitcom Rev. *Journal for Religion, Media and Film* 2 (2): 99–122.

Pym, Barbara. 1978. *Some Tame Gazelle*. Jonathan Cape.

Sachs, William L. 2009. *Homosexuality and the Crisis of Anglicanism*. Cambridge University Press.

Sassoon, Donald. 2006. *The Culture of the Europeans: From 1800 to the Present*. HarperPress.

Sorensen, Sue. 2014. *The Collar: Reading Christian Ministry in Fiction, Television and Film*. Eugene, OR: Cascade Books.

Terrace, Vincent. 2014. *Encyclopedia of Television Shows, 1925 through 2010*. 2nd ed. McFarland.

Wilder, Courtney. 2017. Television Dramas, Disability, and Religious Knowledge: Considering *Call the Midwife* and *Grey's Anatomy* as Religiously Significant Texts. *Religions* 8: 209, 1–23.

Wolff, Richard. 2010. *The Church on TV: Portrayals of Priests, Pastors and Nuns on American Television Series*. Bloomsbury Publishing.

CHAPTER 12

Conclusions: Church, State and Life

The chapters in Part I and Part II moved from non-fictional broadcasting, both great and small, to fictional drama. Because it is the established Church and therefore monopolises the coronation of the monarch and hosts major events of celebration and mourning, the Church of England has been ever-present to television audiences of millions. However, how remote is the institution from these audiences? The 1953 Coronation was discussed above. That occasion was an early landmark of what are now regular intersections of the Church royalty, global broadcasting and celebrity. We earlier saw the initial reluctance, gradually transformed into enthusiasm on the part of the Church to broadcast sacred mysteries and from there the proliferation of television content about the Church. If only viewed in isolation as an entity on a television screen, the Church could seem to be alive and well. National statistics tell another story. Fewer than a quarter of weddings are now in church and adherence falls further each time a census is taken. On-screen, there is a different story, one defined by adaptability, versatility and enduring interest.

In this final section, major forms of non-fictional broadcasting and their policy contexts are surveyed, leading up to the Brexit-era #Vicargate scandal, which shows a curious merging of the fictional iterations of the Church, non-fictional broadcasting and some residual audience familiarity with the C of E.

British broadcasters remain obliged by law and charter to provide certain numbers of hours of religious broadcasting. Comedy and drama that

© The Author(s) 2020

M. Harmes et al., *The Church on British Television*,
https://doi.org/10.1007/978-3-030-38113-4_12

may include clergy and churches are not part of that content; instead the mandated religious broadcasting falls in the realm of non-fiction television. Towards the end of the twentieth century, *Stars on Sunday*, *Songs of Praise* and *Highway* accounted for much of the audience watching religious content. This content was known by surveys to be providing a religious interaction for people who did not attend physically because they were unable to (Viney 1999, 13). Across the early twenty-first century there has been a proliferation of non-fictional broadcasting involving the Church, considering the intersections between television and multi-platforms of dissemination from Twitter to YouTube. The appearance of clergy in reality television, the transformation of *Songs of Praise* from a broadcast church service to a wider and sometimes controversial format (including a broadcast from a Calais migrant camp), the reality television performances of the clergy from *GoggleBox* to *A Vicar's Wife* and the interactions between digital media and broadcasting are some of the Church's most recent appearances in popular media.

Non-fictional programming involving clergy followed patterns of talk and discussion shows more generally, in which the lengthy, detailed formats of earlier decades gave way to the shorter formats of recent years. In non-fictional guise, the Church appeared in the God Slot and both the BBC and the independent companies included talk shows in their 'closed' slot, including *Credo* and *Everyman* (Wallis 2016, 674). As intended by the Radio and Television Council, the Church also staked a claim to appearances in a much wider range of broadcasting. Archbishops in particular expected to producers to call on their services as guests and panellists across a number of talk programmes.

In return, television itself carefully and thoughtfully reciprocated, becoming an intrinsic participant in the life of the Church in areas such as liturgical reform and ecumenical relations. Not simply showing the Church, television actively participated in reform and reflection. In October 1957 the BBC Television Broadcast a service from St Augustine's Church on Langdon Park Road, which premiered Fr Geoffrey Beaumont's Folk Mass. Reactions to the broadcast and the music are telling, as both seemed to reviewers to be in poor taste and beyond the norm of what was already thought of as normal in broadcasts from churches. The *Daily Express* reviewer claimed to have watched a 'disturbing racket' and *Musical Times* said the music 'suited to the fetid atmosphere of a night club or cabaret' (*Church Times* November 29, 2007; Leask 2000, 30). Another instance was the carefully prepared broadcast of an experimental Eucharist on ABC Television on July 27, 1958.

Liturgical reform, meaning the gradual introduction of modern alternatives to *The Book of Common Prayer* occupied the attention of the Church throughout the twentieth century (*The Times* July 12, 1958, 4). ABC's broadcast was a scholarly contribution to these processes, originating with liturgical scholars from the University of Birmingham and included a learned introduction by Dr J.G. Davies, a cleric and academic heavily involved in liturgical reform (*Living Church* 1959, vol. 138, 14).

One significant way to consider how the Church may be present on the screen but remote from people's lives is the broadcasting of these royal occasions, especially weddings. Traditionally royal weddings were private occasions. In 1947 the Movietone film cameras were permitted to capture footage of Prince Elizabeth's wedding to Philip Mountbatten in Westminster Abbey, including close up details such as the entry in the register. In 1960, the marriage of Princess Margaret to Antony Armstrong Jones was a television event and for the first time the BBC broadcast a whole wedding.

Royal weddings became a television commodity from the 1960s onwards, as did the royal family in general after the 1969 documentary *Royal Family* was viewed by a huge audience on both the BBC and ITV (Chapman 2015). Each wedding has brought a Church of England wedding service to a large audience. The reactions to these provide a barometer of how close or remote a wider population became from the Church. Royal weddings of the 1970s and 1980s brought in their wake untidy and scandalous adulteries, separations and divorces, which at times carried religious implications as they tarnished not only the monarchy's reputation but also its relationship with the Church. The clergyman Archdeacon George Austin publicly questioned Prince Charles' fitness to be king, and therefore supreme governor of the Church of England, reasoning that as he had broken his wedding vows by committing adultery, he could not be trusted to follow his coronation vows (Bradley 2002, 175).

His point is a reminder that Charles Prince of Wales appeared twice on television as a participant in a Church of England wedding ceremony; the first was the lavish wedding to Lady Diana Spencer in St Paul's in July 1981 and the second a smaller scale blessing of his civil marriage to Camilla Parker Bowles at St George's Chapel in Windsor in 2005.

On both occasions, the archbishop of Canterbury officiated, successively Robert Runcie and Rowan Williams. For the first wedding, the role of the Church is now cruelly ironic. The characterisation of the wedding of Prince Charles and Diana as a fairy-tale by the archbishop of Canterbury was a comment whose meaning is now inverted, as the marriage became the cause of scandal and tragedy, including Diana's death in 1997. The converse of the fairy-tale wedding of Diana and Charles was another Anglican service, the nightmare of the funeral of Diana, watched by billions of people, again presided over by the archbishop of Canterbury but who found himself overshadowed by a cavalcade of celebrities and the airing of bitter family grievances.

Prince Charles' second wedding ceremony, a blessing rather than a wedding as the couple were both divorcees, shows the gap between the wider public and mainstream Anglican liturgy. Seizing on the fact that both Charles and Camilla had committed adultery, the press suggested the text of the blessing service would include extraordinary admissions of guilt about their adultery. The text seized on this instance was the prayer book's General Confession, which includes phrases such as 'We acknowledge and bewail our manifold sins and wickedness' and 'We do earnestly repent, And are heartily sorry for these our misdoings; The remembrance of them is grievous unto us; The burden of them is intolerable'. The *Independent* characterised the service as including public repentance (April 8, 2005). The *Guardian* said the royal couple chose 'the strongest possible prayer' to offer repentance, although the suggestion overlooks the fact that the confession is a routine and congregational part of Anglican liturgy (April 8, 2005). The *Telegraph* called it the 'strongest act of penitence', which again omits the fact that the General Confession is an ordinary part of the service (April 7, 2005). The use of the powerful Tudor language also registered overseas, with papers such as the *Sydney Morning Herald* and the *New Zealand Herald* calling it a 'bid for forgiveness' (April 8, 2005). These press reports cumulatively suggested that the blessing contained an earnest and extraordinary confession of guilt rather than something quite ordinary, once recited by millions of churchgoers on a weekly basis.

The reactions to the use of the 1662 prayer book emerge from a complex web of ecclesiastical politics, personal preferences, deliberate distortion and, by 2005, a wider public unfamiliarity with the once-universal language of *The Book of Common Prayer*. Some newspapers, reporting that the service would contain the stirring admission of sin and wickedness, did acknowledge that the confession was congregational and not confined to the bride and groom. What these reports did omit however was Charles's personal preference for *The Book of Common Prayer* over modern language service books and his patronage of the Prayer Book Society, making the language used in the blessing indicative not so much of his guilt but his liturgical conservatism. Confusion about the prayer book mingled with ecclesiastical politics with the sudden intervention of the bishop of Salisbury, David Stancliffe, who informed a *Sunday Times* interviewer that the declarations made in the General Confession should be preceded by tangible acts of apology and restitution, such as an apology from Prince Charles to Camilla Parker Bowles' former husband. His comments may have confused in public discourse the distinction between preparatory acts of contrition and the congregational text of the General Confession. Some quarters attributed Bishop Stancliffe's intervention to wider ecclesiastical politics and the need for a conservative leaning bishop to make a conservative statement, in the fall out from a confused debate in the General Synod about same sex relationships (*Guardian* March 29, 2005). The comments swirling around this television wedding are in general a measure of the distance between the wider population and what was once part of familiar discourse.

In time, Charles and Diana's children have married in Church of England ceremonies before audiences of millions. The 2011 wedding of Prince William to Katherine Middleton was traditional, including the traditional liturgical language of the prayer book, an address by the bishop of London, and the music. The 2018 wedding of Prince Harry and Meghan Markle is a study in contrast, including the scene-stealing sermon by an overseas bishop, placing the wedding among emerging discourses of race, multiculturalism and religion in the twenty-first century. The wedding broadcast of a Church wedding opened a space for discussion of multicultural identities and immigration in a way earlier broadcasts had not, because of Markle's own mixed race ancestry, the showcasing of Black British culture and the participation of an African American bishop.

Very few Anglican clergy have becomes memes, meaning in Richard Dawkins's terminology a small cultural artefact that repeats and recreates itself. The exception may be Bishop Michael Curry. His sermon at the wedding in April 2018 lasted longer than normal for preachers before the Queen, and seemed to incur the Queen's visible displeasure, stun Princess Anne's daughter Zara Tindall and leave Elton John unimpressed. However the robust sermon also created a media storm that commentators acknowledged overshadowed the bride and groom, leading Curry onto a whirlwind of global media appearances, a spoof sketch on *Saturday Night Live,* the release of a book of sermons and a broadcasting award. His image also became a meme circulating through the internet.

Curry's sermon intersects with not only British but global audiences. The people hearing him live in St George's Chapel had their reactions caught on camera; many seemed to be not be enjoying it. The vastly larger global television audience responded differently and positively. The response to the sermon also captures a particular moment in time of the Anglican Church's engagement with television. For many, as much as they enjoyed Curry's uplifting messages about love, seemed confused that he was actually Anglican. His race, accent, evangelical fervour and the commonly repeated reference point that he was from Chicago situated him in popular consciousness as something other than Anglican, as something too enthusiastic, Pentecostal and enjoyable than the type of Anglican bishops usually seen on television on royal occasions. As Curry himself acknowledged, the media firestorm around him was also a rare recent instance of television audiences paying particular attention to an Anglican Church leader, or an Anglican having a platform to say something that authentically resonated with a wider audience (*The Guardian* October 23, 2018). Curry instead suggested that where church and faith leaders did command television audiences, they tended to no longer be the mainline type found in the Anglican Church.

One other quieter royal tradition has kept the Anglican Church on screen. The annual Christmas messages by the Queen have become more conspicuously religious in tone and content in the new millennium, even as regular church going has declined. As an annual event for over 60 years, the Queen's Christmas Message is broadcasting history in microcosm, from radio to television, analogue to digital, the BBC to independent, black and white to colour, and more. The format has evolved to include not only the Queen's talking head but a more imaginative and visual manner of presentation. The content however is in an inverse relationship with the presentation. Modernisation of the style has accompanied more conservative content, especially as the Queen has opened up more and more about her own faith, which she presents inscribed within Anglican patterns of devotion and prayer. She has spoken about the inspiration Jesus has provided her and read to her audience from her Bible and prayer book. Rowan Williams, the former archbishop of Canterbury, considers these broadcasts, which are only tiny annual fragments of content, to be a space for explicit religious content that the BBC no longer provides. The historian Ian Bradley (2002) pinpoints the 2000 Christmas Message as a turning point for the Queen's increased religious content, and that came part way through Tony Blair's prime ministership. The Church was often banished from view during the years of 'Cool Britannia', in which Anglicanism gave way to more contemporary forms of national celebration and commemoration. By 2000, the Church's Synod again was debating religious broadcasting and the debate opened up fundamental questions (Viney 1999, 24), including what religious broadcasting had become and if it should still exist at all. The debate and the questions that followed are a useful marker of how the Church was engaging with television and how religious broadcasting had fragmented across genres and in terms of intentions.

#VICARGATE

Royal weddings, the Queen's Message and other occasions of state are irregular occasions, and reactions to them, especially to weddings, suggest an increasing disconnect between audiences and the institution of the Church. However, a recent broadcasting event does show that residual familiarity with the Church of England registers with wider audiences. A cardigan and dog collar can still evoke a distinctively Anglican archetype. The archetype in question is #Vicargate, the name given to a particular guest on the BBC's *Newsnight* and its controversial reception, especially in social media.

Dressed in dog collar and cardigan, the bit part actor Marina Hayter was introduced as the Reverend Lynn Hayter. The internet controversy immediately following her appearance unearthed that Hayter's own denomination was far from mainstream. As a pastor for 'Seeds for Wealth' ministry Hayter wore a striking and outlandish outfit, but not a dog collar. Where #Vicargate reveals its significance is the enduring television 'vernacular' of the vicar as an archetype which retained currency, which still spoke to a wider an unchurched generation of meaning something, and which could cause controversy if they were seemingly misapplied or deceptive.

There are several implications of #Vicargate. One was to see the medium turning back on itself. As tweets on the hashtag #Vicargate cycled through Twitter, a host of TV vicars rose up from broadcasting history to become part of a tweeting storm. Dick Emery's Toothy Vicar, the Reverend Grainger from *The Vicar of Dibley*, the Reverend Farthing from *Dad's Army* and others became sarcastic suggestions for panel members for the next edition of *Newsnight*. More telling was the ambiguous connection between an actual vicar and a television vicar. By 2018, fewer than a million in the general population regularly attended an Anglican service and saw an actual vicar in action. However, a dog collar, a cardigan, as well as a specific unassuming parsonical demeanour remained a functional and recognisable archetype, which is where the *Newsnight* controversy is situated in this study. What William Keenan refers to the 'old dress signs of religious alterity' still contained meaning (Keenan 1999, 390). #Vicargate suggested that a particular archetype or a combination of items such as dog collar and cardigan could still resonate, especially when associated with a comedy grotesque.

AFTERWORD

This study surveyed how the Church has been probed, mocked, satirised and lampooned, when it has been used for dramatic purposes, but also when it has dynamically shaped television content and policy. The Church shaping the medium and the Church shaped by the medium are both relevant here. We began when on television the sole broadcaster was the BBC, itself an institution of establishment status, taken for granted as a Christian institution speaking to a Christian nation (Brown 2012, 345, 350). Decades of television across genres, production companies, channels, and regions and identify the ubiquity of the Church in these decades of television making, the importance of the institution to programme makers, and the ways the Church has been used, abused and presented. From there emerged the impact on the real-life institution of its repeated appearances on the small screen.

In Part I, the chapters showed how the Church swiftly gained a place in television schedules and therefore in people's living rooms. The Queen was crowned in 1953, *Songs of Praise* appeared in 1961 and comedies about vicars and bishops appear by the mid-1960s. Broadcasters become less tentative and more willing to mock and chastise. Comedy became sharper, non-fictional broadcasting asks more demanding questions, and the imaginative potential of religion in broadcasting expanded as producers located televisual Anglicanism in a wider range of programmes.

In Part II, the chapters showed broadcasters delineating specific impressions, from the Church at the grassroots of local communities, be they Dibley or Albert Square, to the Church's leaders moving and shaking with power brokers in Downing St, or caught up in criminal investigations. The dramatic potential of clergy in science fiction peril, the sleazier exploitative potential of vicars doing drugs or having affairs in soaps, or being murdered in crime drama, are all facets of the Church on television. The non-fiction broadcasts of royal weddings, funerals, the Queen's Christmas Message and the aesthetics of reality television complement fictional drama. Although mainstream religion in Britain, especially the established church, has undergone massive numerical decline across the twentieth century, a trend that continues into the twenty-first, the church has remained a prominent focus in broadcasting.

The themes of denominationalism, secularism and genre introduced and framed these chapters. The greatest of these was secularism, as the religious studies scholar Callum Brown points to a collapse in church going from the 1960s onwards, an assertion that seeks to overturn much earlier scholarship on the emergence of an associated urbanised and secularised British society in the nineteenth century (Morris 2003, 968). Television may have partially obscured this secularism. Being a national church makes it a default option for programme makers to show weddings, funerals and baptisms. The Church of England is the central frame of reference for this book, but that may not have been the case for programme makers who portrayed a church service or cleric on the screen.

In Britain, the growth of non-Christian religions and especially the rise of 'no-religion' as a census result, aligned with much of Western Europe. Having a national church can obscure or at least complicate these observations. One bishop described the Church of England as having a 'penumbra' of cultural Anglicans (Rowell 1992, 111), a term re-used and accepted in other commentary. This penumbra is a cultural vestige rather than an active membership. As the theme of denominationalism indicated, the establishment status should mean the Church of England is more than a mere denomination, although recent statistics bleakly challenge the feasibility of still seeing the Church of England as a societal institution. Brown and Woodhead (2016) point out that the decline in regular worshipper numbers in the Church of England matches declines elsewhere in Europe; she also points out the disappearance of even the penumbra of vestigial religion. For instance, the Church of Denmark shares with the Church of England the statistic of about 1 per cent of the total population worshipping on Sundays, but the Danish Church has a far healthier sign of the survival of nominal attachment, such as the numbers who will still marry in church, baptise their children and pay the Church tax. The Church of England's regular worshipping population has declined, but so too have the nominal or occasional interactions with the Church at birth, marriage and death that in earlier decades had been a sign of the societal life of the Church.

Secularism in modern Britain raises significant questions about the Church on television: what aspects of established religion are showcased; why this content remains on the air to viewers increasingly remote from organised religion; and what impressions of the national church are created for people who access it only on the small screen and not via active participation? Creative decisions about what appears on screen point to deeper implications for broadcasting about the Church. What Morrison refers to as the way that religion 'permeated general associations in a manner not possible though its own direct appeal' (2009, 118), means that the visions that programme makers present about the Church are more powerful and more far reaching than anything the Church can do or say itself.

The participation of clergy in major cultural and social changes locates the Church as immersed in secularism and asserting itself in national life and consciousness (Kirby 1999, 328). In providing theological and moral input to major questions such as the legalisation of homosexuality or changes to divorce laws, the actions of churchmen find a parallel in their approach to television. In that domain, churchmen pondered the interaction between the technical and the sacerdotal, the sacral presence of cameras in church and the implications of showing something holy on television. We see a context to this study in the cultural fragmentation that Morrison pinpoints in broadcasting and associates with receding cultural assurances about Christian identity. The mediated visions of the Church presented on television, and the strenuous efforts of clergy to shape those visions, are associated with other changes. The assurances that once underpinned religious broadcasting became subject to shifts and uncertainties, but they are related to the receding influence of the Church and also to its own urgent and dynamic participation in what are often considered landmarks of secular change.

One final point remains about secularism. The 'death' of Christian Britain suggests the rapid decline of Christian belief as a 'commonly accepted moral and spiritual standpoint', signalled externally by a decline in not only attending Sunday services but also in involvement in other activities and works that would have made a parish church the focus of community life. But as Morris cautions, 'death' is not the same as disappearance as there are pervasive and complex ways that Christianity still registers in public life and consciousness. One of these is television (Morris

2003, 975). If Callum Brown's historical trajectory is even partly accepted, the decline to death of Christian Britain from the 1960s onwards occurs inversely with the rise of television as a mass medium expanding from one analogue television service to a multiplatform digital presence. Public and commercial broadcasting undergo regular re-definition, although the requirement for non-fictional religious broadcasting has remained a core legislative requirement (Harrison 2000, 3, 6). However, the decision to make fictional programmes about the Church is a choice. The suggestion the Church may be pervasive is contestable but fascinating, as decline and interest together register when the Church of England appears on television.

REFERENCES

NEWSPAPERS, PERIODICALS AND TRADE PAPERS

Guardian
Independent
Living Church
New Zealand Herald
Sydney Morning Herald
Telegraph
The Times

PRINTED SECONDARY SOURCES

Bradley, Ian C. 2002. *God Save the Queen: The Spiritual Dimension of Monarchy.* Darton, Longman and Todd.

Brown, Callum G. 2012. "The Unholy Mrs Knight" and the BBC: Secular Humanism and the Threat to the "Christian Nation". *English Historical Review* CXXVII (525): 345–376.

Brown, Andrew, and Linda Woodhead. 2016. *That Was The Church That Was: How the Church of England Lost the English People.* London: Bloomsbury Continuum.

Chapman, James. 2015. *A New History of British Documentary.* Springer.

Harrison, Jackie. 2000. A Review of Religious Broadcasting on British Television. *Liberal Theology in the Contemporary World* 41 (4): 3–15.

Keenan, William. 1999. From Friars to Fornicators: The Eroticization of Sacred Dress. *Fashion Theory* 3 (4): 389–409.

Kirby, Dianne. 1999. The Archbishop of York and Anglo-American Relations During the Second World War and Early Cold War, 1942–1955. *Journal of Religious History* 23 (3): 327–345.

Morris, Jeremy. 2003. The Strange Death of Christian Britain: Another Look at the Secularization Debate. *Historical Journal* 46 (4): 963–976.

Morrison, David E. 2009. Cultural and Moral Authority: The Presumption of Television. *Annals of the American Academy* 625: 116–127.

Rowell, Geoffrey. 1992. The Identity of the Church of England: The Legacy of the Past and Problems of the Future. In *A Church for the Nation?: Essays on the Future of Anglicanism*, ed. Allen Warren. Gracewing Publishing.

Viney, Rachel. 1999. Religious Broadcasting on UK Television: Policy, Public Perception and Programmes. *Cultural Trends* 9 (36): 1–28.

Wallis, Richard. 2016. Channel 4 and the Declining Influence of Organized Religion on UK Television. The Case of *Jesus: The Evidence. Historical Journal of Film, Radio and Television* 36 (4): 668–688.

DISSERTATIONS

Leask, Margaret Anne. 2000. The Development of English-Language Hymnody and Its Use in Worship: 1960–1995. PhD diss., University of Durham.

INDEX

© The Author(s) 2020
M. Harmes et al., *The Church on British Television*,
https://doi.org/10.1007/978-3-030-38113-4